MANAGING THE RETIREMENT MAZE

Virginia Edition

Kandi Sterling
Michael Zervas

A Complete Guide to
Retirement Living Issues and
Ways to Maximize Retirement
Years

Published by Dace Publishing
P.O. Box 91, Ruckersville, VA 22968

To all those who have challenged me: "Here's to you......."

Printed in the United States of America
ISBN 0-932045-25-1
Library of Congress Catalog Card Number 98-71437

This book is part of the ***Managing the Retirement Maze* Series.**

For information on inclusion of senior facilities or senior services in subsequent revisions for Virginia, or for other states, please contact:
Dace Publishing, P.O. Box 91, Ruckersville, VA 22968
(804) 985-3603.
For a list of states currently under publication, please contact Dace Publishing or your nearest bookstore.

Acknowledgements

In writing this book we have used help and information from a number of different sources. The Area Agencies on Aging throughout the state, the Virginia Department of Health, the Office of Health Facilities, the Department of Social Services, the Department for Aging and the Virginia Health Care Association have provided information and answered many questions.

A special thank you to Monica Hilary who not only took the time to give us a lot of information on Continuing Care, but edited the chapter! Also Sam Dickinson, who after years in the field, helped with much of the book in terms of information and review. Ester Berg provided material on senior services and was very helpful in answering our many questions. Wanda Cabell, VICAP coordinator for the Jefferson Area Board for Aging, pleasantly volunteered information and material on short notice. Our thanks also to Dr. James Eby for all his assistance.

We also drew upon information from ALFA (Assisted Living Federation of America) and their wonderful magazine, *Assisted Living Today*, The American Association of Homes for the Aging, and the *AARP*. Especially helpful was *McKnight's Long-Term Care News,* a trade magazine for long-term care which we have followed over the last several years. They do an excellent job of following trends and issues in the industry. Also of help was *Provider,* a magazine published by the American Health Care Association.

We would also like to thank the dozens of administrators and service providers who took the time to talk about what is going on in their areas of senior living. They are excited about what they are doing and their enthusiasm is contagious. We hope this work reflects the many good things which are happening in the world of senior living. Any credit for this work is theirs and, of course, any errors are ours.

We have tried our best to provide complete and accurate information in a user friendly way. We do not intend that this book take the place of your own personal investigation and evaluation of living facilities or legal, financial or tax advice from a professional. Each persons situation is so unique that it would be impossible to do so.

Kandi Sterling
Michael Zervas

Ruckersville, Virginia
1998

Table of Contents

Part 1

" The Maze"

We began this series out of frustration. When our editor and his brother traveled to Oregon to help their mother find a nice place to live, they were overwhelmed with confusion, contradiction, and conflicting claims.

Their mother is a widow of five or six years, still mobile and able to drive, but living alone in a small community. Although she has friends in the area, and there is a low crime rate, there is also isolation and she is far from services and activities which she might enjoy. With one son in Alaska and one in Virginia, they are unable to look out for her on a daily basis.

They did not think they would have any trouble finding a good place for her to live, one which would provide her with the services and the social interaction she wanted and yet was still within her resources. In addition, our editor felt he knew what was going on in senior housing because he has a brother-in-law who has worked for years in long-term health care. Hours of listening to stories over the family dinner table made him confident that he could ask the right questions and would know what he wanted when he found it.

After a week of visiting homes, all three brothers and their mother were more confused than ever. Even nightly calls to the brother-in-law didn't help. They were unfamiliar with terms, there was no standardization, they heard conflicting sales pitches, and they had no idea what services and amenities their mother really needed. In the end they gave up. Their mother is still living in her home and still struggling to cope with typical daily home maintenance problems which are sometimes overwhelming to her.

And So This Series Was Born From the Maze of Information

We began our research with the typical material available and by contacting the various associations and agencies. What we found, and what is seldom disputed, is that senior living and health care for the elderly is often a vast, fragmented network mired in bureaucratic pitfalls. The maze of information, sometimes overlapping and sometimes contradictory, is overwhelming. It appears that there is *almost nothing in the field of retirement living which is ALWAYS true!*

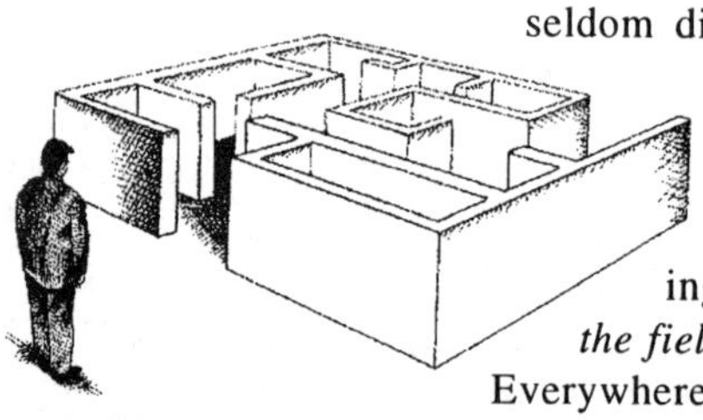

Everywhere there are exceptions, new ways of looking at problems, newly developing programs, and changing terms. No two states use the same terminology or have the same regulations. Even the standard lines between independent living, assisted living, nursing homes, and hospitals are so blurred with facilities taking on new roles or being organized along new lines that they are sometimes almost impossible to segregate. There are new companies coming on the market every month in an all-new field of senior-orientated service providers. And many already existing companies are adding new divisions of senior-friendly products and services. Dozens and dozens of consumer and professional associations are being born or merging with other organizations. Frequently they overlap, but leave gaps which can be confusing.

Throughout this book there will be recognition of the contradictions and sometimes conflicting ideas among service providers. We have tried to point out the different opinions, explain the basis on which they were founded, and the arguments supporting them. Because each individual senior is a unique person, with individual needs and environment, there is no single answer which is best for everyone. This book is intended to make readers aware of the alternatives and present guidelines on how to evaluate what is available.

Often people make decisions because of stereotyped impressions, because they feel it is the "right" decision, or because they do not know what else is available. Decisions based on such impressions may be disastrous. In this book we have tried to provide good information on what is going on in a rapidly changing field and to dispel many of the myths and stereotypes which have shrouded the industry for so many years.

One administrator said that demand drove the companies and providers of long-term care and senior services. The state and federal authorities were behind the curve on regulations and not necessarily in agreement on everything. Behind ***that*** curve is the consumer, who is often confused and frequently unaware of all of the alternatives.

Another administrator indicated that she felt time and planning were the most important factor in senior living and maintaining independence as long and as completely as possible. But she felt that the longer a person waited to make decisions about senior living, the more limited the options were. Most people tend to make decisions when it is necessary — which means that they cannot take time to evaluate all of their options and frequently do not know all of the ramifications of each option. They may not know all of their rights or even the protections which are in place to help them and to help maintain quality of life for their loved ones. If there is a problem, they may not know where to turn. Finally, they may not know of or appreciate what is new in the field since information on senior living is all too often sensational and of a frequently negative stereotype.

> Thanks to strides in health care and the standard of living, lifespans are increasing. Today 43 million Americans, or one in six, have celebrated their 60th birthday.

We hope that this book, and the others in the series, will help provide information which is current, relevant, and clear. Our sources include not only agencies and organizations which serve the senior living industry but also the trade publications which keep health care providers, lawyers, builders, and financiers informed on what are the latest trends, regulations, ideas, and management techniques.

We found tremendous differences between agencies. Although there are twenty-five Area Agencies on Aging within the state, they are extremely different. Some publish a directory of facilities and service providers, some do not. Some provide newsletters, some do not. Some are open and friendly, sending all kinds of information, while others are so guarded that they hesitated to give out the name of their director! Some wanted to send only the information which was directly needed, forcing uninformed callers to know what they want before they can get it! Some work with Parks and Recreation Programs, some do not even know the telephone number of their local recreation program. Some work closely with various Senior Centers, some do not really know what the centers are doing. And Senior Centers can be anything from interesting hubs of interaction and activity to loosely organized groups without a building.

Senior living can range from luxurious homes built around golf courses or well-appointed apartments with a variety of services aimed at seniors, to rooms in a converted school, to rooms in a house. They are run by corporations, privately run companies, families who are very concerned about their residents and look on them as an extension of their own families, to bitter and rude people who are clearly interested only in the money.

We called and personally attempted to talk to the administrator or public relations person for every facility or service in Virginia. We used yellow pages listings for Nursing Homes, Retirement Homes and Communities, Rest Homes, Assisted Living, Continuous Care, and Adult Day Care. Listings were free, but we asked that they answer some questions for us so we could gather data and provide specific information about what was going on in the state. Some of them were excited about what was going on in their field. Some of them were interested in educating the public and keeping consumers informed. Others blew us off, refusing to answer questions, insisting that they were full. This attitude certainly left us with the idea that all they were concerned with was the number of empty beds they had. Some were simply not interested in providing any information about anything which might inform consumers about what was going on. It was obvious that some of them had not made any improvements or innovations in years, preferring to move in a safe but unimaginative groove while others were excited about new changes they were making and challenges they were meeting. We cannot help thinking that these attitudes are reflected in the living situations they provide. We have printed the listing of **every facility which answered our questionnaire.**

Senior Living and Senior Services are Growing, Challenging, and Exciting Fields

In spite of all of this, we want to emphasize that this is a growing, challenging, exciting field with a lot of positive changes and a lot of people working very hard and very earnestly to maximize the level of function for individuals at every level. Senior living is more exciting and more diverse than it has ever been. Not only is life expectancy lengthening with every year, but the *quality of that life is far better than it has ever been before.* Sometimes the choices which are made make the difference in the quality of life and to that end we have endeavored to provide readers with the best possible information and the most complete picture on a regional basis that has ever been compiled.

We also contacted every service provider we could find. We have been amazed at some of the services they provide. We look forward to working with more of these senior-oriented service providers and urge any of them we have missed to contact us. We would love to include you in the next edition of this book.

The History of Aging

In all of life, for all living things, at all times, aging has been a part of life, completing the life-cycle. The French called aging the third age, conceiving that there was a cycle which included growth as the first age, the prime productive years of life as the second age, and the third age was the aging process.

Biologically there are two types of change for any organism, growth and aging, and both can occur at the same time. No one completely understands the aging process. Some scientists doubt that human aging will ever be controlled. Others believe it can be conquered. New theories purport to be able to extend functional life, both physically and psychologically. New drugs are developed every year which extend life and reclaim quality of life which was thought to be lost.

The history of aging developed slowly for many centuries only to gather speed in the twentieth century, and it will roll into the next millennium with speed and power for change that is akin to what the railroad was to the industrial revolution. Those changes will be felt throughout the population in new jobs, new products, and new hopes and expectations for the generations to follow.

Contrary to popular belief, however, long-term care administration did not spring into being after the passage of Titles 18 and 19, which amended the Social Security Act in 1966.

Different societies throughout history have had different ways of handling their aging population. For some, old people have been revered, controlling the family, and making the important decisions. In China, for example, women, especially upper-class women, looked forward to an age when they were free from family obligations and could devote time to their own interests and oversee the family rather than being involved in the day-to-day details of household management. Other societies, some American Indian tribes, for example, revered older men, but turned out old women who no longer had husbands to look after them or sons who were willing to take them in, leaving them to perish with the first cold winter nights.

For most European societies, the older generation was cared for in the home, sometimes with the help of other members of the community. With socialized medicine in many countries, the structure of aging is quite different from that which has developed in this country. In some countries, where housing is difficult to obtain, generations must live together as a matter of practicality. In Sweden, for example, it may take years on a waiting list for newlyweds to get an apartment of their own.

In the 12th through the 15th centuries nearly 700 shelters for the aged, the destitute, and pilgrims were built in England. These institutions housed populations which included the aged, the disabled, and those without homes of their own. Before 1453 all of these facilities were associated with monasteries. In 1536, when King Henry VIII had his dispute with the Catholic Church, all of the monasteries and their health care facilities were closed.

St. Bartholomew's "hospital" in London had been operating since 1123. Interestingly, there are no records of the staff having any medical training during the first 400 years! Pressures to provide care for the poor forced the king to allow St. Bart's to reopen in 1546. But the administrative responsibilities were taken from the bishops and given to appointed local citizens. This was the first step in the process of removing health care from the umbrella of the church. It is said that St. Bart's could accommodate 400 aged, 650 decayed householders (Medicaid-eligible persons), 200 idle vagabonds, 350 poor men overburdened with children (what happened to the women?), and 20 sore and sick persons (where were the state survey teams!). According to today's terms, St. Bart's provided 99% long-term care and about 1% acute care. Over the next 400 years, there would be a slow shift from chronic to acute care.

In 1722 England enacted a new Poor Law that established almshouses, or workhouses, where it was hoped the aged, chronically ill, and disabled could be cared for less expensively.

Until about 1850, there was little distinction between hospitals and what would be considered a nursing home today. Although called hospitals, their functions were more to provide support and comfort, largely due to the lack of medical technology. "Doctors" of the time were practitioners who had a wide variety of training, no standards or boards to pass, and who sold their services such as they were to those who could afford to pay. Doctors were not associated with hospitals until much later. The doctor attended his patient in his home or perhaps in a private clinic or office.

The American health care system, like its legal system, is based on the English system. Throughout the early years of this country and into the nineteenth century, the pattern for aging populations was much the same as in England. Generations lived together, each helping the other. For those who had no relatives, there was the local church to help. For those with no money, there was the "Old Folks Home," a place usually supported by charities. Wealthy people had private nurses who took care of them, poor people died young from the various diseases or hardships of lives filled with unsanitary living and working conditions.

Early in the 19th century, some not-for-profit church, fraternal, and community groups took responsibility, regardless of ability to pay, for their older members. Most early "homes for the aged" in the United States operated as charities. Donations of funds, food, and clothing were common, and sometimes residents had some financial resources that helped support them. In other cases, residents "turned over" their assets and income to the facility in exchange for lifetime care. Today, this practice is uncommon, though opponents of the Medicare/Medicaid system might argue that it still applies, though not in such precise terms.

Home Health Care Versus Institutional Care: A 400-Year-Old Debate

Our governmental view of caring for the aged and chronically ill was much the same as in England. Our federal and state health care programs have their roots in the Elizabethan Poor Law of 1601. Queen Elizabeth I required each local community to care for the poor and disabled. Cash gifts and help were offered to enable them to remain in their homes. For the following century, the major mode of aid and assistance to the elderly, chronically ill, and disabled was to allow them to stay in their own homes as long as possible. That pattern was followed in the New World.

But the English government and our colonial predecessors decided to provide public welfare and health assistance only in institutional settings by the beginning of the 18th century. By that time increases in the number of older and chronically ill citizens threatened to bankrupt state treasuries. It was decided that the cost of caring for these individuals would be less expensive if institutions were developed. Public welfare and health assistance for those who had no private means was therefore relegated to institutional settings. In 1722 Philadelphia opened an institution modeled after the English almshouse, with New York following in 1734, and Charleston, SC, in 1735.

During the early part of the nineteenth century, the pendulum swung back toward provision of in-home assistance for the aged. In England this was known as the Speenhamland System and provided a minimum annual income which was guaranteed to everyone. In this country it is often termed a "safety net" through which no one should be allowed to fall. But such programs are expensive and the pendulum began to swing back.

By 1830 it moved back to institutionalizing those who looked to the government for help and care. But this trend included two interesting innovations. First, they had infirmaries for the ill. These were the origins of the early public hospitals. Secondly, these institutions, often referred to as "workhouses," began to move toward specialization. One location would take the aged while another would take those who were out of work; yet another would take children and those who were caring for them. Those who were sick were sent to an institution focused on medical care. The Almshouse founded in Philadelphia became one of these institutions, and by 1903 it became known as Philadelphia General Hospital. In New York, the Publick Workhouse of 1734 added medical facilities in 1825 and medical personnel including a resident physician. The name was eventually changed to Bellevue Hospital.

The nursing home industry was further molded by the Social Security Act (1935) which generated financial support for older persons. The evolution of America from an agrarian society to a highly industrialized society made growing old more visible nationally. The aged in rural areas were cared for by their families, but in urban areas the family structure could not always support an elder family member. Pressures of living space and income often left the elderly without resources. The Great Depression of the 1930's focused attention on the aged and indigent. Who could forget the *Grapes of Wrath*'s depiction of grandma, dying without medical attention.

In 1950 federal matching money was made available to states to pay for medical care for persons on public assistance. This was the predecessor of Medicaid, which did not come into being until 1965. Although there were several additional steps in the evolution of medical assistance, it was the 1965 Title 18 which created Medicare and Title 19 which created Medicaid. In 1967 amendments were added which called for the licensing of nursing home administrators.

Attitudes and Care Change in This Century

Some of the facts we do know about aging have greatly influenced the nature of senior living in the United States. There is agreement that aging involves both environmental and hereditary factors. And the average life-span of Americans has increased considerably over the past half century and continues to increase. On an average, women outlive men across the categories of lifestyles, economic levels, race, education, and professions.

Not all societies define old age or senior citizens the same way. For many in the United States 65 is used as the beginning of old age because full Social Security benefits begin at that time. However, by law, no company can force a worker to retire until the age of 70. Senior discounts or senior associations such as the AARP begin to serve people as young as fifty or fifty-five.

In other societies, old age may be determined by the birth of a grandchild, the appearance of grey hair. Or the handing over of title or possessions to a child may signify the beginning of old age.

The percentage of senior citizens is rising rapidly as the Baby Boomers move into their fifties. Not only are they aging, but many of them are faced with aging parents who are in their seventies or eighties and who need care or can no longer cope with living independently. In 1900 only four percent of the population was 65 or older, and that constituted a group of 3 million. By 1980 that percentage has risen to eleven percent and the number has increased to 25.5 million. By the year 2000 there will be over 30 million people who are 65 or older.

Many people have a negative attitude toward old age. But the attitudes are changing as the Baby Boomers grow older. Because of their numbers this demographic group has influenced the nation throughout their entire lives. During the 1960's and the 1970's, their youth strongly influenced everything from products to advertising campaigns, putting the emphasis on youth. During those decades, people who were entering retirement often felt pushed out of the market by the younger generation which was perceived as more in touch with the market.

During the 1980's the perception changed as the Baby Boomers began to enter the establishment. By the end of that decade, attitudes on aging were changing considerably. More emphasis was being placed on remaining active, eating healthy, exercise, and keeping an interest in life. As they approach the age of senior living, their expectations are very different from those of their parents, and they are likely to exact many changes because of their numbers.

Finally, there is another change in senior living which is due to the changing nature and number of seniors. A new class of affluent, or at least financially comfortable, seniors is changing the market. The Baby Boomers are

At each stage of life, "Baby Boomers" — people born between 1946 and 1964 — have challenged existing structures and resources. They put pressure on hospital maternity units when they were born. They overflowed the public school system, leading to record construction, overcrowded classrooms, and sometimes double shifts of classes. They gave a huge boost to college enrollment, and they created an "echo boom" of births when they reached childbearing ages. They traveled through the country's life course in what has sometimes been described as "a pig in a python." As the oldest Boomers began to turn 50 in 1996, the media took up the cry that demographers and those who work in the field of aging had been voicing for many years. "What is going to happen when the Boomers reach retirement age?"

more educated than any generation before them and include more professional people who have worked at a higher wage most of their lives. They qualify for more Social Security benefits and are more likely to have planned for their retirement. Also, changes in corporate tax laws in the last decades have led more companies to develop retirement plans. Many of tomorrow's seniors will have retirement incomes which will provide them with the means to have more control over their lives and living conditions. This new class of affluent seniors attracts more private companies into the field and encourages development of new facilities to meet their needs and their desires.

In this century senior living has changed due to several factors. First, medical and technological advances have not only increased life expectancy but also the level of training and cost of equipment used to maintain acute and subacute patients. Drugs frequently need to be administered in very precise dosages and timed specifically throughout the day. A combination of drugs may necessitate close monitoring of the patient to watch for side-effects or adjustments. This is frequently something that family members either cannot handle without special training or are unable to handle because of pressing schedules and conflicting obligations.

Second, two-career families mean that the daughter or daughter-in-law who would have been the primary caregiver is not in the home. She may be overwhelmed already with a job and childcare. In addition, the modern woman may not see herself as a caregiver to the aging generation, especially if it does not share her views.

High divorce rates and reconstituted families increase stress in relationships which no longer break along clear-cut lines of family loyalties and allegiances. New mates may bring new children who do not view the elder family member as having a place in the home. Divorced elder parents who did not get along in their younger years certainly do not wish to end up both living with the same adult child. And, people married later in life may not share the same commitment to elder parents they have only recently met and barely know.

> If the United States considered gray hair as the indication of old age no one would be old. According to *Men's Health Magazine,* the sale of men's hair-coloring products has grown from $27 million in 1986 to $86 million in 1995.

Privacy becomes a consideration as family time becomes shorter and fewer and fewer older people live with their children than in the past. Although more than half the people over 65 live near their children, few actually live with them. Privacy is also important to the older person, who may feel very uncomfortable in the home of a child who has a much different living pattern than the one he or she was raised to accept. A woman in her 70's may be critical of the career choices of her working daughter and very uncomfortable with the more open discussions and show of affection which characterize many of the Boomer families who grew up during the sexual revolution.

Mobility in the last half of this century has also reduced the number of seniors who live with their children. Families no longer live in the same neighborhood for generations. Adult children may be spread across the country, far from the place the senior regards as home or where they feel comfortable.

Finally, seniors themselves are increasingly independent. They want to travel, they want to make their own decisions, they want a group of friends with similar interests. They are healthier than the generation before them, being more aware of the role of nutrition and exercise. The generations which follow them will be in even better condition, both physically and mentally as they enter their retirement years.

All of this means that fewer seniors are living with younger family members, and those who do frequently make use of home health services or adult day care which extends the function of the family. Overnight respite services offer beds for overnight stays of seniors to allow their caregivers to go on vacation, have an evening out, or just get a respite from caregiving.

A host of new services is growing. Ten years ago no one had heard of some of the businesses which flourish today. Elder law is now a specialized field, recognized by bar associations and with its own national organization of practitioners. Visitation services allow adult children who live far away to be assured their parents have visitors who will check on them and take a personal interest in their welfare. Construction companies are specializing in home renovation to make daily living easier for seniors who choose to remain independent.

Seniors join clubs, do volunteer work, get into politics and travel. They do more walking and socializing. Groups like the Gray Panthers have become involved in what is going on in the country. The American Association of Retired Persons has become more active and grown, moving into many fields and broadening their activities. The federal government has encouraged groups such as SCORE (Service Corps of Retired Executives) which attracts many retired business people who enjoy serving as advisers for community organizations and small businesses. Men and women over 60 join the Retired Senior Volunteer Program (RSVP) and work in hospitals, libraries, schools, and other institutions. Congress has developed a Senior Intern Program which offers a chance for seniors to discuss issues and work side-by-side with those who develop national policy. The Foster Grandparent Program (FGP) uses senior citizens to help care for children from poverty-stricken families. And 1.3 million children have grandparents as primary caregivers, frequently because their parents are part of a generation which suffered from a high rate of drug addiction and cannot care for their own children. About 20% of men over 65 still work, while only about 10% of women over 65 still work.

By the 90's, the parents of the Baby Boomers were beginning to get to an age where they could not continue to live alone. They could no longer do the cleaning and home maintenance which is required for independent living. They were having trouble driving, especially at night, which limited their mobility, and they had medical problems which made it unsafe for them to live alone.

THE FUTURE:

America's older population will grow and change rapidly. By the year 2030, those 60 years old and older will more than double to 85 million. Those 85+ will triple to 8 million.

More and more seniors are beginning to recognize that living among other seniors has some advantages. In 1980, fewer than 10% of the nation's senior citizens lived in special retirement communities, and only about 5% lived in nursing homes or other institutions. Over the past fifteen years that percentage has grown. Senior communities have developed and broadened their activities; assisted living facilities and nursing homes have become big business. Corporations have entered the market, and mergers and acquisitions have increased each year and are expected to continue into the next century. Seniors often feel more independent and secure in retirement communities which provide recreation and social activities, contracts for housekeeping and medical care, and leave seniors with more time to pursue their interests instead of trying to cope with day-to-day living.

> Although aging Americans present many challenges to society, they also offer many opportunities. They represent a great reservoir of talent, experience, and knowledge which can be used to better their communities and the nation. New programs are being developed which will promote intergenerational programming. Older persons are serving as pre-school workers, as tutors in school and after school programs, as mentors, role models, and surrogate grandparents. Through the Eldercare Volunteer Corps the talent of a half million volunteers, many of them older persons, assist in service programs. As much as these programs provide to the community, they also ensure the dignity and independence of older Americans.

Along with this, the state and federal governments have stepped up their inspections, licensing procedures, and guidelines. Social, occupational, and physical therapy have begun to play important parts in what is expected of senior housing. Safety has improved with handrails and restraint-free buildings. There is more emphasis on providing home-like, comfortable atmospheres. Therapy dogs, birds, indoor gardens, and snacks are part of many facilities now, even nursing homes. The emphasis is shifting toward rehabilitation instead of accepting hopelessness.

The federal government administers Medicare, a medical insurance program for senior citizens that pays part of the expenses for physicians, drugs, and hospital care. Medicare also pays a portion of the cost of medical services at home or in a nursing home after an elderly patient has been discharged from a hospital. Medicaid has expanded into other areas such as managed care programs.

For those who do live alone or with families, there have developed a wide variety of programs and companies, and even technological advances, which help make their lives and the lives of their caregivers easier. Hospice programs, home health care companies, private nursing companies, and adult day care centers help families cope with their busy work schedules and the needs of an aging parent who needs care. Pagers, portable phones, medical alert buzzers, and riding chairs which run along stairways help seniors who live or spend time alone cope with emergencies and limitations. Elder law specialists have emerged within the last decade to help people plan for the future and evaluate their financial options. Geriatric Care Counselors help families and seniors evaluate their options. And monumental breakthroughs such as cloning and freezing, which were once only science fiction, are now possible, at least to some level. What they will bring, ethically and practically, is still very much unknown.

So fast is the field of senior living changing and emerging, it is fair to say that by the end of the first decade of the next century there will be more new companies, new discoveries, new patterns of looking at the aging process, and new developments to meet the needs of the senior market than we can possibly imagine now.

Changing Attitudes on Aging

As the population in the United States grows older, senior living is taking on a new look. It is not uncommon to see such well known names as Marriott and Hyatt as the owner or manager of a property. Dozens of big companies own retirement homes in communities across the country, and hundreds of facilities are owned by local investors, hospitals, and development companies.

Only a decade ago the senior living industry was largely a group of independently owned properties. Acquisitions and mergers have rapidly changed that picture. Terms used to describe services provided and types of living situations have changed. Requirements, licensing, and regulations have grown and proliferated so rapidly that in some cases no one is quite sure what they say. One administrator we talked to said she was on the committee which wrote the latest regulations. Because these regulations had to get past a committee with representatives from a wide variety of services and providers, the wording was frequently a compromise and a compilation of the goals and imperatives of the individual committee members rather than a strong, smoothly written document with clear, well defined structure. Certainly everyone is concerned with the welfare and dignity of the senior population, but there are wide differences of opinion as to ***how*** to accomplish those goals and even as to ***what*** is most beneficial for seniors.

Although it is sometimes frustrating, there are several bright spots to hang onto in the search for the right place to retire to and the right housing for you or your family member. Within the last five or six years, federal and state agencies have begun to pay particular attention to the needs of the aging population.

> **Change is one of the few constants in long-term care these days. — *McKnight Long-Term Care News,* July 1997**

People over fifty-five are beginning to become a voting block, one which will grow at a steady pace within the next two decades, and government regulatory agencies are already alert to the shift. In many ways, these government agencies, and the senior housing facilities — both private and public — which function under their guidelines, are much more attuned to the needs and diversified goals of seniors than are their own families.

While the idea of aging is frightening to a population which once proclaimed, "Never trust anyone over thirty!," and children are not comfortable with a shifting role of adult child into that of the caregiver for parents, those who have worked with the aging have long ago adapted a much more positive attitude and have set goals to support those attitudes.

Senior housing is often a way to extend the useful years of life, not a place to go simply to die. Literally dozens of different programs have been developed at all levels to keep seniors involved in life, active, and feeling useful at every level of care. Within the past half dozen years, federal and state guidelines have been enlarged to include social activities, recognizing that these are as important as physical care for the well-being of the senior resident. Vocational therapists and activities directors have flooded into the field. Inspection (termed "survey") teams which regularly visit all licensed facilities not only want to check the kind of medical care each resident receives, the nutritional balance of the meals served, the care with which records are kept, and the cleanliness of the building; they also look to see if each resident is receiving encouragement and support in maintaining quality of life and maximizing the use of his or her skills.

For years research in all fields has proven that a positive mental attitude extends life and promotes recovery. Support groups extend the lives of cancer patients. Patients who feel they still have something to give, something to do which is of interest to them, have a higher rate of remission and the periods of remission last longer. Patients who have had knee or hip replacement surgery recover more quickly and more completely with physical therapy and social activities which support recovery, such as sharing their recovery challenge with others who have similar experiences.

Nursing homes are now extending their concept of recovery and rehabilitation. Even skilled-care units set goals and plans for returning their residents to a more active life-style. Each year a larger percentage of their beds are filled with patients who have a recovery and rehabilitation plan. No longer is the view of aging that of a one-way street, downhill. Now there are plans and programs to bring back quality of life at all levels. There are skilled, trained personnel available to deal with reversals and depression as well as the physical problems of aging.

Staffing has changed over the past several years. Most facilities have qualified activities professionals, people who have completed a 90-hour course on directing and motivating residents to extend their skills and increase their interest in life. This special certification is necessary to meet current nursing home regulations. A recreational therapist is another person who meets these requirements. This four-year degree in recreation is designed to develop a highly skilled professional to deal with the disabilities now seen in long-term care settings.

Facilities are also now using the term "pro-active" which means that care is taken so that the residents have the feeling they have control over their own lives, even when they need constant care. The Residents' Bill of Rights was adopted to guarantee basic rights to residents and to promote the feeling of control and continuation of quality of life.

VOTING IN 1994

	Registered	Voting
18-24	42.2%	20.0%
25-44	57.5%	39.1%
45-64	71.0%	56.0%
65 and over	95.6%	60.7%

Senior citizens were 22.3 percent of all 1994 voters. They are 16.4 percent of the voting age population, meaning that they register and turn out to vote in exceptionally large numbers. Seniors are becoming very well informed about issues which are important to them.

In 1987 Congress passed a landmark federal law changing forever how states and the federal government oversee nursing homes. OBRA '87 has helped upgrade care to the nation's 1.7 million nursing home residents. Among the law's most notable achievements are increased resident autonomy, better care plans, reduced use of chemical and physical restraints, and importance of maintaining accurate records as a critical part of patient care. It paved the way for tougher inspections and huge fines for facilities who do not meet the requirements.

But even something which seems so positive has produced criticism and disagreement from those who actually support its goals of improved patient care. While it has required major changes and upgrading of patient care, it is often controversial, considered by some to cause almost as many problems as it solves. Supporters say it is achieving its intent by focusing on residents and promoting their optimum function and care. Others say the new survey process is frustrating in its inconsistencies and too often focuses on details which are not directly related to patient care. Frequently administrators complain that the excessive documentation which is required takes time away from the real issue, which is care of the patients. For most facilities it takes the equivalent of a full-time nurse to do the paperwork. For the same dollar, many administrators complain that the nurse would be better used providing direct care for the patients.

Consumer groups often feel that the conditions must be bad before surveyors will even note that a deficiency exists. They feel the law has been instrumental in improving resident care planning and assessment. Administrators and other providers disagree, feeling that survey teams may cite by the letter of the law rather than from a reasonable approach.

In every university in the country, basic business and economics classes are teaching that the United States is rapidly becoming a country whose economy is based on service rather than production. As such, any shift in consumer demographics will cause a shift in the economy to meet those shifting needs. As more consumers reach the age where they need senior-oriented services, companies of all sizes are changing to meet the demands. A wealth of new services is growing, forming a secondary level of businesses designed to make life easier for seniors. Major companies such as banks and power companies are instituting programs to make them elder-friendly.

And the emergence of a new group of seniors has changed senior options. There is an emergence of an affluent senior class. Although these people may not be "rich," they are well above the poverty level which has previously entrapped the majority of the country's senior population. For years, services were aimed at taking care of a group of people who were almost without resources. Government agencies and senior service providers developed programs which provided services at the lowest economic levels. Today's seniors, and those right behind them, have worked longer, been paid better, are more educated, and have resources that the depression and war generation did not have. They worked for companies who had health plans and retirement programs. They have invested in retirement plans. They have collected resources over their lifetimes. And they know what they want. Government and groups previously geared to low-income seniors are now revising their attitudes to include services and programs for seniors of all economic and education levels.

Healthy, active life-styles mean that not only will they enjoy longer lives, they will have a better quality of life in advanced years. These consumers are driving a new kind of senior economy which will continue to be so for the next ten to twenty years, depending on what figures are used.

There is a growing need for workers at all levels, from administrators and nurses to daily caregivers. Salaries are gradually increasing to compete with other industries and draw talented people into the field. OBRA regulations drove some providers and caregivers out of the field. Many feel that those who left were not flexible enough to meet the changing market. Today, for the most part, employees across the industry report that they are satisfied or very satisfied with their work. The industry is recognizing that the attitude of their staff makes a big difference in the quality of life for their residents, and many companies are taking steps to promote employee satisfaction in a tight labor market. **The old image of the residential staff with the personality of Cinderella's stepmother is simply not true.** Most senior residences, from independent living to nursing homes, are staffed by employees who are interested in the people they care for and who enjoy their roles in a growing field.

Patient satisfaction has reached an all-time high. Patient satisfaction surveys found that patients rate facilities using such factors as staff sensitivity, concerns for privacy, and technical skills of nurses. Interpersonal issues such as attitude, interactive skills, and caring behavior dominate the factors most closely associated with overall patient satisfaction. Although the temptation to present senior living facilities of all kinds in a sensational light has often contributed to a negative outlook on senior long-term care, even Ann Landers' column is reflecting the change. A recent letter from a woman who was considering suicide rather than enter a nursing home was answered by a rabbi who was 86 years old. He supported the quality of life offered in a nursing home he had been in for a while, and (as is becoming more common all the time) he had used the facility for a recovery period, returning to independent living. The new emphasis is on recovery and rehabilitation; yet even when a patient is terminal, the attitude of dignity and respect are ever-present.

The demographic shift to an older population is fueling unprecedented demand for senior housing over the next three decades. The current market demand is 1.78 million people, but the figure could be as high as 3.7 million people by 2030. Public stock offerings by the corporations serving the senior market have made some of them large solid entities which entice investors and mutual funds, whose investors may be some of the very seniors who live in the facilities or who use the services. This is not an industry which is driven by normal business cycles. The stability of the senior housing demand is driven by demographics. Senior housing, long-term health care providers, and health services are changing from the charity-based programs run by churches and other nonprofit organizations to market-driven health care companies, attracting institutional investors.

> Assisted Living and Nursing Homes are becoming places which serve more than one function. Patients recovering from surgery such as hip or knee replacement may check into a facility which offers physical therapy and closely monitored recreational activity until they are past the critical point in recovery. Patients who live at such facilities where they are supervised and encouraged to be active and participate in their recovery are much more likely to have a successful outcome and full recovery than those who remain home where they may be allowed to postpone physical therapy or limit it to a few visits a week. In this way long-term care facilities are beginning to be places of hope and recovery.

The fastest-growing age group remains individuals age 85 or older. In nursing homes the average age resident is 86, but that age is rising slowly. This is not only because of the increased life-span but also because assisted living facilities are moving into some of the special care areas which once mandated a move into a nursing home. Residents may therefore remain in their living situation longer and enjoy the continuity of friends and familiar surroundings.

In the latest survey of the fifty largest providers for assisted living, residents had an average age of 82, which was down from 84 as an average age in 1996. There were no figures available for independent living senior communities because they cover such a wide range, but the age for people entering independent living situations and those entering continuing care communities are younger than ever, with residents reaching down into their late fifties or early sixties. The reason for this is that more and more people are choosing to consider retirement living opportunities earlier.

Changing attitudes in the population in general have also contributed to changing attitudes in senior housing. Smoking policies have been a matter of controversy. With smoking so heavily linked to health problems, even for those who are exposed to secondary smoke, the rights of smoking residents have come under attack. Over 20% of facilities across the nation have taken some steps to restrict smoking within their buildings. But facilities must also address the rights of residents who have smoked in the facilities for years, before the smoke-free policies were adopted. And there are the rights of residents who have smoked all their lives and do not wish to quit. Many facilities that choose to eliminate all indoor smoking among residents allow those residents who fall under a "grandfather clause" to continue to smoke in designated areas such as a lounge. And with more facilities available, smokers may simply choose a facility which continues to allow smoking.

A growing number of facilities seek youthful exuberance. Intergenerational programs are based on uniting generations. At Virginia Tech, the Alpha Phi sorority has initiated a "Senior Prom." Each year the girls and their dates deco-

These young dancers get a chance to perform in front of an audience and seniors get a chance to visit and enjoy programs which help add variety and interest to their daily routine. Each group benefits .

rate and host a dance for senior residents which has become one of the highpoints of the year for both groups.

In Charlottesville, the Wilson School of dance visits a senior residence. The girls in the junior dance troop have a chance to perform before a live audience and to practice new material, and the residents enjoy the entertainment and the enthusiasm of the girls. Some facilities have developed more formalized programs where youthful volunteers, much like the old hospital candy-stripers, visit each week.

Intergenerational programs increase patient satisfaction, provide a base within the community for acceptance and appreciation of seniors and the facility, and make the facility more marketable. These programs increase staff satisfaction and help retain staff and can even improve care quality. Although many facilities still resist change, and visitations can cause problems in scheduling for administrators, those administrators who have initiated such programs see children and seniors as a natural fit. The interaction of generations takes the facilities back in a full circle to the interaction of generations which was part of the family in the past and makes the facility seem more like a family. One administrator laughingly said that Christmas carollers were his biggest nightmare. Adjustments in meal schedules had to be made, patients had to be moved for better viewing, and routines were interrupted every time a carolling group visited. He had five such groups in a one week period. But, he said, the residents loved it, the staff was happy to do the extra work required, and the community developed a positive attitude toward the facility and its residents. All this made it more than worth his scheduling problems.

Another consequence of the market-driven senior living trend is reflected in plans for renovation. Most long-term providers plan to renovate or remodel within the next five years. Residents' rooms and public gathering areas are the targets. This suggests that residences are more and more concerned with the quality of life and the environment and that images of bare rooms and austere living have gone the way of the great institutional orphanage. "Shady Pines" of the *Golden Girls* exists in fiction along with the *Oliver Twist* orphanage.

Finally, new kinds of architects and designers have begun to emerge. In an effort to design physical environments which help residents function at their highest possible level, interior designers and architects have begun to specialize in senior residential designs. Their innovations blend in the needs of the seniors without drawing attention to declining abilities. They understand regulations and needs and maximize the available opportunities. They strive to open up the environment and make it into a significant life experience for both the residents and the staff.

Retirement in Virginia

Virginia, known as "The Old Dominion," was one of the original colonies. In fact, it is the site of Jamestown, the first permanent English settlement in the New World. Today it attracts tourists from all over the world and is famed for its historical significance as an early colony, for its role in both the Revolutionary War and Civil War, for its proximity to Washington D.C., and for its many splendid natural resources, which include such features as Natural Bridge, numerous caverns, scenic drives such as the Blue Ridge Parkway and Skyline Drive in the Shenandoah National Park, lovely sand beaches, and the quaint old life-style of the eastern shore and Tangier Island. Virginia's appeals today are as broad and diverse as its geography and as abundant as its nearly four centuries of history. Stretching from the Atlantic Ocean to the Blue Ridge and Allegheny mountains, Virginia is a mixture of exciting cities, small towns, historic homes and villages, and as much varied beauty as you would ever want.

> Within it's boundaries, Virginia serves up nearly 400 years of history and heritage, miles of beaches, some of the most famous mountains in the country and a tradition of southern hospitality at its finest.

"Virginia is for Lovers," and "We have it made in Virginia" have both been used as slogans. Pride runs high, and there is a lot to be proud of. Both visitors and new residents are welcomed. But in spite of the influx of people from all over the country, and, in fact, from all over the world, the commonwealth maintains a much slower and more gracious life-style than its northern neighbors and is much more traditional than Florida. Virginia is for lovers of mountains and beaches, history and culture, natural wonders and man-made delights, vibrant cities and postcard-perfect towns.

The climate of Virginia has four mild seasons. The winters seldom drop into the single digits; the summers seldom climb above the low nineties. The mountain regions are a little cooler, the piedmont a little warmer, and the coastal areas a little milder in both winter and summer. Spring generally comes early, and the spectacular fall with the dazzling fall foliage hangs on until early December. Only January and February are always cold, and only June and July are almost always hot. Snowfall is usually limited from a few days a year to a few weeks, and a twenty inch snowfall is considered record setting. For those from colder climates who do not wish to give up the white stuff completely, Virginia is an ideal place!

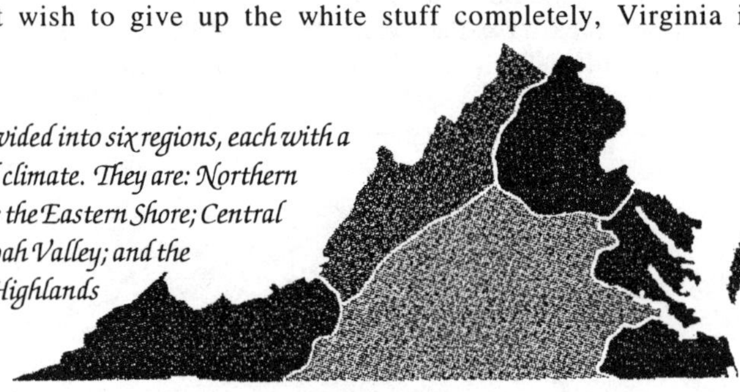

Virginia is generally divided into six regions, each with a distinctive flavor and climate. They are: Northern Virginia; the Tidewater; the Eastern Shore; Central Virginia; the Shenandoah Valley; and the Southwest Blue Ridge Highlands

REGIONS OF VIRGINIA

The commonwealth is generally divided into six regions, each with a distinctive character. The climate, mild through most of Virginia, is different for each region, and each offers a slightly different flavor. Though all have a characteristic pace and pride, a resident would be well served to consider the attractions of each so that the search for a retirement area could be narrowed to one or two areas.

Northern Virginia

Close to Washington, D.C., this area offers proximity to two large international airports. Travel in and out of the area is excellent. Trains link Washington, D.C., with the northeast on several direct routes. If travel for the retiree or visiting family is important, Northern Virginia has a distinct advantage. Dulles Airport is in Northern Virginia to the southwest of Washington, D.C. Located near Reston, it has flights to all major cities in the U.S. and abroad and direct, easy access in and out of the airport area. Reagan Airport, located just outside the beltway of Washington, D.C., along the banks of the Potomac, is busy and crowded, but serves the corridor of Interstate 95 into Northern Virginia and south toward Fredericksburg and Richmond.

Washington, D.C., has everything. Skyscrapers, modern high-rises, upscale shopping centers, historical and cultural events, and some of the best museums in the world — many of which are free or very inexpensive. The parks are plentiful throughout the region and offer peace against the background of one of the most active cities in the world.

> Northern Virginia has an abundance of everything and a variety unrivaled by any other state. The largest concentration of stores on the East Coast outside of New York resides in Northern Virginia. The scenic beauty of the area is spectacular. Houses and historic places date back to the earliest years of the country and include important sites from both the Revolutionary War and the Civil War.

Throughout, Northern Virginia is rich in Civil War and Revolutionary War era sites and battlefields which bring history alive. Painstakingly restored homes and plantations are maintained in the best tradition. Exhibits and tours provide a glimpse of the past and many are aimed at seniors. All of the arts abound, from drama to concerts. Historic and international festivals and music provide different entertainment almost every weekend. Fine dining, antiquing, and places to watch skilled artisans at work in almost every field balance against golf courses and fine fishing. Nature trails, most equipped for the handicapped, are a part of many parks. Potomac Mills is one of the largest outlet malls in Virginia and is located between Fredericksburg and Washington, D.C., along Interstate 95.

Alexandria, the place where George Washington lived, and slept, and danced is still alive with that tradition. Scottish and English traditions are everywhere. Alexandria is where an old town and a new city are one. Fifty percent of the seniors in Alexandria live in high rise apartments. The city, which was once thought to have reached its growth capacity, is now experiencing a new boomtown feeling as two large areas have been torn out and are being redeveloped for modern needs. Citizens watch out for each other and services are abundant.

Further into Northern Virginia, housing for senior citizens ranges from suburban to semi-rural. There are several excellent senior retirement communities which offer an excellent life-style for the actively retired.

The Tidewater

Rich with history and home of beautiful beaches, the Tidewater area of Virginia offers a mild climate. Seldom seeing snow because of the warmth of the Atlantic waters, sea breezes also keep it cool in the summer.

Naval yards, both modern and historic, dominate the Virginia Beach area. Tidewater is the most populous area of Virginia and spreads across several counties, enveloping large and sprawling cities such as Hampton Roads, Norfolk, Virginia Beach, Newport News, and Portsmouth. Much of the population is working middle-class, with retired naval personnel and shipyard workers making up a large part of the senior population. There is a wealth of services for seniors in this area.

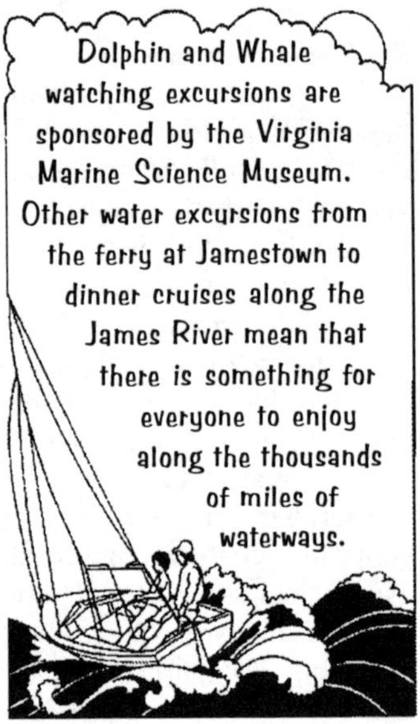

Sports enthusiasts can enjoy a minor-league baseball team and the world's largest natural harbor, public golf courses, and even a sports hall of fame. Twenty-eight miles of the Atlantic coast and miles and miles of canals and rivers are a joy for water lovers. The Elizabeth River leads to the inland waterway along which a small boat can travel all the way to Florida. The area provides recreation from whale-watching to fishing. Virginia Beach is the world's longest resort beach, and the James River stretches back toward Jamestown and Williamsburg with a host of plantations open to the public, providing exhibits of 18th-century life and crafts. The Revolutionary War ended and the United States began at Yorktown. Scenic drives and nature walks are part of at least four different tours of the area.

Museums abound, from fine art collections to the Virginia Marine Science Museum. The latter incudes a bird aviary, 3,000,000 gallon open ocean aquarium, seal and river otter habitats, and a nature trail with handicapped facilities.

Shopping ranges from outlets to the Waterside, a collection of fine shops and restaurants overlooking the mouth of the James River. All types of cruises are available from dinner and sight-seeing to inexpensive watertaxi trips from Norfolk to Portsmouth.

The Eastern Shore

By contrast, Virginia's pristine Eastern Shore beaches are filled with rare and beautiful seashells, charter boats, guided tours, quiet coves, and lazy lagoons. It is a place that time passed by, where life moves slowly, away from the pressures of the city and the hum of industry. It is flat, filled with natural marshlands and the wildlife that has made the Chesapeake famous. It is a haven for thousands of migratory birds.

No large shopping areas invade the area. No large museums filled with fine art, no plays and concerts by national and internationally known companies, and no skyscrapers are to be found here. This seventy-mile peninsula is dotted with quaint towns and secluded barrier islands. The climate is damp, for the land is narrow and surrounded by water — the Atlantic Ocean on one side, the widest part of the Chesapeake Bay on the other.

Attached to Virginia only by the twenty-one mile Chesapeake Bay Bridge-Tunnel, it is remote and isolated. Only one main highway bisects the two counties and the other roads are sometimes not much more than lanes which wander from town to town. The inhabitants are fishermen, craftsmen, and people who enjoy small village life. Place names like Kiptopeke, Nassawadox, Onancock, and Pungoteague are reminders of the Indians who once lived in the region and whose pastoral way of life has remained. Crafts also reflect the way of life; duck decoys are an art form here, along with other reminders of the sea.

The local festivals are of seafood and honor the region's watermen such as the oyster and crab festivals. Only Chincoteague, made famous by the children's books by Marguerite Henry, attracts tourists in any large number. Summer brings the roundup of the ponies of Assateague, and millions of children of all ages catch a quick breath at the thought of *Misty* and the other members of the pony and human families who truly lived on the two islands. Today nature trails, bike paths, and beaches fill the area, and, though the summer is filled with visitors from Labor Day to Memorial Day, the islands slip back into harmony with the surroundings for most of the year.

> We were most impressed by the personal friendliness offered by those we talked to from the Eastern Shore. This Area on Aging has pioneered a number of unique programs including one of only twenty senior literacy programs, a Thrift Shop which opened in 1990, and a craft co-op store called "Country Makin's"

Tangier, accessible only by boat, is a voice of the past. The older residents still reflect their Elizabethan dialect and preserved lifestyle from an era long past. Debtors' prison, a lighthouse, and one of the oldest general stores on the East Coast bring alive a time gone by.

Today, life on the Eastern Shore is dominated by church and local activities more like those of New England villages than like its busy tidewater neighbor to the south across the Chesapeake Bay Bridge. Time moves in harmony with the tides and nature and blends evenly from one century to another. Two country clubs, both private, serve the area. Both have yacht facilities and golf courses. But there is only one hospital, and it has limited services. The nearest large hospitals with full services are to the north, in Salisbury, Maryland, or over the bridge to Norfolk on mainland Virginia.

Central Virginia

With a climate milder than that of Northern Virginia, storms from the west are often diverted by the Shenandoah and Blue Ridge Mountains and frequently tend to veer north, bypassing Central Virginia. Although only 100 miles south of Washington, D.C., it is often without snow when the capital is clogged with snowy roads. But, being further inland, there are more definite seasonal changes and more temperature fluctuations than in the coastal tideland area. Central Virginia is protected by the mountains, but not warmed by the sea.

Life in Central Virginia has prospered for centuries. To the west, the Blue Ridge Mountain foothills rise into the Shenandoah National Park. Gleaming cities and country towns can provide almost any life-style. Many of the nation's greatest founders and leaders lived in Central Virginia, including three U.S. Presidents and the president of the Confederate States of America. Lewis and Clark were boyhood friends in Charlottesville. Many of their homes, as well as those of other patriots, are open to the public.

> So popular is central Virginia with seniors that builders in the area frequently design homes with first floor master bedrooms and other features which appeal to retirement living owners.

Much of the Civil War took place in Central Virginia. Richmond was the capitol of the Confederate States and the White House of the Confederacy is open to the public. Petersburg is the city subjected to the longest military siege in U.S. history. Danville was the last capital of the Confederacy, and Appomattox Court House was where General Robert E. Lee surrendered to Union General Ulysses S. Grant.

The area is filled with variety. Richmond, today the capitol of the commonwealth, offers all of the amenities of a large city though its population is only about a quarter of a million. The James River provides activities from the annual "Plastic Duck Race" for charity to the lunch and dinner cruises on the Annabel Lee Riverboat. The fine art museum is outstanding and has hosted such major exhibits as the Fabergé collection. Notable people from Edgar Allen Poe to Arthur Ashe have left their influence. Richmond offers almost everything from shopping to senior activities, from history to festivals, and from sports to drama. But the pace of life is slower than that of Washington, D.C.

South of Richmond the city suburban sprawl reaches to Petersburg and Hopewell. Along with historical plantations and the Petersburg National Historic Site, the area boasts a 1920's neighborhood of Sears, Roebuck and Company Houses by Mail. Diverse examples of unique Sears cottages and homes connect the colonial plantations and Civil War battlefields with the present.

Directly west of Richmond, separated by some sixty miles of mostly undeveloped countryside, is Charlottesville. Home of Thomas Jefferson, Charlottesville was a crossroads of Central Virginia. But it is set off from Northern Virginia by more than sixty miles of small towns and counties. To the south, its closest neighbor is Lynchburg, reached by an hour's drive through rural country.

Though isolated, Charlottesville is both traditional and progressive, taking its cue from the University of Virginia. Founded by Jefferson as the first publicly-funded full university in the United States, UVA influences Charlottesville. Its Medical Center is one of the best in the world, its students come from all fifty states and dozens of foreign countries. Students and professors bring ideas from almost every nation, blending their cultures and traditions with the tradition of the heart of the Old Dominion. People of every major religion worship there and restaurants include almost every type of food. Local theater and artists have a strong tradition, and the city has attracted the rich and famous from Anna Anderson, the woman who claimed to be Anastasia, to William Faulkner. Charlottesville is both one of the largest small cities and one of the newest and most progressive old cities in America. In 1997 it was rated one of the ten best places in the United States to raise a family. It has the highest per capita number of newspapers and lawyers in the nation. Although it has a low rate of unemployment, the popularity of the region attracts many college graduates and professionals. It is often said that you need a masters degree to be a bartender there. Therefore, many who come to school there, and fall in love with the town, must move out of the area to find jobs. But when they retire, they retire there. Charlottesville is one of the most popular areas for active affluent seniors, and its senior programs are excellent and stimulating.

Lynchburg, by contrast, is the home of conservatism. Jerry Falwell and Liberty University have figured largely in the city's culture and laws, and the main shopping mall was closed on Sunday, even during the busiest shopping seasons, until state laws outlawed local blue laws only a few short years ago. Lynchburg is an old city, located high on the James River, and a site of early manufacturing.

Danville, home of the Dan River Company, was an early mill town. Located along the banks of the river which once powered the looms, Danville stands on the Virginia-North Carolina border and still has the feeling of a southern mill town.

Aside from these towns, the rest of Central Virginia is mostly rural counties and small towns. Wineries sprinkle the area as Virginia is one of the leading wine producing states and her vineyards date back to the time of Thomas Jefferson. The Virginia wine industry has grown in the last two decades and wineries have now taken some top awards in national and international competitions. Small farms and cattle ranches fill the remainder of the landscape of Central Virginia, and much of the area is as it was (frequently even owned by the same families) a century ago.

The Shenandoah Valley

Shenandoah is an Indian word meaning "daughter of the stars." Glorious mountains line the expansive valley and create some of the most beautiful scenery and relaxing resorts in all of the United States. It has been termed Virginia's crowning glory, and in it nature has created such phenomena as the Natural Bridge, Natural Chimneys, and numerous caverns. Golf courses abound and festivals of all kinds from outdoor theater at Lime Kiln and Blue Grass celebrations to regional delights fill most weekends of the year. The spring features the Apple Blossom Festival in Winchester at the upper end of the valley. Fall foliage events punctuate the colorful end of the year and complete the continuing celebration of life in Virginia.

> **"I look with infinite joy...when I shall...be in the midst of my affections, and free to follow the pursuits of my choice."**
> — Thomas Jefferson, commenting on his retirement.

The scenic Skyline Drive, The Blue Ridge Parkway, and National Forests are the parks for this area instead of city-style, well tailored parks created by man. Even the cities of the area are more like oversized towns, with a town feeling. It is colder in the Valley than in Central Virginia. Snowfall comes earlier and stays on the ground in patches for much of the winter, though it seldom covers the ground completely for more than a few days at a time. Spring comes later and summers are cooler than to the east, with the nights having a crisp air except in the very peak of the summer. By late August there is a feeling of fall in the evening air.

This was the breadbasket of the Confederacy. Food crops have always been grown by German immigrants who moved down from Pennsylvania — often bringing with them their Mennonite religion and way of life. Buggies can still be seen in towns such as Harrisonburg. Farmers Markets sell produce and baked goods from local farms. The P. Buckley Moss Museum exhibits the artist's paintings of the area and its inhabitants. Dozens of small towns with narrow main streets and antique shops fill the area and Virginia's covered bridges are part of the area's charm.

> During the Civil War this was the "breadbasket of the South." Sherman marched through the Valley leaving it so desolated that "a crow flying the length of the valley would have to bring his own rations." Today it is an area filled with natural beauty, dramatic change of seasons, antique shopping, golf courses, and horse activity. Small towns invite discovery of the past, outdoor festivals and plays make use of the natural beauty and history, and easy transportation and cities offer access to up-to-date health care.

From Belle Grove Plantation, built in 1794 at the upper end of the Valley, to Lexington, the historic home of VMI and Washington and Lee University, the Valley abounds in reminders of George Washington and Confederate Generals Robert E. Lee and Stonewall Jackson. As a young man, George Washington worked on a survey crew in the Valley and left his initials carved at Natural Bridge.

There are no sports teams here except for the high schools and colleges, but the Virginia Horse Center offers a glimpse of some of the best competition in the field. Classic cars can be found at a shop in Staunton, and the Virginia Transportation Museum is in Roanoke.

The largest city in this region is at the southern end. Roanoke and its neighbor, Salem, have over one hundred thousand people and a strong middle-class base.

Southwest Blue Ridge Highlands

Climbing into the mountains, the Southwest Blue Ridge Highlands give way to a Tennessee flavor. This was the earliest jumping off place to America's westward expansion. Daniel Boone, a Virginian by birth, led settlers on the Wilderness Trail through the Cumberland Gap in 1775. Unspoiled natural beauty, small towns, and the feeling of highland living abound and permeate life in the same way the watermen and their culture dominate the flavor of life on the Eastern Shore. Square dancers and cloggers are at almost every local celebration and the hauntingly beautiful mountain music fills the air. Crafts such as quilting fill the numerous shops and craft shows.

Scenic roads and byways are dotted with streams and breathtaking overviews. Natural marvels such as the 850 foot long limestone tunnel, Virginia's highest peak (5,729), and a gorge that has earned the name "Grand Canyon of the South" are but a few of the natural marvels. The pioneers and settlers are alive in exhibits of log cabins, grist mills, the sounds of handcrafted banjoes, fiddles, and dulcimers. Two regional outdoor dramas run during the summer, but winter is a quiet season and colder than Central Virginia.

Blacksburg, home of Virginia Polytechnic Institute and State University (Virginia Tech), offers a glimpse into campus life and some outstanding, nationally-ranked football. In Bristol, a city situated on the Virginia/Tennessee border, the world's fastest half-mile track for NASCAR events can be found. And, of course, the area abounds in swimming, fishing, and picnicking. In the Clinch Mountain Wildlife Management area wild ponies roam free. Clayton Lake State Park offers a 472-acre lake, created by damming the New River in 1939. A cruise affords an excellent way to enjoy the area.

In this area Virginia borders West Virginia, Kentucky, Tennessee, and North Carolina. It is a short trip into any of them. For those who like to shop, there is Tennessee's Pigeon Forge, with one of the largest collections of outlet shopping malls in the country.

Virginia is a Leader in Maximizing the Senior Years

With their love of life and the land as a foundation, Virginians developed the feeling that retirement was a time of freedom from the demands of the working years. It is a time to be looked forward to, to be appreciated for the luxury of time, good thought, the exchange of ideas with others who have lived life and learned from its experiences. Retirement was never looked at as a time of useless decay. It is a time to explore nature, to appreciate gardens and parks, birds and animals. Retirement brings time to read, write, paint, and sculpt.

So Virginia has been a leader in developing quality of life for seniors. Active Senior Centers organize trips of all kinds designed for enjoyment by those who can afford to take a slower, more careful look at the world around them.

State Agencies provide all types of assistance for seniors, at every level. Family support groups reach out to adult children. Merchants offer senior discounts, and newspapers in many towns and communities produce senior supplements once or twice a year. State offices in each jurisdiction offer public presentations designed to reach senior citizens, and there are publications for persons interested in information about aging such as *Silver Linings*, a newspaper aimed at seniors.

Quiet living, bluegrass music, old fashioned values and country crafts mark this area of Virginia.

Retirement in Virginia is not a slide into death, but an opportunity for life with the state and communities actively reaching out to seniors and inviting their participation and residence.

Diverse Housing Possibilities

Housing alternatives in Virginia cover a wide range of options. They are from modest to elegant, from completely independent to some of the finest skilled nursing facilities available anywhere. There are choices of detached houses, condominiums, apartments, and even boarding houses. Some are new; others are converted homes of great age and graciousness that echo a bygone era. Many communities provide access to scenic lakes for fishing, swimming, and boating. Everywhere there is lovely countryside, nature trails, and country roads which wander through picture postcard towns and villages. Golf courses abound, as do trails for walking or horseback riding. Physical fitness facilities provide exercise for the body day or night in any kind of weather. Educational, employment, and volunteer opportunities provide a continuing challenge for the mind. And everywhere in Virginia there is an opportunity to see, meet, or be a writer, painter, or musician.

Analyzing The Situation

One of the most important things for seniors of all ages to do is to take a good look at their situation. People enter their senior years at different times. A person who is in the military or working for a company which offers retirement after twenty years may think of themselves as approaching their senior years when they are ready to retire. This may put them only in their early forties. Others may begin to think of themselves as seniors when they realize that they are eligible for senior discounts at theaters (usually 55) or when they get an invitation to join the AARP at age 50. Many people will continue to work until they are 65, but professionals or self-employed people may continue to work long after that. Whether the person is just entering the senior years (at whatever age that might be) or already considers himself a senior, there is a time when each needs to analyze carefully. It is best to begin early and reevaluate on a regular basis or at least every time a major change take place in life.

Retirement is not the only major change in life. Some people take the opportunity of evaluating their situation when the last child moves away from home. A change in health, even when there is full recovery, may be enough to make a person aware that it is time to do some planning. For older seniors, a realistic evaluation of financial, emotional, and environmental resources can go a long way in developing a plan which will have optimum benefits both now and in the future.

Taking time to plan and evaluate choices does not mean resigning oneself to an idle life of old age. It is simply another step in a process most people have been doing their entire lives. People often evaluate their careers, financial options, and social situations when they begin to think about getting married. Planning a family is another example. Moves made for career advancement, planning for a child's education, going back to school for further education, loss of a job, or even moving up the success ladder are all examples of times in life when people are likely to take a good look at their options before they make decisions and plans.

> " I now contemplate the approach of the moment of my retirement with the fondness of a sailor who has land in view."
> — **Thomas Jefferson**

Planning is the Key

Today's seniors are interested in maximizing their independence and remaining active as long as possible. Planning can increase the length of time that is possible. In addition, a wide variety of facilities have been developed with that goal in mind. Many places offer continuing education classes, craft classes, travel developed for seniors, and short trips to local community events and performances. No longer does senior living mean simply going into a nursing home and being forgotten.

More and more frequently we see actors such as Walter Matthau and Jack Lemmon doing delightfully popular movies at an age when others are simply sitting. Together, this team has brought senior years to life in an example of the

new attitudes on aging. Four out of five of the Best Actor Academy Award nominations for 1997 went to older actors; two were over 60. (Jack Nicholson, winner, age 61; Dustin Hoffman, age 60) Gloria Stuart had an Academy Award nomination for Best Supporting Actress at 87. John Glenn is going into space once again at 76. Not all of our aging population is going quietly into the night, and we can expect the generation behind them to be even more active.

Every Senior is Unique and No Single Choice is Right for Everyone

There is no single choice which is best for every individual. That is one reason why so many different choices have developed. A person who has lived in one area all of his or her life and has family in the area is very different from the person who has moved several times throughout a lifetime and who has family spread over several states. A person who has been married for years may have very different needs than one who is single or someone who has been married several times. As our population has become more educated and more mobile, growing expectations and less attachment to one geographic location has dramatically altered the retirement picture. The best choice can only be made by critically looking at all of the options. There are a number of people such as geriatric care managers, financial planners, elder law practitioners, and social service professionals who can give guidance and suggestions based on particular resources and needs. But each of them will need to be provided with personal information before they can make recommendations.

Physical

Although health is the first thing that comes to mind when a person thinks about analyzing physical resources, it is equally important to think about physical condition and life patterns. People who are at risk due to life-style need to consider that statistically they will need services sooner than the average person. Smokers, for example, may be in good physical health at age 55, but statistically speaking they will need care and medical services within the next ten years. Those who do not have a family history of certain diseases and who do not smoke have a lower chance of needing long-term care within that period of time.

Physical condition is important, not simply because those who exercise on a regular basis are statistically in better health, but from the fact that better physical condition makes daily living easier. Those who are overweight, do not exercise, and are inclined to be involved in sedentary activities for most of the day will experience deterioration of muscle tone and coordination faster. This necessitates eliminating things which require lifting or physical labor at an earlier age. In an area of the country where there is snow, for example, shoveling snow may be not only a physical problem but a life-endangering exercise. Maintaining a private home requires physical activity on an erratic basis. Repairs and maintenance are very necessary at the time they occur and may demand physical activity, but they do not happen frequently enough to condition the body and keep it ready to perform the activity.

In contrast, for those who enjoy recreational activity such as swimming, golf, or even exercise in a gym, retirement communities may make these activities more convenient. The ironic part of the traditional idea of maintaining independence is that it is frequently associated with continuing the same life-style we have had all of our lives when, in fact, a change in life-style may promote more independence.

Eyesight is another consideration. Often seniors have trouble driving at night. This will inhibit mobility and increase the feeling of age. What about lighting in the house? Squinting or struggling to see is exhausting and contributes to the difficulty of even simple tasks and pleasures. An investment in better lighting will do a lot to make daily living more pleasant and keep from feeling old.

Environment

Staying at home may work for some, but the daily care of a home often becomes difficult and consumes more time and energy than the senior may wish to invest. Retirement in senior communities offers amenities such as security, home maintenance, cleaning services, and floorplans designed to eliminate stairs and offer other features to fit the retirement life pattern.

Not all private homes are convenient for seniors. They may be far from doctors or be in neighborhoods full of noise or even crime. Seniors can be easy prey for burglars since they often have a lifetime of collected valuables and little defense in case of a break-in. Burglar alarms and other security devices frequently make entrance, exit, and daily living in the home difficult for seniors who may not have the dexterity to punch in security codes, set locks, or even fasten gates. Parking may not allow for direct entrance to the house. Neighbors may be far away, or because of work schedules not able to keep an eye on the house or its inhabitants. Even such things as garbage pickup may require lifting which can be difficult for seniors.

One of the saddest things today is the senior who hangs on to independence at the cost of good mental health. With so many options available, with so much potential to enjoy life, seniors can often maximize their lives by letting go of their negative attitudes on aging and looking toward many of the positive advances taking place in connection with this rapidly changing time of life.

For a senior who wishes to remain in the family home, the home itself can make a difference. Are the bedrooms downstairs? If the master is upstairs, is there a downstairs bedroom used as a study or guestroom which can be switched with the master bedroom for easier accessibility? Is the home in good condition or is it old enough to need constant upkeep?

How is the home furnished? Lots of clutter makes housekeeping harder. The more overwhelming the task, the less likely it will be done. Are there some items which can be removed, given away, packed away? By evaluating and sorting things collected over a lifetime a little at a time the trauma of eventually moving can be reduced. Take the time to sort through the stored memories and items while still young enough to enjoy the process. This does not mean getting rid of everything dear, it simply means reducing the nonessential so that everything can be seen and important things can be found. Anyone who has lived in a home more than five years has collected things they don't really need. This excess fills space and prevents seeing or enjoying the things of importance.

Is the home in a safe neighborhood? Older people may be perceived as easy targets. Feeling vulnerable decreases self-esteem and feelings of being in control, contributing to the feeling of aging. What are the neighbors like? Does the senior still have anything in common with them or has the neighborhood changed over the years? Do the neighbors know each other? Is there a neighborhood watch? How much interaction is there between neighbors?

Is the house close to a doctor, to friends, to a store? Does the senior entertain frequently? How convenient is it for guests, who may also be aging and may not like to drive on dark roads at night?

Rural living may be more difficult with age because of maintenance, driving distance, and isolation. Are the roads good? Is there a lot of heavy work which is required around the property?

How available is help and how expensive is it? Is the home close to services and programs which are community-based and will help maintain independence? How close are family members and how much are they willing to help?

Are there pets? Animals are wonderful companions, but they also need care. Housing may be influenced by the desire to keep pets. Seniors who wish to move to apartments or retirement communities should find a situation where pets are allowed if that is an important consideration. Some facilities are very pro-pet, others are not. Even at the level of nursing homes, some facilities keep dogs and cats in the building as companions to their residents while other buildings do not have an interest in the role of animals. If the elderly person has been an animal lover and a pet owner for years, it might be very important to find a residence where there are animal companions.

> *Age does not make us childish, as they say. It only finds us true children still.*
>
> Johann Wolfgang von Goethe

Other considerations are important. Does the senior like to play loud music? How about gardening? Are there a lot of vehicles which need to be parked or an RV, a boat, a trailer, or snowmobile? Is there a need for space for a hobby? Will he be working late in a shop which may make noise? Does she take care of grandchildren?

Financial

Evaluate the financial situation. Know what programs are out there to help and how expensive it may be to provide for future health or housing needs. The local Area Agency on Aging can advise what services are available in the area such as home health care, support systems, and facilities. Become familiar with Medicare, Medicaid, and any private insurance plan. Take a good, long look at assets, both in terms of cash and in holdings such as a family home. Decide what kind of disbursement is best under a variety of circumstances and where the vulnerability is in terms of finance.

Since there is no way to predict the future exactly, nor future needs for care, this is one of the most difficult areas to analyze. Some of the following chapters will discuss these considerations in detail. It is important to be educated on options before care is needed because decisions made out of necessity may be very costly. The longer a senior waits to address some of these issues the more limited options will be.

Make Choices Early

A recent study from UCLA had some interesting ramifications for consumers. About one third of the seriously ill adults in the study were willing to die rather than spend the rest of their lives in a nursing home. Another 26% were seriously unwilling to spend the rest of their lives in a nursing home. However, those who were better educated, desired more aggressive treatment, or who were familiar with a facility were much more willing to enter a nursing home. More interestingly, only about 37% of the families and only 18% of the physicians were able to identify what the patient wanted and where he or she wished to go if there were options.

What this tells us is that choices need to be made earlier, before a choice is forced upon the senior by an emergency or made by family or the physician. People who are at risk of needing skilled care within the next five years, either because of existing medical conditions, life-style, family history, or because of age should take the time to investigate their options while there is still a wide range. How far will home care serve the individual and is it the best alternative? What companies are in the area and will they be able to meet projected needs? Most importantly, time should be taken to visit, investigate, and tour assisted living and nursing home facilities which are of interest.

For people of all ages, there is much less fear and apprehension if the future is known and if there has been a chance to be pro-active in the decision. Why should seniors be any different? By taking time to consider options, by educating the senior and the family about skilled long-term care, and by finding a facility which matches the needs and personal preferences of the patient the transition into the nursing home is much easier and positive.

Problems Common Among Seniors

Every phase of life is subject to problems. Adolescents must deal with acceptance and learning who they are. The years of working and raising a family are filled with stress. Likewise the senior years have their own particular problems. Understanding what these problems are is the first step in recognizing and avoiding them.

Isolation and Depression

One of the most common problems for seniors, even those in good health, is the growing feeling of isolation and depression. Again and again studies have shown that the more active seniors stay the less likely they are to suffer from these feelings. Depression is fed by the feeling of helplessness which occurs as seniors find it harder and harder to cope with daily housekeeping and maintenance chores which are necessary in any private home.

Because seniors who live in their homes tend to get out of the house less frequently than those who live in senior-oriented communities, they experience a sense of isolation from friends and families. Even young seniors, newly retired from the daily working routine, are likely to be at a loss on how to fill their days.

Geriatric care providers and social workers are recognizing now that it is important to mental health for retired people to continue to interact with others and to develop new interests. They may become more involved with hobbies they previously had time only to dabble with before retirement. For many travel is an enjoyable pastime.

Regular exercise programs are also a must to maintain flexibility and mobility. At every level of function, there are exercises which can improve health and well-being. If the neighborhood is safe and pleasant, seniors may walk on a regular basis. If not, they may have to drive to a park or place where they can walk. Developing the motivation to exercise at home, even when equipment is available, may be somewhat less successful than developing an exercise program at a regular time with friends or people their own age who have similar needs.

Folk artists and photographers have chronicled for decades the simple pleasures of elders sitting and talking around a checkerboard, at a quilt, or simply sitting on a bench in a park or taking a walk with others of similar years. But for those who do not live in a small town where access to others is easy, these kinds of pleasures are unknown. The *camaraderie* of people with a shared history, such as depicted in *An American Quilt,* is not available to most of today's seniors. The mobility of the middle class, the breakdown of the "neighborhood" in cities, and the decrease of multigenerational living have all attributed to the isolation of seniors who try to fulfill traditional ideas of remaining "young" and "independent."

Based on typical ingrained thought patterns, seniors who like to think of themselves as "young" will often say things such as "I don't want to join a senior center, attend senior classes, or move from my home because I don't like to be around 'old' people. I'm young." While this may be true for some of these people, for the majority these comments are based on ignorance. If they attended some senior programs, went to the senior center, or found out about senior services offered, they would see that their preconceived idea of what is happening in the senior world could not be more wrong. A wide variety of programs, designed to appeal to almost every interest, are funneled through and provided by the Area Agencies on Aging and Senior Centers. There are so many interesting things going on that it would take a very negative person not to find something which appeals to them.

As in any stage in life, a positive self-image is important to both physical and mental well-being. To develop and maintain a positive self-image we need positive feedback. Those who live at home need to make a conscious effort to develop interests, become involved in activities, or work with one of the many volunteer programs. There are many jobs for people of retirement age which require short hours, allowing people to enjoy the leisure of retirement, but also the interest of interacting in the working world. People with nothing to think about beside their failing ability to cope with chores — which were once easy — are almost certainly going to be victims of depression.

America is filled with communities from single-family housing to apartment complexes which provide central community centers where residents can meet and interact. It seems only reasonable that this pattern should be extended to senior living. Communities developed and devoted to seniors often provide a community dining room. Even if it is only once a week that the resident takes a meal there, it allows both the escape from cooking and the interaction with others. Where meals are not provided, common exercise areas, meeting rooms, or periodic health screening can bring members of the community together over common concerns.

Living with Family Members

One alternative to living alone is for elder family members to move in with, or near to, other family members. This has a wide range of success, sometimes providing love and support for all members of the family but often creating stress, guilt, and financial burdens to all generations.

The success of this kind of living depends more on such factors as the size and even floorplan of the home, the relationship and living patterns of the younger generations, the flexibility of the individuals involved, the openness of communication, and financial security than it does on the love which is shared between an adult child and an aging parent. Some of the factors to be considered are:

1) The availability of services for the senior member, how close they are, and how well they meet the social, medical, and recreational needs of the senior member(s) of the family is important.

2) The home situation must be considered carefully. The spouse of the adult child may not be as enthusiastic about bringing additional family members into the household. The personality and pattern of the family, the acceptance of

the senior member(s) by those already living in the household, and the relationship between the husband and wife and between any children living at home and their parents make a big difference in how successful the move will be. Frequently, past relationships between family members and efforts which have been made to understand each other throughout the lifetime of the relationship will determine the success of such a plan.

In a situation where a senior has not made any effort to develop a relationship with the spouse, has been openly critical, or may have tried to exclude the married partner from events, there is likely to be resistance to a move into the home. On the other hand, if there has been a good, strong relationship from the beginning of the marriage between both generations and a genuine bond has developed, it can be very rewarding.

With stepparents, reconstituted families, and children from previous marriages — all of which are common today — there is often a lot of stress revolving around family relations. Statistics show that the divorce rate for second and third marriages is 60%, higher than the rate for first marriages. The largest single reason for such breakups is children. Extending the family to another generation may cause friction in a pattern which is already stretched to the limit. For example, a child from a previous marriage may resent the time, money, and space required by the parent of the new partner even if the spouse is willing to extend care to the aging parent.

3) The attitude of the senior member has a lot to do with the success of a merged living situation. The feeling of loss of control that often comes with moving from independent living to living under the roof of a child causes the senior to try to regain control of their own lives by restructuring, over-advising, or even criticizing others within the existing family. This can sometimes be part of a personality pattern developed from the childhood of the adult child. It can also be subconscious on the part of the senior parent. It can be no more than simply the fact that the senior is moving into a new pattern and is trying to adjust to the new environment and make the new environment into something where he or she can feel comfortable and familiar. For whatever reason, stress is frequently the overall product, even in the most loving and well meaning families.

4) The physical layout and size of the home is a factor. Houses with a lot of space, a room and bath on the first floor, or a wing where seniors can have some privacy and where the family can maintain some privacy work out the best. But often that is not the case. Aging parents may displace a child from his bedroom or take over a home office which may have been either needed or has been a luxury the family has become used to. Resentment can easily develop. New rules about noise, late night visitors, phone calls, or even visiting friends may need to be put in place. They may not be easy to accept, especially for teenagers who are trying to deal with their own new discovery of freedom and self.

5) There can be a lot of pressures on time. The time needed to cope with a new family member, to make them feel part of the family, to help them with tasks they cannot do by themselves, and even to simply shop with them may be difficult to fit into the schedule. Even the time needed to clean, cook, and do laundry for additional members of a family may put a burden on the adult child who may already be taxed to the limit with pressures of a job and family. Every parent

knows how hard it is to arrange the schedule of an active family and how difficult it sometimes is to fit something else into that schedule. Work schedules conflict with school activities. Children must be dropped off or picked up from day care or activities. Social engagements of every member of the family often put one parent going in one direction and the other going in the other direction. Ask any single parent how difficult it is to keep conflicting schedules working smoothly. When a senior is added it may make scheduling even more difficult. Seniors need care, they need time to talk and interact, they have doctor's appointments, and sometimes medication must be monitored. They may need help bathing or getting ready in the morning. All of this can cause an overload of stress.

Often, it is the woman who takes on the new role as the caretaker. She may do it out of feelings of guilt or the perception of what she "ought" to do. But she may then feel guilty because she does not have the time for her job, for the children, or for her husband. In such a trap the woman will feel guilty no matter which road she chooses, and it is a lose-lose situation for everyone concerned. Working women, or those who truly do not have the time, must be able to call on such services as adult day care, home health care, respite care, or senior programs if the move is to be successful. In addition a woman must be able to recognize her limits and not feel guilty about them.

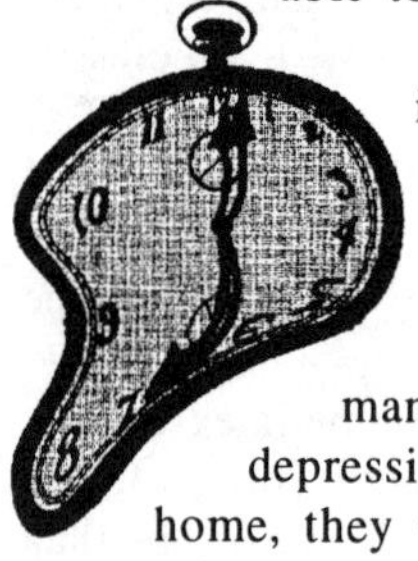

Seniors left alone all day may experience the same feelings of loneliness, isolation, and depression as they would if they lived alone. To feel valuable, they may drive themselves to do something around the house, to help "pay" for their care. But instead of taking care of cleaning and maintenance for only one or two elderly people, this may be the more demanding work connected with an entire family. If the former is depressing, the latter is overwhelming. And, when the family arrives home, they want to have time to talk and be included. Statistics indicate that although many families still share a family dinner hour there are many who do not. When family members come home from work or school only to rush off in different directions, it may leave the senior feeling even more isolated and alone than before.

6) Unrealistic expectations may cause friction. Not all members of the family may have the same ideas about the roles of other members. An adult child may expect that the aging parent will provide after school child care for young children. This may not be something the senior member wishes or feels comfortable coping with. The aging parent may expect to be consulted about family decisions, or included in family trips or activities, while the family of the household may look at these times as a chance to get away. Painting, yard work, housekeeping, and even auto care can easily become points of conflict. Remember, in most cases, the two generations have had years of independent living and decision making, free from the advice and criticism of the other. Even simply sharing chores and assigning activities which are appropriate for the abilities may be difficult. A parent may not be willing to admit that they can no longer do something, or they may feel that because of their age they should not be asked to do anything.

7) A critical element is the financial situation. With so many families relying on a two-person income, reduced work time to meet the needs of a senior family member may cause pressures on the budget. Even the simple decision about going out to dinner or to the movies with one or two extra people can

become a financial problem. Extra food, sometimes the demands of special dietary needs, home renovations, and the need for such things as help with housekeeping or yard work because there is no longer the time may put pressures on a budget, even of a middle-class family.

These are some of the things which can make moving an aging parent into a family more difficult than first imagined. The love of a parent and the desire to do the right thing for them often overshadows practical concerns. Failure to be able to keep everyone happy, stress within the family, and added burdens often result in guilt and anxiety. No matter how completely issues are discussed ahead of time, it is sometimes impossible to foresee problems which arise. Careful consideration should be given to all alternatives, from all angles, before a parent is moved into the household.

Studies have shown that the best arrangement is a separate living facility on the same property. In some areas a trailer or a garage addition will pass zoning codes and allow for privacy for both generations. But this often ignores the needs of the senior in terms of feelings of isolation, helplessness, or depression. Seniors need interaction and activities of their own to maintain their self-worth.

If it does not work out, all members of the family must realize that it may not be a measure of love or commitment. It should not be a source of guilt or accusations from the adult child if the rest of the members of the family cannot cope.

The Trauma of Moving From Home

One of the most common problems of moving to retirement housing is the trauma of moving from a home which has been part of the senior's life for many years. Some seniors see the move away from the home they have occupied for years as the beginning of a slippery slope toward a bleak future. Others do not want to leave the memories of a family which once occupied the home. For some it is simply the feeling of loss of independence. And for some it is simply the problem of trying to fit the possessions of a lifetime into a smaller living unit.

The key to success, as with most of senior living, is that the senior focus on what is being gained instead of what is being lost. The knowledge and experience of a lifetime should teach that nothing is ever all positive or all negative. Every gain involves some loss. From the choice of a job, to marriage and children, to the purchase of a home there are always things which must be given up in order to reach the desired goal. Seniors who continue to experience life by realizing that change is a part of living have the greatest success in maximizing their retirement years.

Women outlive men in every racial and economic category. At ages 65+ there are overall 20 million women but only 13.9 million men. At ages 65-69 there are 120 women for every 100 men, but by age 85+ this ratio increases to 257 women per 100 men. Because of these figures, older men are much more likely to be married than older women. Half of all older women are widows and there are five times as many widows as widowers. Divorced older persons represent only 6% of all seniors, but their numbers have increased three times as fast as the older population as a whole since 1990. Research has shown that men's brains shrink due to aging much faster and at an earlier age than do women's brains!

This resistance to moving causes concern for adult children who may fear that an aging parent is overtaxed at home. The possibility that the elder person may fall or have an attack in the middle of the night and not be able to summon help is a concern. Adult children often begin to notice that the overall care and maintenance of the home is slipping as the senior is less able to perform housekeeping chores. Frequently seniors begin to rely on quick-fix foods or may neglect eating on a regular schedule. If special diets are necessary for control of medical conditions this can be a particular concern.

It is extremely important to realize that moving into senior housing at an earlier level is easier than moving into it at a later level. Services, care, convenience, and social outlets give a senior **more independence not less.** The senior community helps keep people more active, enjoying life longer. It keeps them from dwelling on problems because there is nothing else happening in their lives. It keeps them from letting the daily problems of living loom out of proportion. And it preserves positive self-image which is eroded when the aging parent must impose on family members or outside help to do something they could once do for themselves.

The earlier the issues of moving can be addressed and the more positive the attitude is about the move the better. If a person waits to move into a senior living situation only after they are completely unable to live on their own it will necessarily take on the air of defeat. This attitude often robs the senior of years of enjoyable living and leaves them bitter about their situation and sometimes even against the loved ones who have participated in organizing the move.

It is far better to take the time to look into areas for retirement, housing which is available, and opportunities it offers when seniors are still young and active enough to make decisions on their own. When people wait until poor mental or physical health dictates a move, choices are made under emergency conditions, or by other family members, and the seniors have even more feelings of loss and lack of control over their own lives.

If done ahead of time, planning can enrich the sharing between generations. A family home can be sold, taking the time to maximize profit. Plans can be made for the best way to accomplish the move, and careful selection of a facility can maximize the quality of life today while planning for the needs of tomorrow.

There is nothing more difficult than having to move a senior into a nursing home suddenly. They cannot close their own home. They have no say over what happens to their things. They have no real choice between facilities. If done before a crisis arises, the move is certainly a letting go of one part of life, but it is a chance to enjoy new opportunities with the elimination of some of the day-to-day chores which have made demands on their time for many years. It is a chance to make new friends at a time in life when old friends may be slipping away. And it is a chance to share and enjoy new opportunities.

Keeping Active

Sometimes small things can make a big difference in terms of feeling old. Mental attitude has a lot to do with well being and things which promote a positive attitude can help seniors stay active longer.

Studies have shown over and over again that recovery, even from major illnesses like cancer or stroke, is affected by mental attitude and by the physical condition of the person at the onset of the illness. The older a person gets the more important it is to pay attention to physical condition and mental well-being.

Begin with small things. Take a look around you and begin to notice things which you might not have paid attention to before. Lighting is an example. Seniors require more light to see than younger members of the family. If lighting at home is increased to accommodate eyes which do not adjust as well as they did in the past, there is the overall feeling of being able to cope and function. Poor light can be exhausting and it contributes to the difficulty of even simple tasks and pleasures. This enforces the perception that one is too old to do things, reduces self-esteem, and contributes to an overall impression that things are progressing in a negative manner. An investment in better lighting will do a lot to make daily living more pleasant and keep from feeling old.

The same is true when a senior travels. Typically hotel rooms have low watt bulbs to reduce power bills when guests leave the lights turned on. By bringing along additional lighting, or even a few 75 or 100 watt lightbulbs, a hotel room can be much more inviting and make the senior traveler feel much younger.

Use-It-or-Lose-It!

The older a person gets the more the old adage "use it or lose it" applies. Both mental and physical exercise and challenge become more and more important in maintaining the maximin level of function. Aging accelerates when people cease to learn, to be interested in things and people around them, and to evaluate what is happening in their world.

As we grow older and retire our lives take a turn in the opposite direction. During the working years, those which encompass raising a family and caring for a house, we are often faced with so many challenges simultaneously that we cannot help but be overloaded. This stress can take its toll on health and mental outlook. Relaxation and other techniques help us handle stress and unwind and are a very important part of our lives.

But once people reach retirement they often find themselves in the reverse situation with no familiar pattern of how to cope. The need to take time to relax and eliminate or reduce stress is turned around. The family has grown up and children are out on their own, managing their own families. The job is left in the hands of others. The stress and tension of daily worries has greatly reduced. At this point the problem is no longer eliminating or managing stress, which requires relaxation, but in finding a challenge or an interest which will keep a person active and maintain feelings of self-worth.

This need to remain active and challenged is widely accepted and is the basis of most senior programs today. Whether it is a window garden brought to a very infirm patient in a nursing center, a discussion of the current news topics at a senior day care center with Alzheimer's patients, or a volunteer program for active seniors run by a senior center, the philosophy is the same. When seniors stay active, interested, and interacting they do more to keep themselves young than any medical treatment available can do for them.

One of the saddest things is seniors who have a negative outlook on programs, senior centers, and interaction with other seniors in general. Their belief that they are remaining "young" simply because they live in their own home may be a poor evaluation of their situation and completely counterproductive to that end.

Contrary to popular mythology, it is often not the aging and deteriorating seniors who sell their homes and move to senior living communities but those who are the most active. Seniors who are still very active may prefer to sell their home for a good price, without doing any senior remodeling, and move into a community designed and developed to serve senior needs. There they will have a ready-made group of people who enjoy many of the same things and who talk on the same level as they do, instead of living in a neighborhood full of children. They will have easy access to social events which appeal to them, travel groups, and volunteer programs which make use of their knowledge and experience. Because these communities often include routine home maintenance, seniors can spend time on hobbies or activities which interest them.

Having other people around to interact with can do a lot to maintain a positive outlook. People who have been isolated or had few friends for most of their lives have more risk of becoming depressed with age. Sharing life experiences, interacting with people who are interested in the same things, and knowing there are others who are experiencing the same problems and challenges goes a long way to keeping the problems of aging in perspective. Casual gatherings for conversation, a game of bridge, a partner for dancing, or a companion for lunch make a big difference in maintaining a positive attitude. Shared laughter does more to keep a person young than almost anything else.

As an example let's take three couples. They are in their mid-70's and in reasonably good health. Mr. and Mrs. Thompson have lived in their home for several years. They live within driving distance of their children. Their home is twenty miles from town, on a winding, two-lane road. They are having trouble maintaining the house now. They must call someone in for tree removal after a storm. They cannot get out of their home, which is on a hill, when it snows. They appreciate a program provided by the garbage collector, who comes up their driveway to get their garbage because they are seniors. They have a well, with a filter which must be changed and they find it confusing. Frequently they must call someone to look at it because they have trouble maintaining the system. Last year they had bats in the attic and had to spend a lot of time finding an exterminator. They have bottled water because they like the taste better than their well water, but they must get someone else to lift the bottle onto the cooler because it is too heavy for Mr. Thompson to lift. Mrs.

Thompson is having trouble keeping the house clean and sometimes gets very frustrated with the mess. She gets tired of cooking for just the two of them and frequently falls back on frozen dinners. These meals are often high in sodium which aggravates several medical conditions, including high blood pressure and some heart problems.

They will not visit the senior center or entertain the thought of moving because, as Mrs. Thompson puts it, "I don't like being around all those old people!" But they spend most of the day at home, thinking about how frustrating it is because they cannot do many of the things they used to do. Because of busy schedules family members do not visit more than once a week. When they do, Mrs. Thompson is fussy, complaining that they never see anyone. Visits there by family members are often put off because they are never short. When a family member tries to cut a visit short, Mrs. Thompson fusses that the visitor "just got here" or "...you never want to spend any time." The problem is that in truth a visit is a welcome change of pace for her and she does not want it to end. The effect is that family members often find themselves putting off a visit because of the pressure to stay.

They have no hobbies or interests. Their recreation consists of watching old movies, TV, or going for aimless drives. Last year it was recommended that Mrs. Thompson have knee surgery because she can only hobble with the use of a cane. Due to the distance from town, the doctor suggested that she go to a nursing home for recovery so that she could get frequent physical therapy. She decided not to have the surgery because that would leave Mr. Thompson alone in the house. They have been married almost 60 years during which time she has never worked. As a homemaker, she has done all of the cooking and running the house. Her fear that Mr. Thompson might not even be able to get his own meals is probably well-founded. They have missed the graduation of their grandchildren from high school and college within the past few years because Mrs. Thompson has trouble walking a long distance. Because she is not exposed to other seniors, and has not taken the interest to learn how to solve problems caused by age and develop new adaptions, she does not realize she could easily rent a wheelchair (although she does not need one at home) for the graduation and use the handicap access to have a wonderful view and participate in the big day. They are becoming more and more isolated every year, not only from the world and the community, but even from their family.

Early this year, Mr. Thompson had some heart problems which required him to be hospitalized. Mrs. Thompson does not drive much and it was very difficult for her to visit him. She got lost several times trying to find the hospital, even after family members had driven her there several times.

Every year their world gets smaller and smaller. At Christmas they focus on whether this will be their last Christmas. Their old friends pass away and their world gets smaller with even fewer people to call on the phone, or as Mrs. Thompson puts it, "Every year my Christmas card list gets shorter and shorter."

Compare this with Mr. and Mrs. Finley. They have also been married for over fifty years. They live in town. They are very active in the senior center. They have meetings with others about things of interest in the community. Mr. Finley is very interested in the proposed laws which would limit driver's licenses for seniors. He is on a committee which has met with State Representatives and DMV officials.

Mrs. Finley attends a group which makes crafts which are for sale in the senior center shop. She also teaches craft classes to students for a special project run by the city. Sometimes they go to lunch with friends, and last year Mr. Finley helped put on the Womanless Fashion Show and lunch which was part of the Senior Center fund-raiser. He was not interested in being one of the men who dressed up in outrageous women's fashions, but he contacted local businesses for donations of raffle prizes and had the tickets printed at a local printer.

Their children drop by and visit. There is always a lot to talk about. Sometimes Mr. Finley will become quite animated about what the state is proposing. Two of the grandchildren attended the Fashion Show and thought it was very funny.

When Mr. Finley went into the hospital because of his high blood pressure, Mrs. Finley used the transportation for seniors which is set up in town. The nutrition center is now helping her plan meals which will help control his blood pressure and several times a week they eat at the senior center congregate meals program. This means Mrs. Finley doesn't have to cook, and they can visit others and talk with friends.

Their home is small enough for them to take care of without much trouble. The Senior Center keeps a list of people who will do work for seniors or organizations which will help with larger projects. Last year their porch roof came off during a bad storm. The storm also kept them inside. The local senior services made sure they had medication and food until the snow could be cleared. The outreach services helped them file their insurance claims and find someone to fix the porch. Because of unexpected medical expenses the Finleys were short of money during that winter and the local energy program made sure they had fuel for heating in spite of their financial problems. A legal aid official is helping them apply for benefits which will cover these additional medical expenses.

Finally there are the Sheldons. They live in a retirement community. Mr. Sheldon likes to spend time in the community work shop. He and several friends he made there enjoy working with wood, and he has learned several new techniques. Mrs. Sheldon goes with several other women on the shopping trips run by the community. This saves her from driving and she enjoys the conversation on the way. Mr. Sheldon has never enjoyed shopping, even for groceries, and he is very pleased that he does not have to keep her company. Last week they went to the community playhouse, and Mrs. Sheldon is still talking about the trip the group took to the Carpenter Center in Richmond where they saw a production on its way to New York. These trips were organized through the retirement community. This fall they are planning on going to England with a group of seniors from the community.

They have a garden this year, but they traveled most of last summer, and the community took care of the yard and their home while they were gone.

Last year, in spite of the flu shot she had received at the community health center, Mrs. Sheldon went into the hospital unit of the community with a bad case of flu. When Mr. Sheldon visited her he walked to the center and then went to the community dining room for his meals because he hates to cook for himself. Besides, he needs a special diet for his diabetes and, although the center has helped Mrs. Sheldon plan meals for him, he finds it easier to stay on his diet by using the dining services. After she came home and recovered from her illness, Mrs. Sheldon felt weak. She attended exercise classes designed to help her regain her strength and she now she feels just like her old self. Last year two of their good friends passed away. One left a wife and the Sheldon's have provided a lot of support for her. They have also become good friends with several younger seniors who have recently moved into the community. One of them is a single man and Mrs. Sheldon is trying to get him interested in the retired schoolteacher who moved in last year. Mr. Sheldon says she should leave the poor man alone!

Neither the Finleys or the Sheldons suffer from more than occasional depression, while the Thompsons are depressed frequently. While the Thompsons went through Christmas focusing on whether it would be their last, the other two couples went to parties at the community center or senior center. They visited friends throughout the season. Mr. Sheldon made several gifts in the workshop and was very pleased with the outcome. While baking by herself is quite a bit of work, Mrs. Finley got together with several other women and they baked cookies while they talked and visited. Mrs. Thompson didn't do any baking this year. In fact, she didn't do much decorating. It seemed so hard and she says she "just couldn't get into Christmas this year." The Finleys went to the Senior Center for a wonderful performance by the High School chorus. It included several of their favorite pieces. The Thompsons went to the *Nutcracker* with a group.

Programs are out there for everyone. They work. Keeping fit physically is important for the body, but keeping active socially and intellectually is important to keep the mind fit. Aging is not what it used to be. Senior living is changing every year. Health care professionals, social workers, state and federal agencies, and community programs are extending not only life but functional, useful, enjoyable life for thousands every year. Seniors who are open-minded enough to reach out and make use of these dozens of programs will be well rewarded.

One activities director who works with people in their mid to late 80's and 90's is pleased to report that many of them are making great efforts to stay mentally alert and active. They are interested in current events, news stories, and special reports. Not only did they watch such stories, listen to them on the radio, and read about them, but they enjoy talking about these events with each other and with the staff. Many residents keep their minds active by playing bridge, working crossword puzzles, doing jigsaw puzzles (either individually or as a group), and watching quiz shows on TV.

Exercise classes are well attended. Seniors who begin an exercise program and stick to it with some regularity will almost always enjoy increased mobility, strength, and flexibility. It is important for seniors living at home to remember that simply walking around the house or doing simple chores does not constitute an exercise program nor will it give the benefits. But exercise must be designed for the level of function. Almost everyone, even those with severe physical limitations, can enjoy some kind of regular exercise which will help them maintain or even increase their mobility.

More and more seniors are being encouraged to write or record their family history. Computers, video cameras, and tape recordings have made this easier for those who may hesitate to sit down and write. When complete, a copy donated to the local historical society may find a place in scholarly work of the future. Family histories do more than educate the next generation about those who have gone before. They record life experiences and are capsules of time for all generations to follow. One of the most important programs to come out of the New Deal was the recording of personal histories. Although it was seen at the time as a way to provide employment for the interviewers, these collections of recollections have become invaluable to historians and scholars who strive to understand the forces and influences of the past. It is sometimes amazing what people have stored in their minds which will indicate to later generations what was going on in a particular period and location. The well-known *Little House* series by Laura Ingalls Wilder was originally a family history of life in the 1870's and '80's and a rich first-hand record of pioneer life, and they have become some of the most popular books ever written for boys and girls. Helen Hooven Santmyer published her novel *...And Ladies of the Club* in 1982 through Ohio State University Press. It was an account of the life of women in a small Ohio town and reflected the time and the sweeping changes of modern life on women of the period. Although she had been working on it for decades, she was 88 years old and in a retirement home when she finished it. In 1984 it was picked up by G.P. Putman's Sons and became a best-seller. She completed one more work before she died.

Even at advanced age and with physical limitations, many residents are volunteering in the community. They feel they still have something to give and the work supports their self-esteem. Programs are available for almost everyone from working at local libraries to volunteering as a peer provider to homebound seniors. Most senior centers use senior volunteers for their lunch programs. The Foster Grandparents Program is one of the largest and most successful. Each weekday seniors leave their homes and head out into the community to give love and support to at-risk children. They work in Head Start programs, in schools, at day care centers, hospitals, treatment centers, battered women's shelters and anywhere there are children who need someone to love.

For those who might doubt the effectiveness of the Foster Grandparents Program, the Capital Area Agency on Aging printed this poem written by a terminally ill young girl about one of her Foster Grandparent volunteers!

Often I look in the mirror and I see,
That in my eyes where tears used to be
Shines a single sparkle, only because you know how to love me.
You showed me the true meaning of love.
And when it's done right, it feels like it's from above.
What you've given to me, I could never return.
You were so patient and willing, to teach me all the things I needed to learn.
You understood me when no one else could understand;
Made me feel relevant and wanted, eager to lend a soothing hand.
You taught me how to bring out all the powers I possessed.
How to use it to my advantage, be enduring and sexy with finesse.

Buzzwords, Lingo, and Categories

The long-term care industry, and other senior care or senior living options, use conflicting terms, many of which overlap and almost none of which have well defined parameters holding true in all cases. Part of the reason for this is that the industry has developed slowly over the years, being patched and padded as it expanded rather than growing to maturity in a short time with well defined goals.

In times past medical technology was not so well developed that there was any real question of prolonging life. No technological advances demanded skills beyond compassion and comfort. Care and love were about all that was available, and when it failed life ebbed away.

Today that has changed dramatically. There are many life and death questions which simply did not have to be answered half a century, or even a decade, ago. As life-prolonging technology has developed, there are always questions about when to let go. Hospitals, nursing homes, and acute care centers are necessary in many cases because the care required by the patient demands trained staff and expensive, sophisticated equipment.

But not all seniors need that level of care. Some of them need daily care or have conditions which mandate that they should not be living alone in case of emergency. Some of them are simply forgetful about medication, or the medication schedule may be too complex for them to manage. Diversified needs have resulted in diversified facilities and companies.

To answer the changing needs of the elderly the government has developed regulations and agencies to monitor medical and daily care of residents. Lawyers, who were a well established profession (writing the Declaration of Independence and the Constitution) at a time when medical doctors were still using leeches and did not need a license to practice, are now on the back side of the curve, trying to regulate and monitor medical practices developed within the lifespan of a single judge!

Traditional Categories of Facilities

Probably the most confusing thing about senior living is trying to understand the basic categories of facilities. Take heart. In some cases even people within the industry cannot reach a consensus on what category a facility should fall into.

In addition, states vary considerably in how they define and regulate facilities. For example, assisted living housing is just that in Alabama, *assisted living.* In New Mexico such residences are classified as *adult residential shelter care homes.* In Virginia they are classified as *Homes for Adults,* and are termed in the regulations as *Adult Care Residences.*

Independent Living

Traditionally, *Independent Living* means residences for seniors who are in good health and able to live on their own. These communities are different from seniors who are *living independently* in the general population. Those who are living independently simply remain in their homes, in the same neighborhoods where they have been living. Or they may have sold a home which had become too large for them and purchased a more appropriate one in a location which appealed to them in a neighborhood with mixed age residents.

Naturally Occurring Senior Communities develop without planning simply because the neighborhood remains stable. Usually this happens in areas where a group of homes have been built at one time and sold to young families. These families age, the children grow up and move out. But, if the neighborhood is appealing and provides services and an atmosphere which is pleasing, if it is perceived to be safe, and particularly if property values have not skyrocketed to the point that seniors feel it is in their best interest to sell for the capital gain, many of the residents may remain in place. This makes the community as a whole a senior community. Because of that, when property is sold, senior buyers are attracted to it. Realtors are reporting this phenomenon more and more.

Elsewhere independent living communities have been built and developed from the onset as senior communities. Within that group is a wide range of situations. In Northern Virginia there are a number of high-rise apartments and condo buildings which are designed for seniors. In central Virginia independent living could mean a community of homes grouped around a golf course which is designed to appeal to seniors! In Scottsville, Virginia, a school has been renovated to give housing to low income seniors, while in Richmond a church has been converted into a home to accommodate seniors. In Virginia Beach a trailer park, owned and operated by a private individual, has a section set aside for seniors. The owner is a young man who likes seniors as tenants and who performs services for them because he considers them part of his "family." He has been successfully providing good deeds and a helpful hand to his older tenants for many years and has enjoyed the company of seniors from dozens of different states.

HUD and other subsidy programs provide low income housing for seniors who qualify. At the other end are expensive communities with golf courses and country clubs where seniors buy their homes, and can sell them, making a profit if the property values have increased.

Today many seniors who would have once been living in *residential homes* are in independent living properties, sometimes because of new trends and an extension of services provided by these independent living communities. These residents do not need much help, but they may have some physical or mental impairments and require a little assistance with the activities of daily living. In the past, if older people could not completely maintain themselves and their property, they were considered candidates for residential care. Now most senior living communities make maintenance and housekeeping available along with other amenities such as security and transportation. At the far end of this category are properties which have contracted for medical or daily living assistance for their residents. When services which were formerly associated with residential communities are provided by senior living communities, they do not need to be licensed, although they must of course comply with local and state building codes and real estate laws.

When we were contacting facilities for this book we found that many of these residences fell into a third category. Especially in older or rural areas group homes have developed. They can almost be termed a kind of cottage industry. These properties do not really have a director. Residents are able to function and perform daily activities. There may be a common kitchen and sitting room with a TV. Residents may have assigned chores for the common area. These are like a boarding houses which caters to seniors. The phone is often answered by a resident. Sometimes cleaning or cooking is provided.

In many cases the owner or director may be almost as old as the other residents. Usually there is only one property for the owner, and he or she may live in the building; occasionally there are two or three properties owned by the same person. This pattern is typical of many senior properties of a decade or more ago. We regret to report that many of them were rude and uncooperative with no interest in providing the consumer with information. Often all of their residents were local people who knew about the home. None of this kind of facility replied to our questionnaire, and they are not reported in this book in the directory section. Even if you or a family member are local to this kind of property, take the time to look at other options. Just because you are familiar with a property there may be places more interested in offering services and a philosophy much more likely to provide a high quality of life.

Assisted Living

The next traditional category is *Assisted Living.* These facilities care for seniors who need some help with daily life. At one extreme it could simply mean that these seniors are no longer able to care for their home and maintain it. Or they may need a reminder for medication, help with a bath, cooking and meal supervision, or dressing. At the other end of the category, many assisted living facilities are now opening units for Alzheimer's patients or units for people who need more critical care. Many of the services which were once handled by nursing homes are now being handled by assisted living facilities. Skilled care may be available, allowing a senior to stay longer at one facility or allowing a senior who has a temporary need for a higher level of care to receive it without moving to another location.

Residential Living, Assisted Living, or *Residential Homes* are all the same as far as being interchangeable terms. They are not, however, the same from property to property. In the past these residential living facilities were called *Old Folks Homes, Rest Homes, Retirement Homes,* or *Elder Care Homes.* All of these terms are no longer in common usage, although some phone books still use **Rest Homes** as a listing. When the term is used, it usually applies to a private house or a residence sponsored by a group, in many cases a church.

These properties need to be licensed if they provide maintenance or care of four or more adults who are aged, infirm, or disabled who are not related to the caregiver by blood or marriage. Residential or assisted living facilities are licensed and regulated in the state of Virginia under the Department of Social Services. They are not regulated or supervised as rigidly as *Nursing Homes.* Today, however, many of them provide services which were previously associated with nursing homes. When they do provide such services, they still operate under their social services license and provisions.

Many of these properties are owned by private individuals or groups of investors who own fewer than five properties. More and more of them are being built or acquired by corporations each year.

Services may vary greatly from state to state and from facility to facility. According to one survey, assisted living commonly includes assistance with activities of daily living, transportation, laundry, activities and/or recreation, arranging health-related services, housekeeping, medications management, and health status monitoring. The average age for assisted living is 82, which is down from the previous average of 84. One reason for the lower age, in spite of the fact that people are living and remaining active longer, is that assisted living facilities are expanding their programs to include social and occupational programs making them more appealing to residents. Individualized goals for each resident promote quality of life and have helped seniors focus on the positive benefits of such senior housing.

Many of these assisted living facilities are adding Adult Day Care Centers. Since they already have the staff and the program, it may be a simple thing for them to adapt an area or build an addition which will allow them to expand their services to a wider range of people without having to add additional services or skills. Empty beds, sometimes in a special area, may allow them to offer respite care.

Nursing Homes

Nursing Home, or *Long-Term Care Facilities* provide skilled care. These residents need specialized help. Like assisted living facilities, the range of nursing homes is evolving. Many of them are adding subacute units or specialized units to serve patients who once would have needed to remain in the hospital. Nursing home beds are more cost effective than hospitals and moving subacute patients to nursing homes frees up the hospital beds for more seriously ill patients.

These properties are licensed under the Department of Health, Office of Health Facilities Regulations. Their regulations are very stringent.

Continuing Care

Continuing Care or *Life Care,* communities are one of the oldest forms of planned senior communities. Seniors who are in good health move into the communities, usually paying an entry fee and a monthly fee. As they need more care they are moved to assisted living or nursing home units which are part of the community. The practice of having all senior care in one community is what gives rise to the name.

Adult Day Care

Adult Day Care means exactly what it says. Seniors who need or want help with daily living chores, need supervision, or monitoring of medications may attend an adult day care center. This is a low-cost alternative for people who have care from family in the evening. It allows them to remain with their families, but it gives family caregivers the ability to continue working or to have time away from the responsibility of continuously caring for the dependent family member.

Respite Care

Respite Care is usually associated with adult day care centers. When a family is traveling, or simply needs a night off, the elder person in their care may stay overnight if the facility offers respite care. Meals and overnight supervision are provided on a temporary basis until the caregiver can take over the job once again.

Terms for Professionals and the Regulations Governing Senior Care

An **Administrator** is the licensee or person designated by the licensee who oversees the day-to-day operation of the facility, including compliance with all regulations for licensed adult care residences or nursing homes. By contrast, the **Director** may be the manager of the facility, but is not necessarily licensed by the state.

Qualified Activities Professional is a person who has completed a ninety-hour course and is then acceptable to meet the Nursing Home Regulations requirements of providing activities on an appropriate level for residents. A **Recreational Therapist** is a person who has a four-year degree in recreation. They are highly skilled and trained to deal with the many levels of disability now seen in the long-term care setting. Both of these staff members are part of a new concern in the industry to rehabilitate people of all ages who suffer from disabilities. An **Occupational Therapist** works with redeveloping skills used in everyday living.

Ombudsman is an appointed official who assists patients and their families with concerns of patient care; serves as a link between patients and staff; lends an ear for patients who wish to express problems and concerns of a financial, social, family, or legal nature; provides families and patients with information about rights, governmental benefits, and other agencies and services. The Ombudsman program was set up in 1979 and expanded in 1983 by the Virginia General Assembly to include homes for adults and community-based long-term care services.

Qualified assessor means a person contracting with the Department of Medical Assistance Services to perform nursing facility pre-admission screening or to complete the uniform assessment instrument for a home and community-based waiver program, including an independent physician contracting with the Department of Medical Assistance Services to complete the uniform assessment instrument for residents of adult care residences, or any hospital which has contracted with the Department of Medical Assistance Services to perform nursing facility pre-admission screenings.

ADL refers to activities of daily living. This is defined as bathing, dressing, toileting, transferring, bowel control, bladder control and eating/feeding. A person's degree of independence in performing these activities is a part of determining appropriate level of care and services.

IADL (Instrumental activities of daily living) means meal preparation, housekeeping, laundry, and managing money. A person's degree of independence in performing these activities is part of determining appropriate level of care and services.

Individualized service plan means the written description of actions to be taken by the licensee to meet the assessed needs of the resident.

UAI, the Uniform Assessment Instrument, was passed in 1996. This code of evaluation provides a guideline for patient assessment in a number of different areas. It is designed to promote uniformity and uniform assessment patient-to-patient and building-to-building. Its goal is to match patients and their needs with facilities and the services they provide.

Surveys are state inspections of long-term care facilities. A **survey team** is a group of state or federal inspectors who enter a building unannounced and inspect records, patient care, menus, medication administration, and other aspects of the facility which are mandated by state or federal regulation. When problems are found, appropriate action is taken which can range from a warning to a severe fine and withdrawal of state funds until the problem is corrected.

OBRA refers to the Ombudsman Budget Reconciliation Act of 1987. This was a nursing home reform act which greatly changed much of senior living. The field of Elder Law was an outgrowth of new issues in financing, eligibility, and residents' rights which were provided in the bill. On the other side, OBRA required long-term care facilities to develop a residential care plan and documentation which supports that plan for each resident.

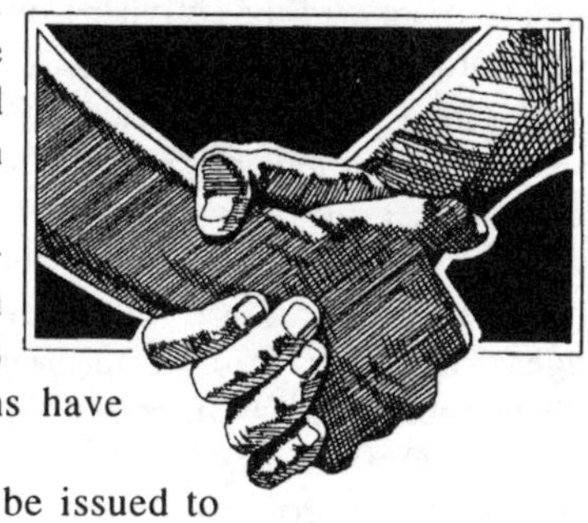

HCFA is the Health Care Financing Administration. This is the agency dealing with Medicare and Medicaid. It is under the auspices of their funding that survey and evaluation teams have developed.

License refers to the permit which must be issued to allow a facility to operate. Nursing homes, assisted living facilities, adult day care, home health care companies, and continuing care communities (the nursing and assisted living part of continuing care, not the entire community) must have a license to operate. The license covers the physical plant. In order to operate the facility must be in compliance with fire codes, have proper control of drugs and medication, comply with Safety Regulations, Sanitary Codes, and Food Service Health Codes.

Certification refers to what is needed to qualify for Medicaid and Medicare money. If a facility has only one patient under Medicare or Medicaid, it must be certified. Such certification involves providing **Interdisciplinary Care Plans** for each patient to provide for all aspects of the patient's needs. Activities, social interaction, nutritional needs, and interaction with family are important as well as medical care. Records must document all care and treatment given to support that plan. Inspections of the facility are done twice a year when a facility is certified.

Terms Used By The State of Virginia

Virginia defines *assisted living* as a level of service provided by an adult care residence for adults who may have physical or mental impairments and require at least a moderate level of assistance with activities of daily living.

Administer medication means to open a container of medicine or to remove the prescribed dosage and to give it to the resident for whom it is prescribed.

Ambulatory refers to anyone who is physically and mentally able to exit the residence without assistance in an emergency and who can ascend or descend stairs if present in any necessary exit path. A person may also be considered ambulatory under certain provisions if they require limited assistance such as a wheelchair, walker, cane, prosthetic device, or single verbal command. *Independently mobile* is another term which is interchangeable with ambulatory.

Case management means multiple functions designed to link clients to appropriate services. Case management may include a variety of common components such as initial screening of needs, comprehensive assessment of needs, development and implementation of a plan of care, service monitoring, and client follow-up. A **case manager** is a person who is qualified and designated to develop and coordinate plans of care.

Continuous licensed nursing care means around-the-clock observation, assessment, monitoring, supervision, or provision of medical treatments provided by a licensed nurse.

Chemical restraints are drugs used to keep residents from falling out of bed, wheelchairs, or from wandering around a nursing home when they are no longer able to control their bodies or make appropriate decisions. *Physical restraints* mean the resident is strapped into a bed, chair, or wheelchair. In 1997 the state of Virginia put a particular emphasis on making all nursing homes *restraint free.* This means that such restraints are not in use.

Direct care staff means supervisors, assistants, aides, or other employees of a facility or home health care who assist residents in their daily living activities.

Discharge means the movement of a resident out of the adult care residence or hospital. Before a resident is released to return home (for example, after a fall or accident) the case worker or social service worker, or other qualified assessor, should prepare an assessment of needs and a **Discharge Plan.** This includes the level of care which is needed to function in the home and who will provide it.

Independent physician means a physician who is chosen by the resident of the adult care residence and who has no financial interest in the adult care residence directly or indirectly, as an owner, officer, employee, or as an independent contractor with the residence.

Maintenance or *care* means the protection, general supervision, and oversight of the physical and mental well-being of the aged, infirm, or disabled individual.

Maximum physical assistance, moderate assistance, or *minimal assistance* is a rating of the individual according to how many of the seven activities of daily living there is need for assistance according to the uniform assessment instrument. This in turn is used to develop an assessment of needs and a care plan. You have a right to ask about such plans either as a resident or for a family member.

Nonambulatory means a resident of an adult care residence who by reason of physical or mental impairment is unable to exit the residence in an emergency without the assistance of another person.

Residential living means a level of service provided by an adult care residence for adults who may have physical or mental impairments and require only minimal assistance with the activities of daily living. This definition includes independent living facilities that voluntarily become licensed.

Buzzwords

Current buzzwords focus around **maximizing the highest level of function.** In simple words this means keeping people from declining as long as possible.

Facilities are also now using the term **Pro-Active** which means that care is taken so that the residents have the feeling that they have control over their own lives, even when they need constant care. The Residents' Bill of Rights was adopted to guarantee basic rights to residents and to promote the feeling of control and continuation of quality of life.

Outcome Driven Process refers to the way state and federal inspectors evaluate nursing homes. The goal is for each resident to be happy and healthy to the maximum of their function. If there has been some deviation from regulations or the care plan, but the resident is happy and functioning well, a warning will be issued but there is a limit to the fine which can be imposed. When the outcome of the deviation has been detrimental to the resident, there is a much more severe consequence. This is an attempt to humanize and individualize a rigid regulatory process.

To age in place means to stay in the same location. For some, it means remaining in their homes (sometimes through senior-friendly renovation to the premises) and for others it means to remain in one facility as with a continuing care or life care community or in an assisted living facility which will accommodate those needing nursing care.

Terms Involving Payment

Veteran's Administration Contracts allow patients eligible for VA benefits to receive care at facilities other than specific VA facilities. Although the VA maintains several of its own facilities in every state, it also contracts care to private facilities. Usually this is because the veteran is in a location some distance from the nearest VA facility, or because he or she requires special care which is not part of the VA facility in the area. Occasionally it is because there is simply no room at the VA facility. Private facilities may provide care if they have a VA contract. Not all facilities have a VA contract and acceptance and renewal of such a contract, which runs for a limited period of time and must be renewed on a regular basis, is at the option of both the VA and the facility.

Managed Care refers to a payment method. In this type of agreement, a facility negotiates a contract for the care of the patient under managed care. The contract is all inclusive, with no additional charges allowed. The managed care provider who negotiates the contract with the facility may be a private insurance company, an HMO group, or in many states the state Medicaid program. The contract is between those who are responsible for the payment for care of a resident and the facility, and it may vary within a wide range depending on the patient's needs, the location of the facility, and the services provided.

Elder Law

Elder law is a specialty which has developed within the past ten years and is growing rapidly as a field of specialization. Like so much in the field of senior living, it was a result of rapidly changing options and regulations. The growing pressure from the increasing number of seniors in the country has put demands on the federal and state governments to respond to their needs and concerns. Legal issues that affect the elderly are growing in number and becoming more complex. Actions taken by seniors may have unintended legal effects which can create significant problems or issues in future financial or health care matters. In response, the number of attorneys specializing in elder law and recognizing the various legal and financial interrelationships is growing.

As with most general descriptions, such as personal injury or family law, the actual practice of elder law encompasses many and varied disciplines. Everything from contracts, real estate law, taxation, insurance law and financial planning; through governmental assistance issues and claims; to conservatorships and guardianships, wills, trusts, estates, disability law, age discrimination, elder abuse or fraud, and retirement issues are sections of the law pertinent to the practice. An attorney specializing in elder law must have at least a working familiarity with all of these and other bodies of law. An elder law attorney must also take into account the potential problems associated with aging, both physical and emotional.

That is not to say, of course, that you will be involved in all, or even more than a few, of these legal areas. But the complexity of the body of law involved in most of these specialties dictates caution in trying to do it yourself. Although many of the controlling laws are Virginia statutes, there are an equal or greater number of federal statutes, rules, and regulations that control how and what is done. There are federal acts which dictate to a state what it can, or must, prescribe in its laws. Additionally, these laws are constantly in flux and what may be true today will most certainly change tomorrow.

To add more confusion to this mix keep in mind that seniors, especially the very elderly and seniors stricken with Alzheimer's Disease, have often been the subject of predatory practices by different businesses or individuals. Not all of the victimizers have been street con-men, but, in some instances, agents of supposedly honorable companies. The salesman selling multiple insurance policies with overlapping and expensive coverage, the contractor selling unneeded or shoddy home improvements door to door, or the telephone solicitor promising fantastic deals which actually **are** too good to be true. Most people are aware of these widely publicized activities, all of which are now closely and specifically regulated and monitored. All of them are responsible, in part, for the ever-burgeoning legal system detailing the rights and remedies of seniors as well as the legion of service organizations designed to provide assistance and counsel to the senior.

Obviously this, and the following chapters (and this complete book for that matter), is not intended to be and certainly should not be used as a substitute for professional legal or financial advice. Neither should it be construed as

a comprehensive or all encompassing listing of elder law topics. Instead, it should be used as a general guide to legal issues facing senior Virginians.

In few other areas of the law is the maxim that "the man who represents himself has a fool for a client" more apt. Doing it yourself may save money in the short run, but such attempts may result in the dissipation of the quality of life, the wasting of a lifetime's worth of assets, the denial of a rightful claim, or the ultimate disposition of your property in ways that you don't want. Knowing when legal help is necessary is the key. The following chapters outline matters of legal consideration which are those common to most seniors as well as areas of law which are, perhaps, less common but vitally important when needed. Understanding these issues is a beginning point and with the application of common sense and the assistance of an attorney in areas where required the elderly Virginian can live with self-assurance and dignity.

There are certain matters, such as estate planning or litigation, where an attorney is clearly advisable and it would be unwise to proceed without such counsel. Other issues, such as the preparation of an advance medical directive, may not require the formal intervention of an attorney but may be readily handled by the senior, especially if done in conjunction with one of the many support and advice organizations available. Virtually all of those groups can be accessed through Virginia's Area Agencies on Aging which are listed with telephone numbers in the directory section of this book. Additional help and information may be available to members through the American Association of Retired Persons (AARP). After contacting your agency or the AARP you may be able to resolve your problem or know what to do and how to approach an issue. Of course, if there is **any question regarding the necessity of legal help, spending some time in consultation with an elder law attorney is well worth the relatively minimal investment.**

Once a determination is made that legal assistance is necessary finding an elder law attorney is not difficult. The Virginia State Bar has a state-wide referral service, the members of which will provide a thirty minute consultation for twenty-five dollars. Additionally, a few regional bar associations within the state operate their own referral services. Your local Area Agency on Aging can provide the telephone numbers and locations of those local associations or the closest legal aid office which can offer low cost or free legal services to qualified persons. Perhaps, however, the best source of referrals are friends who have had occasion to utilize an elder law practitioner's services in the past. Or ask an attorney you know for a referral. An experience registry, by state and by the area of elder law specialization, is available from the National Academy of Elder Law Attorneys at 520-881-4005, for twenty-five dollars.

VIRGINIA STATE BAR LAWYER REFERRAL SERVICE

1-800-552-7977

Like most broad specializations, the practice of elder law has its subspecialities. It is important that the lawyer you choose has a detailed and up-to-date understanding of the problems or tasks you present as well as a broader understanding of the social and financial ramifications of the contemplated actions. For example, rather than merely adding your adult child as a joint tenant on the deed to your home, does the lawyer know enough to advise you about its potential effect on your estate taxes; does the lawyer understand the rules against impoverishment when a spouse is required to go to a nursing home? Will changing your marital status help preserve your assets? Is the use of a trust or gift necessary or appropriate to reduce or eliminate probate costs or estate taxes and how will that affect governmental assistance for long-term health costs? These issues arise all the time, and it is important that the individual you select as your lawyer is one who regularly deals in your area of concern and has a current and complete awareness of the results of the actions he is advising.

As in most areas of the law, experience is paramount. This is especially true in the elder law area. An experienced attorney will have developed both formal and informal networks to handle all the aspects of a senior's distinctive needs. When calling to set up an initial appointment find out what the lawyer's primary specialty is and how long he or she has been involved in elder law. Is the attorney a member of the Elder Law Section of the Virginia State Bar? Does he or she belong to the National Academy of Elder Law Attorneys and, if so, in what fields has he or she achieved certification? If a trial may be involved, does the attorney do trial work or will it be turned over to another lawyer?

It is also important that you are comfortable talking to and dealing with the person you select to represent you. Don't hesitate to seek another attorney if you are not satisfied that you will have open communication. At the initial meeting with your prospective lawyer make sure that all questions about your matter are fully answered. The appointment should include a discussion of alternative approaches to your problem and the benefits or detriments of each, including the anticipated time and money involved. If appropriate, an interdisciplinary approach involving available social services, governmental benefits, long-term care decisions, asset preservation or transfer issues, disability planning, and estate matters should also be discussed. Be sure to bring all supporting documents to the initial meeting. Take the time to outline your problem or needs so that you can present them in a concise way. This saves time and makes it easier for the attorney to evaluate your situation.

It is essential to have the services to be rendered and the fees established and agreed upon before you begin. A written agreement is always best as it will limit or define the services and costs for which you are financially responsible. Fees for legal services may be charged by the hour, at a flat rate, or on a contingency basis. With an hourly charge a retainer may be required. This retainer will be placed in a trust account and the attorney will provide you with a periodic statement detailing the services rendered and expenses paid on your behalf, and will then draw payment from the trust account. Phone bills, charges for copies, mailing or delivery expenses and filing fees are part of the costs which will usually be added to the bill. In an extended matter the attorney may ask you to replenish the funds in the trust account as required for future services.

Some services which are fairly simple may be provided at a flat rate. This means that the attorney will look at your requirements and agree to provide everything for one fee which is agreed upon before the service is performed. Such fees may or may not include costs and it is important to come to an understanding of how such expenses are to be handled before hiring the attorney.

Contingency cases are those taken for a percentage of any recovery or settlement received from a lawsuit or claim. The lawyer will only be paid a fee if he succeeds in recovering money on your behalf. Not all types of cases are appropriate for a contingency fee and there are ethical prohibitions against taking other cases (such as domestic relations matters) on a contingency basis. In governmental claim cases (*e.g.,* Social Security or Veterans Administration claims), there are limits to the percentage the lawyer can charge. Again, an understanding of how the costs, if any, will be handled in a contingency fee case is fundamental. Will the lawyer pay the costs along the way or will you be responsible for them as they are incurred?

Whatever the case or the fee structure, the attorney you hire has an ethical obligation to maintain open communication and diligently pursue your claim or perform the services for which he has been hired. Most lawyers, especially those who have chosen elder law as a specialty, are not sharks as they are usually portrayed in the movies, but are compassionate human beings. However, like most professionals, they do have time limitations and conflicts. They are not always available immediately upon demand and often simply do not have the time for casual conversation. Consideration of your lawyer's time and his reciprocal consideration of your needs will hopefully result in a mutually satisfactory professional relationship.

Living Wills and Guardianships

Pursuant to the Virginia Health Care Decisions Act of 1992 (and earlier incorporated legislation), Virginians are able to direct their own medical treatment — even if they are unable to communicate their wishes at that time — through the use of an advance medical directive. An advance medical directive actually consists of two distinct parts, a ***living will*** and a ***durable power of attorney for health care***. The two parts are mutually exclusive and either may be independently created. A third, closely parallel, document is a ***financially-related durable power of attorney***, and it too may be created without regard to the existence of either part of an advance medical directive.

The Living Will — In the event of a terminal illness or accident, you may be unable to tell your treating physician what your wishes are regarding the use of life-prolonging treatments. A living will describes what treatments you would like to withhold and which you want to have provided to you at such a time. To take effect there must be a determination by an attending physician that a terminal condition exists.

Although there is no particular form which must be followed to create a valid living will, the Virginia Legislature has approved certain language which specifically provides for the withholding of treatments that would only serve to artificially prolong life. It also provides that all necessary medical treatments and medication designed to alleviate pain be administered. The form itself is relatively simple to fill out and is readily available from multiple sources. Your Area Agency on Aging will have the forms or will provide you a source for the forms upon your request. Additional information is available through the Virginia Health Quality Center at 800-545-3814.

The Durable Power of Attorney for Health Care — As a part of the same form, provisions are made, if chosen, for the appointment of an "attorney-in-fact" or agent to speak for you if you are incapable of making an informed decision about medical treatment but are not suffering from a terminal condition. The determination of incapacity is made by the attending physician as well as a second doctor, or a licensed clinical psychologist, after an examination. The conclusion must be certified in writing before — or as soon as practicable after — treatments are begun and before treatments are withheld.

The legislative form provides that, when making health care decisions, the agent will follow, to the best of his knowledge, the medical treatment preferences, religious beliefs, and basic values of the incapacitated person. He also agrees to be guided by information provided by the treating physicians and — in the absence of knowledge as to what the incapacitated person would want — to make decisions which he believes are in that person's best interests. The agent is not responsible for any medical costs merely because he authorizes treatment in accordance with the power of attorney.

The approved language provided in the form allows for some or all of the following powers to be given to your agent:

1. The power to control the type and extent of medical procedures used as well as the power to consent to the administration of higher than normal amounts of pain medication;
2. The ability to obtain and disclose any medical information or records;
3. The power to hire and fire health care providers;
4. The right to authorize the admission, discharge, or transfer to or from any medical facility; and,
5. To do anything legally necessary to further decisions made under these powers.

Because of the potentially broad scope of the powers of this type of agent it is extremely important that some time and thought go into selecting the appropriate person. In fact, you should consider selecting two people, one to act as an alternate. Equally important is to discuss your plans with them after you have discussed it with your doctor (see below) and insure that you have their understanding and awareness of your wishes. They should be fully advised as to the choices they may be called upon to make and be fully aware of the emotionally charged nature of those choices.

The Advance Medical Directive — Both the living will and the health care durable power of attorney are found on the legislatively approved form. If you do not want to include one or the other of the sections, merely strike a line through it before signing the document. If you wish to add procedures or treatments to the living will, restrict the powers of your agent, or otherwise change the form, it is permissible to do so.

In order to be valid the advance medical directive must be witnessed properly by two people who are not related to you and a copy must be provided to your doctor. The witnesses must watch you sign the paper. Other than that, there are no specific formalities required to create a valid living will or durable health care power of attorney. Although a **written** directive may be prepared at any time before it is necessary, it may be done **orally** provided a terminal condition has been diagnosed and your treating physician is present with the two witnesses. The more prudent course, obviously, is to prepare or have it prepared, in writing and in advance, since it may not be possible to verbally communicate your wishes when necessary.

In addition to your doctor, copies should be provided to your agent(s) and family members or appropriate friends. Keep the original in a safe place and let people know where it is in order to locate it if necessary. Also keep a list of the people to whom you have given copies so you may retrieve them if you wish to modify or revoke the document. Although a later-dated advance medical directive will control, it is better practice to destroy earlier documents to avoid problems or confusion.

To revoke an advance medical directive, which can be done at any time, you must advise your physician. To be absolutely sure there is no mistake gather up and destroy or cancel all copies and the original. If that is not possible, you may sign and date a statement to that effect, have the original directive cancelled in your presence by someone else at your request, or merely state that you want to revoke it. In any event, it is essential that your request be communicated to your doctor as soon as feasible, as the revocation will not be effective until that is done.

Although it is not necessary to use an elder law attorney to prepare a living will, it is highly recommended that a doctor be consulted for information and particulars on available treatments and all options. It is also important that all parties be in agreement with your directive since there is no obligation to honor your requests if your treating physician considers them to be medically or ethically improper.

If you decide to substantially change the legislative form — to provide for specific treatments or change your agent's powers, for example — you may feel more comfortable having a lawyer involved to insure that all changes are made accurately and appropriately. Also, if you have retained a lawyer for another matter such as a will, it is a simple and relatively inexpensive process for an advance medical directive to be prepared at the same time.

If you are unable to make informed decisions about health care, including medical treatments, and have not previously appointed an agent, then a guardianship proceeding, with its potential expense and conflict, may result. Further, without an advance medical directive, Virginia law provides that decisions about artificial life support will be left to others if you become incapacitated. If a guardian has been appointed for you that person is charged with the obligation to make those decisions; if not, your family — spouse, children, parents, siblings, and so on, in descending order of blood relationship — will be responsible. While these may very well be the people to whom you would look in any event, and even assuming they agree, do they really know what it is that you would want? Also, keep in mind the emotional burden such an involuntary process would place on close family members. Alternatively, do you really want to have a distant cousin making your choices even though that person may be able to approach the issue dispassionately?

There may be no way to create a purely objective decision-making process and still insure that the person making decisions on your behalf knows you well enough to express your desires. However, by talking to those close to you, including those you have selected to be your agent(s), it is possible to minimize their anguish and still maintain your personal outlook on medical treatments. Issues to be discussed may include your feelings about organ donation; the maintenance of family or religious traditions; the use of artificial life support systems, including hydration and nutrition, and when and to what degree they should be used; spending your last days at home; and whether you would prefer to have increased amounts of pain medication or to be alert and perhaps physically uncomfortable, and to what degree. Only through detailed and ongoing communication will your family and agent(s) be able to act on your behalf with the comfort of knowing your wishes are being met and, in that way, perhaps lessening their burden.

The Durable Financial Power of Attorney — As a corollary to an advance medical directive you may wish to create a durable power of attorney for your financial affairs. There may be many circumstances where a standard power of attorney is adequate, such as the necessity of having someone handle your bills or take care of household matters while you are on vacation or otherwise temporarily unable to conveniently do so. But such a power will usually terminate upon your return, or other date you select. If you are incapacitated a general power of attorney usually becomes ineffective. A **durable** power of attorney, on the other hand, remains in force in spite of your disability. If you have more than a modest estate you may also wish to consider an *inter vivos*, revocable trust to accomplish the same objectives. (See the Trust section of the Estate Planning chapter.)

Your "attorney-in-fact" under a financial power of attorney may have greater or lesser authority to act on your behalf depending upon the powers you allow in the document. Powers may include anything you could do, including buying or selling real estate or personal property; investing money; negotiating contracts; hiring or firing legal or financial counselors, or others; or merely making deposits and paying bills. Obviously, a broad grant of power should be given only to a person you implicitly trust to handle your affairs appropriately since you will be bound by his actions. However, powers that are too narrow may not avoid the necessity of a guardianship proceeding with its required judicial finding of incompetence. Due to the specific language essential to a power of attorney to insure that all of your concerns are resolved, an attorney's advice and help in drafting the document is highly recommended.

Guardianships and Conservatorships — Simply put, a **guardian** is a person who is charged by the court to handle the affairs and make decisions for another person who is unable to do so. A guardian may be appointed in one or several areas of concern, such as financial or health and medical. A guardian of the financial affairs of an individual may also be called a **conservator**, or sometimes the **guardian of the estate**. A person for whom a guardian has been appointed is called the **ward**. A ward may have both a guardian and a conservator, or a single person acting as both; or he may have multiple guardians and conservators operating jointly as co-guardians or co-conservators referred to as a committee.

A guardianship may be necessary if the senior is deemed incompetent. Competency, however, is a matter of degree. Mere forgetfulness, the onset of a degenerative disease, or even a mental or physical impairment, without more, does not constitute incompetence. Incompetency also may be transitory or a person may be competent in some areas but not others. But when matters progress to the point where an elderly person is not capable of making basic life decisions, handling daily financial affairs, or understanding and taking actions to keep safe and healthy, it may very well be time to consider a guardianship proceeding. Seniors in Virginia may be able to avoid the emotional trauma and expense often resulting from a guardianship proceeding by exercising their rights under Virginia's Health Care Decisions Act, or by completing a financial durable power of attorney as discussed.

The process of guardianship, in Virginia, may be initiated by the filing of a petition with the court by any adult person. The senior who is the subject of the petition has the right to an appointed representative called a **guardian *ad litem***, who insures that the rights of the senior are preserved. Those rights include the right to be notified of the hearing, to present evidence, to have a jury, and to appeal an adverse decision.

If the court, after hearing the required medical and social services evidence, determines that the senior is not capable of handling personal, health care, or financial decisions, it will direct an individual, usually a family member, to act as guardian for the senior. Regardless of the relationship, the guardian must periodically report to the court about the affairs of the ward and is required to be bonded.

Due to the complexity of these proceedings it is recommended that an individual involved in a guardianship matter seek the assistance of an elder law attorney.

Estate Planning

Estate planning consists generally of the establishment of financial and testamentary goals and the preparation of documents, or taking actions, or both, designed to achieve those goals. Such plans can be fairly simple or incredibly complex depending upon the size of the estate and the family involved. A couple with a modest estate and no children will have far different goals than a family with children or grandchildren, or one with extensive financial resources.

A simple estate plan may consist of nothing more than a will. A complex plan may involve different kinds of trusts, gifts, endowments, annuities, title transfers, and the like, as a part of, or in addition to, a will. It may even involve a change in marital status or the execution of marital agreements. All estate planning, no matter how complex or simple, should take into consideration any existing or potential long-term health care questions as those can dramatically affect not only your life-style but your financial well-being. Due to the intertwining and intricate issues posed in estate planning for seniors, it is suggested that the services of an elder law attorney be retained for most matters. Depending upon the size of the estate perhaps an accountant, financial planner, tax advisor, or long-term health care specialist should also be consulted. The cost of such experts may very well be more than worth the money in terms of what can be saved in taxes or asset preservation, not to mention peace of mind. Whether the goal is to preserve as much as possible for children, to protect a surviving spouse, or insure the maintenance of your life-style and health needs, there are perfectly legal and financially sound ways to accomplish those goals.

Wills

Almost every adult Virginian should have a will. Without one, the probate court will appoint an "administrator" (an "administratrix," if female) to distribute your property according to the laws of descent and distribution of the state. While those laws do a reasonable job of anticipating the classes of people to whom most of us would like our property left, they are incapable of "personalizing" that distribution. There may be certain close relatives that you would not want to share in your estate, for example. Or, suppose you would like to leave something to a close friend. The laws in Virginia that control the distribution of your assets when you do not have a will would allow your relative to share and would cut out your friend, exactly the opposite of your wishes.

The appointment by the court of an administrator may also cause problems. Suppose you own an economically valuable but non-divisible asset — a piece of jewelry, perhaps — wanted by multiple heirs who have equal rights to claim that asset and do not wish it to be sold. An administrator may not fully appreciate your heirs' desire to keep the asset, or more likely, may not know specifically to whom you would like to leave it. While most conscientious administrators will listen and try to adhere to family requests — and most probably is a member of the family anyhow — it may work out. However, the potential for conflict is high and, if a fight breaks out, the time, expense, and emotional upheaval associated with a prolonged probate can be damaging, both at the time and for long afterward. And the court may order the asset sold, in spite of its sentimental value, to resolve the problem.

The presence of a simple will directing the disposition of assets can insure, with one main exception (discussed below), that your property goes to whom you want it to go. A typical will provides for specific gifts to specific people with the balance of your estate going to your spouse or children, or perhaps grandchildren. Once again with the one exception, you may establish the percentages in which the balance of your estate is divided. If you want to give unequal shares — you may have a child that has greater need than the others, for example, and wish to make special provisions — you may do so. Also, preparing a will allows you to personally appoint the person in charge of distributing your estate. That person, the "executor" (or "executrix"), may be anyone you designate but for obvious reasons should be someone you trust. By virtue of the position, your executor will pay your debts and taxes out of your estate and distribute your property in accordance with the will all under the guidance and control of the probate court.

Specific gifts do present some challenges that are worth considering. For example, you may want to leave your old, but precious, pickup truck to your friend's son, Ryan. Without a will, the court appointed administrator has absolutely no authority to give the truck to anyone not formally an heir under Virginia law. With a will, so long as Ryan is listed as the beneficiary, your executor may give him the truck. But what if it has been sold or destroyed; or perhaps Ryan lives in Oregon — what about the shipping costs? Or, what happens if you give your child your shares in ABC Corporation but the stock has been sold prior to your death, or perhaps the stock has split, or maybe the company has declared bankruptcy and the stock is valueless? What if the real estate you gave has been sold or is subject to a contract of sale? All of these matters may be addressed and remedied in a properly drafted will or left to the laws of Virginia which may or may not be what you prefer.

Giving the balance of your estate to several people, your children for example, also needs fine tuning beyond merely stating "All the rest and residue of my estate I hereby give, devise and bequeath to my children in equal shares." If one of your children has predeceased you, will his share go to his children (your grandchildren) or be split among your surviving children? If your grandchildren do get a share, do they divide up what your child would have gotten or do they take an equal share with your remaining children? For example, if you have two children, each would take one-half of the estate. If one of your children dies before you and he has two children, do they take nothing, or share your deceased child's half, or is your estate divided equally among your two grandchildren and your remaining child so each gets one-third? What happens if a grandchild is born after your death but before distribution under your will? Again, there are laws controlling these issues but will they accomplish what you want?

There are many software programs and generic forms for wills (not to mention contracts, trusts, powers of attorney, and advance medical directives) available on the market today. Many of them may be perfectly adequate for your purposes, but care should be taken in selecting and modifying such forms. All that is required in Virginia for a will to be admitted to probate is that it be properly witnessed, dated, and signed — or if it is handwritten that the whole document be in your handwriting. While Virginia is not particularly strict on what can be admitted as a valid will, the real danger lies in your actual intent not being clearly stated. For all its arcane complexity, the legal phrases and stilted language of the law, if used properly, do serve to express as clearly as possible the real expectations of the person making a will. Absent that clarity, the probate court is left to decipher what you really wanted and is subject to the laws providing for such cases which once again may not result in the desired disposition or treatment of your assets.

With some thought and a properly drafted and executed will you will be able to resolve any question and dispose of your estate as you see fit with the exception mentioned earlier. Unless there is a valid marital agreement permitting it, you may not disinherit your spouse, who may chose to take up to one half of your estate — depending upon the number of surviving children and their relationship to you and your spouse — regardless of the language of a will. Also, if you chose to disinherit a child, it is much better practice to give that child a nominal testamentary gift, since there are certain, particular circumstances where you will not be able to disown a child (including an illegitimate child) by merely neglecting to mention him.

Also regardless of the existence or language of a will, certain jointly owned property will pass to the surviving partner, outside of probate. The most common type is real estate held as a "tenancy by the entirety" or a "joint tenancy," which requires specific language in the deed to create a "right of survivorship." In addition to jointly owned real property, there are other types of interests that similarly may pass outside probate. For example, joint bank accounts of most types belong to the survivor, and life insurance proceeds, individual retirement accounts, some mutual funds, and pension plan death benefits go directly to the beneficiary you have designated on the company form. Those beneficiaries may be changed at anytime by merely signing a new form.

Changing your will is a bit more complex and requires a formal amendment, called a "codicil," which complies with the same statutory requirements of the original will (*i.e.*, dated, signed and witnessed). Or, you may merely redo the whole will, making sure to destroy the first will (and all copies) and stating that all prior wills are revoked in order to avoid a will contest. In Virginia, merely having a later-dated will does not necessarily revoke a former will unless the intention to do so is clearly manifested. Either redrafting your will or preparing a codicil will serve to modify your estate plan to conform to your present wishes.

In that regard, a periodic will review is recommended. What if the truck you wanted to give to Ryan has been sold, ABC Corporation has merged with XYZ, or the real estate has increased in value tenfold? Should you give something else, change the beneficiary of the gift, or merely drop it? Also, life changes such as marriage (see above), divorce, or relocation may cause you to revise your will. If divorced your will is still valid except for the provisions pertaining to your ex-spouse. But, unless a new will is drafted, the court may have to rely on Virginia's statutory distribution for the part of your estate that your ex-spouse would otherwise have taken.

A relocation to another state does not effect the provisions of a will. Every state in the union will admit to probate a will legally prepared in another state. But laws regarding the qualifications necessary to be an executor (usually residency issues), the form of probate, and other procedural matters do vary, and the new state will insist that its laws be followed. A consultation with a lawyer in the new state, and perhaps a new will, may avoid unnecessary expense and time in probate.

If you have property located in more than one state it will probably be necessary to have an estate administration proceeding, or probate, established in each state. (See the Estate Administration section below for a method to avoid this.) Needless to say, that can be burdensome on your executor, not to mention your beneficiaries, and the cost to your estate can be significant. Furthermore, without a will, the laws of each state relating to the distribution of the property will control, which may lead to unexpected results. For example, unlike Virginia, some states do not recognize adopted or illegitimate children as heirs resulting, perhaps, in your adopted child sharing in some of your property but not all. While these problems can be resolved through *inter vivos* (during your life time) gifts, trusts, or sale of the assets, there are potential ramifications that may effect your qualification for governmental assistance programs which should be considered. (See the chapter on Medicaid.) Therefore, consultation with an elder law specialist is recommended prior to making any significant gifts or sales, or preparing a trust instrument on your own.

Special Instructions

Although a will details the general disposition of your estate there are many practical issues which may remain unresolved. If property is not given by a specific bequest, then it becomes part of the "residue" of the estate. Often many of those items are of little economic consequence such as furniture, photos, personal effects, or family memorabilia but may have significant meaning to one or more of your beneficiaries. To attempt to list each and every item in a specific manner in a will would be burdensome to say the least and would increase the cost of will preparation to astronomical proportions. The task of equitably allocating and distributing the residue of the estate falls upon your executor and if he is faced with no further instructions than appear in the will —"I hereby give, devise and bequeath all the rest and residue of my estate in equal shares to my children" — it could be a difficult job indeed.

There are several ways to help your executor make the right decisions. Some seniors discuss with their families and/or their executors which items each beneficiary should have relying on the memory and good faith of each person involved. Many people "tag" items of furniture, mementos, photo albums, and the like with color-coded stickers or name tags designating which beneficiary is to have that particular item, which can be messy, expensive, and inefficient. Both methods are somewhat helpful but are subject to the stated limitations. Perhaps a better way to handle these matters and accomplish much more at the same time is to prepare a written document expressing your wishes for the division of your personal property. There is no particular form which has to be followed; no legal or other experts need be consulted; it can be as detailed as you wish; it may preserve family harmony; and it can be used for multiple purposes. The downside: like the other methods, **it is not legally binding**. But it gives family members and your executor an idea of what you would like them to do. If the family is prone to disagree or if there are different points of view about who should get a particular item, the more detailed the instructions the better. Having discussions with your executor and family members about the instructions will assist you in preparing the document and will assist in the harmonious distribution of the property involved.

In addition to a list of personal property and effects your special instructions may include information about business or personal records and locations or codes to access them; a list of bank accounts and investments; instructions on how to care for property or pets; and the names and telephone numbers of people to contact to let them know of the situation, which may include doctors, lawyers, financial advisors, or brokers and, most importantly, friends, especially those living in different areas. You may wish to include any special instructions regarding memorial services, the maintenance of family traditions, or any other matter of importance to you. Finally, you might include personal messages or thoughts in this, or in another personally addressed and more private letter.

There is no need to retain a lawyer to compose such a paper. But since it is not legally binding, care should be taken that anything involving items of value or costs to the estate be included in the will and not just in the special instructions. Perhaps you have some expensive jewelry or a valuable coin collection. Rather than allowing it to be part of the residue of your estate — and potentially sold or broken up — give it as a specific gift in the will. Suppose, further, that you have a dog. Your letter instructs your daughter to take care of Rover, but he needs special medical care and a special diet. If you intend to provide money from the estate to pay for his care, it must be specified in the will, even though it may also be mentioned in your special instructions.

Trusts

There are basically two types of trusts relevant to estate planning. A **testamentary trust** is created in probate as a result of a will which sets forth the terms and conditions of the trust and provides money or property to fund it. An *inter vivos* (during life) trust, also called a **living trust**, is created, and all terms and conditions are set by a trust instrument prepared during your lifetime. A living trust should not be used as a substitute for a will but as an additional element of your estate plan. A living trust may be **revocable** or **irrevocable** and, as the names imply, one may be modified or terminated whenever you choose and the other may not.

Testamentary Trusts may be used for one or many combined specific purposes. For example, it can be used to hold and maintain assets for the education of your children, grandchildren, or others. Or, you may wish to prevent the distribution of money to your beneficiaries until they reach a certain age. You may provide in the trust for a disbursement in a lump sum to be made when that age is met or, if you wish, provide for partial disbursements on a periodic basis or distribute the income from the trust to certain persons and the assets in the trust to others. You may even create a "spendthrift trust" designed to keep the trust assets away from your beneficiary's creditors.

BEWARE OF ESTATE PLANNING FRAUD

Several states have filed suit and issued consumer warnings against unscrupulous companies selling "fill in the blank" revocable living trust documents through "free" seminars and high pressure sales tactics. These dubious documents not only failed to comply with the state laws but could not accomplish the probate savings claimed and may actually have resulted in higher estate taxes. There are many legitimate do-it-yourself books and software products in the market, designed to handle simple estate matters, but they will specify when an expert should be consulted.

A testamentary trust allows you to maintain full control over your assets during your lifetime and provide whatever reasonable conditions on the use and disbursement of those assets you direct in the trust portion of your will. The use of a testamentary trust provides a tremendous amount of flexibility in estate planning; however, to amend the trust in any way requires a formal amendment of the will. Although the assets provided by your will to fund the trust are subject to probate, a testamentary trust may be a valuable tool in reducing or eliminating estate taxes for larger estates while maintaining your estate plan. (See the Using Trusts section below.)

A **Revocable Living Trust** is created by an instrument totally separate and distinct from your will. Such a trust may be used for many of the same purposes as a testamentary trust, but also has certain unique characteristics and uses found by virtue of the time frame of its establishment.

For example, a person suffering from a progressive, debilitating disease, such as Alzheimer's, may establish a revocable living trust prior to the onset of cognitive impairment, designed to have a trustee take over the management of his affairs when necessary. A trust of this kind will help prevent involuntary guardianship proceedings and allow the person establishing the trust to specify how his assets are to be managed when he is no longer capable of doing so. Although the legal control over the assets is transferred to the trustee in accordance with the trust instrument, it is a revocable trust, and until the disease has progressed actual control may be maintained since the trust may be terminated at will. If full actual and legal control of the assets is desired until it becomes inappropriate, consider establishing the trust as a shell to be funded by your agent under a financial, durable power of attorney. (See the Living Wills chapter.) In that fashion your assets will not be placed in trust until absolutely necessary. In that regard also, you may establish reasonable tests or conditions to establish incapacity — such as requiring your physician and/or others to make a specific finding of incapacity — before the durable power becomes effective or the trust is funded.

> **In Virginia, unless the power of revocation is expressly reserved, the trust will be deemed irrevocable and cannot later be revoked or amended.**

An interesting hybrid is a "pour-over" trust which is created before, or at the same time, as your will but in a completely separate document. It may be nothing more than a shell and, although it may be partially funded, like a testamentary trust, it is not totally funded until probate with assets which pour-over from the will. Unlike other living trusts, it does not shelter the pour-over assets from probate, but it may be utilized to save on estate taxes, which may or may not be important depending upon the size of the estate. The advantage of a pour-over trust is that it is amendable at any time without the necessity of engaging in the formalities of will modification. So you may change the trustee, the beneficiaries, or the purposes of the trust without having to redraft your will. Also, except for the pour-over assets —which require a will modification to change — you may reconsider and revise the amount or type of trust property. Cancelling the trust should be done with some caution, however, since, at best, the pour-over property allocated to the trust will become part of the residue of your estate and, at worst, the will may be declared invalid.

An **Irrevocable Living Trust** is a highly specialized tool which should be utilized only after significant thought and legal or financial counsel. Once it is created, it may not be changed in any way nor may it be cancelled. In order to take advantage of the potential estate tax benefits accruing from an irrevocable living trust, the person establishing the trust must forgo all control over the assets placed in trust, may not be a trustee or a beneficiary of the trust, and the trust must be established at least three years before death. Perhaps the most common purpose to which an irrevocable trust is put is to shelter property likely to appreciate in value (or, in some cases, life insurance proceeds) from estate taxation.

Estate Administration & Taxation

Estate administration, commonly called **probate**, is simply the collection and protection of the estate assets followed by their distribution to the appropriate people. Although simple to state, the actual practice is fairly complex and may be time-consuming and expensive. The administrator or executor, working with the estate attorney, have to follow specifically detailed laws describing how different assets are to be handled or protected, and to whom and when they are to be distributed; what is to be done with any income derived from estate property; what priorities are to be established for the payment of debts; and what assets are to be used to pay those debts and which are exempt. Finally, he must prepare and file the Virginia state inheritance tax return as well as comply with federal income and estate tax requirements.

There are summary administration procedures for very small estates (less than $5000), but the typical probate in Virginia will take about eighteen months. Creditors have one year to submit claims against the estate and the subsequent inventory and accounting required of the administrator or executor, coupled with court submission and approval, will usually take another six months. Administrative fees, which must be approved by the "Commissioner of Accounts," a representative of the probate court, will include payment to the administrator or executor. There are no hard and fast rules about such payments but a figure of five percent of the value of the personal property and three percent of the value of real estate is normal. These amounts will vary depending upon the size and complexity of the estate.

Assets placed in a testamentary trust are included in the probate estate as is property which "pours-over" from the will into a living trust. If a living trust is funded during life, however, the assets are not part of the probate estate since they are not legally owned by the decedent but by the trust. Similarly, if you own property which is located in more than one state, establishing a living trust and putting that property in trust will eliminate the necessity of multiple estate administrations since the property is not legally yours. Note that life insurance proceeds — as well as other types of death benefits, gifts, and property with an associated right of survivorship — are not normally considered part of the probate estate unless the estate itself is the beneficiary. Any assets which are subject to probate will become a matter of public record by virtue of the necessary accounting and inventory performed by the executor or administrator.

The property that is considered part of the probate estate may be significantly different from that which is cumulatively regarded as potentially subject to estate taxes. Although probate can be fairly expensive it may pale in comparison to the estate taxes which will be paid on an estate which exceeds the nontaxable base. With federal estate tax rates going as high as fifty-five percent it obviously makes sense to do what you can legally do to reduce or eliminate those tax obligations.

Briefly stated, your estate, for the purposes of the federal estate tax, includes the value of all property in which you had an interest at the time of death. An interest in property is broadly defined and includes many items which are not owned outright and for which legal title is held by another person or entity such as a trust. The right to collect income from your own trust, the right to give the property away, or the right to possess or use the property are all considered, in various circumstances, an interest in property sufficient to bring the full value of the property into your gross estate.

For example, all the property you placed in a revocable living trust, although not subject to probate, is includible for the purposes of estate taxation. The value of property placed in a testamentary trust or which pours over from a will into a revocable living trust is part of the probate estate and is also part of the potentially taxable estate. A portion of the value of property held with another as joint tenants, or as tenants by the entirety, is included, and life insurance proceeds are included if they are payable to your estate or if you owned the policy. Any property you transferred during your life, for less than full value, is included if you kept any interest at all in the property. Finally, certain transfers you made and any gift taxes you paid within three years of death are includible.

Once the value of your gross estate is determined it is then reduced by the debts you owed and the costs and expenses of probate. If you are married, the value of virtually all the property that passes from your estate to your surviving spouse is also deducted (the marital deduction), which may serve to reduce the taxable portion of your estate below the amount generating tax liability. However when the surviving spouse passes away — unless remarried — there is obviously no marital deduction.

In 1998, estates of less than $625,000 (up from the previous limit of $600,000) are exempt from federal estate taxes —the tax credit which creates this exemption is a unified gift and estate tax credit, so these figures may not be entirely accurate in your situation, but for this discussion the full exemption will be used. Even better news is the $625,000 limit will increase to $650,000 in 1999, and will continue to increase until 2006 when there will be an allowance of $1 million which may be left to heirs or beneficiaries without paying any federal estate taxes. Family farms — which traditionally have been hit hard by the estate tax — and family businesses, which are passed on to family members, may now be eligible for a reduction of up to $750,000 from the fair market value of certain qualified real estate providing even greater estate tax protection for those groups.

If your estate is close to or beyond the exempted amount, serious consideration should be applied to retaining the services of a qualified elder law practitioner, tax accountant, or other estate planning professional. It is much easier to exceed the exempted amount than most people realize. If you combine the value of your home and other real estate with the amount of your life insurance, bank accounts, stock portfolio, and other investments, you may be closer than you think. Also, keep in mind that any taxable gifts you have given (even if you did not file a gift tax return) will cause a reduction in the unified gift and estate tax credit, resulting in a decrease in the amount of the exemption which can be applied to your estate. Given the incredible complexity of the federal estate tax laws, coupled with the virtually infinite number of asset combinations, family situations, and estate planning goals, it is difficult, at best, to draw generalizations or provide information common to all seniors. Suffice it to say that there are estate planning mechanisms which, in particular circumstances, may provide relief from estate taxation.

Using Trusts & Maximizing Exempt Property

Assume that Dave dies in 1998 with an estate valued at $1.5 million. He is married to Tina and decides to leave her his whole estate. Since the marital deduction covers everything, Dave's taxable estate is zero. However, Tina's estate is now increased by $1.5 million and if she dies in 1999, leaving that amount to her children, she will be taxed on $850,000 out of Dave's original estate after using her $650,000 exemption.

If, instead, Dave left $625,000 to the children, and the balance to Tina, his estate would still avoid liability for estate taxes because of the 1998 exemption of $625,000, and the marital deduction (in this case $875,000). Tina's estate would increase by $875,000, and when she died her 1999 exemption of $650,000 would leave a taxable estate of only $225,000, rather than the $850,000 if she had been left Dave's whole estate.

If Dave wanted his total estate to be available for Tina's use, he could give the children $625,000 through a testamentary or living trust, subject to certain rights to Tina during her life, such as the right to income or small principal reductions, and give the balance of his estate to Tina outright. Caution needs to be exercised here, however, since the rights given to Tina through the trust must not be significant enough to cause the trust property to be included in her estate. It is also important to understand that the assets transferred to the trust must be Dave's separate property and not assets held jointly with Tina, since joint assets will automatically be transferred to her.

If part of Dave's estate consisted of property which was expected to gain significant value over a number of years he could have used an irrevocable trust to shelter the increased value of that property from estate taxation. For example, if Dave owned real estate worth $110,000 in 1994, which appreciated to $300,000 in 1998, the year of his death, his estate would include the full appreciated value of the property. But, if he had placed the real estate in an irrevocable living trust in 1994, no part of the value of the real estate would be included in his estate which would then be worth $1.2 million. Since the transfer of the property to the trust in 1994 is a gift, he would use $100,000 — $110,000 less the $10,000 annual gift tax exclusion discussed below — of his unified credit, leaving an estate tax exemption of $525,000. Giving that amount to the children would leave $675,000 which, if given to Tina, would be excluded from the estate tax computations because of the marital deduction. When Tina then died in 1999, her tax credit exemption would shelter all but $25,000 of that portion of her estate. As previously noted, to achieve tax benefits from an irrevocable trust Dave must not have any rights remaining in the property, including any right to control it as a trustee or any rights to the use, enjoyment, or income of the property, and if not done more than three years prior to his death, the full amount of the trust will be included in his estate.

Taking Advantage of the Stepped Up Basis & Capital Gain Exclusion

Simply put, when property is purchased, the cost to the buyer becomes his **basis** in the property. If he later sells that property, his taxable gain is the difference between the basis and the sales price. When an interest in property is transferred to another through an estate, the basis of that interest is **stepped up** to its fair market value. For example, if a piece of land has a basis of $60,000 and is sold for $100,000, the taxable gain on the sale is $40,000. If that same property is given through an estate, the basis is stepped up to $100,000 and a subsequent sale would result in no taxable gain.

Assume Sam and his wife, Katherine, are not as financially well off as Dave and Tina. In 1998, their assets consist primarily of their home worth $400,000 (with a basis of $100,000); two or three bank accounts totalling $40,000; some life insurance on Sam's life with a face value of $100,000; and some stock worth $60,000 which was originally purchased for $30,000. If the property, totalling $600,000, is all held in Sam's name alone and he dies in 1998 there would be no estate tax payable since the aggregate value of the estate is less than the 1998 exemption of $625,000 (not to mention the marital deduction for property left to Katherine). However, all of the assets, except the life insurance, would be subject to probate. If the property were all jointly owned by Sam and Katherine, with a right of survivorship, the probate estate would be very small since none of the assets would be subject to estate administration but would transfer outside probate to the surviving joint tenant.

However, only the interests that were transferred to Katherine would have a stepped up basis. If Sam owned all the property and willed it all to Katherine, her basis in the house would be $400,000 and her basis in the stock would be $60,000. She would, of course, receive the value of the life insurance and the bank accounts with no tax effect whatsoever. So, even though most of the property had to be probated, she could now sell the house and the stock with no taxable gain (or, if the stock lost value, with a deductible loss).

If the property were held in joint tenancy, Katherine's new basis in the house would be $250,000 — the basis of Sam's 50% share would be stepped up to $200,000 and Katherine would retain the original basis of $50,000 on her half. A sale of the home for $400,000, would then result in a realized, but nontaxable, gain of $150,000. (See below.) The stock would have a basis of $45,000 — the $30,000 stepped up basis of Sam's share and Katherine's original basis of $15,000. If the stock were then sold, Katherine would have a taxable gain of $15,000. Therefore, although probate has been avoided through the use of joint ownership, there is still a potential taxable event. Do the savings justify the increased income tax situation?

Two things should be noted here. First, a change in title of property between spouses is usually not a gift subject to taxation. Therefore, if Sam and Katherine decide that it would be better to change title to Sam's separate property to a joint tenancy, or if it makes more economic sense to change title from a joint tenancy to separate property, it can be done without tax ramifications. Secondly, under the new regulations for home sales, any gain from a sale after May 6, 1997, is not taxable unless the gain exceeds $250,000. That provision is applicable to everyone and may be used once every two years, provided you owned and lived in the home for at least two out of the five years prior to the sale. If you are married and file joint income tax returns, then each spouse is entitled to the exclusion resulting in the ability to shelter up to $500,000 in capital gain.

Therefore, as a part of estate planning for a couple whose primary assets are real estate — and other capital assets such as stocks, bonds, or mutual funds — an evaluation should be made as to whether it is better to shift title to one person and contend with probate and estate tax considerations and costs, to gain a stepped up basis for the whole property; or whether holding the property as joint tenants and only gaining a stepped up basis for one half will be offset by the savings created by avoiding probate. If your home is your primary asset, you may also want to consider selling it while both partners are still alive in order to take advantage of the full $500,000 exclusion. In all likelihood, a combination approach may be best, but an evaluation of your individual situation by an estate planning professional is recommended.

Additionally, caution should be used if you are considering placing some third party on title as a joint tenant with you. It seems fairly common for an elderly person, or couple, to decide to add adult children on their bank or brokerage accounts or place them on title to the home. At first glance, doing so seems perfectly reasonable to provide security for the senior and to insure that the property automatically will be given to the children, but it may have several potentially adverse affects. First, the transaction will very likely be a taxable gift, thereby reducing the amount of the available estate tax exemption. Secondly, adding a third party to a joint tenancy mandates that the full value of the property be included in the estate of the first joint tenant to die, unless you can prove that the surviving owners purchased their shares for full value. Conversely, even if you are able to prove the "extent, origin and nature" of the surviving owners' interests thereby reducing the value included in the estate, it will likewise reduce the portion of the property to which a stepped up basis is applied.

Another fairly common situation occurs when a senior deeds his or her home to an adult child, without receiving payment, with the agreement — whether legally enforceable or not — that the senior can continue to use the home for life. The full value of the home will very likely be included in the senior's estate under those circumstances. If not, a taxable gift has probably occurred with the commensurate reduction in the available estate tax exemption and no stepped up basis will be applied to the property. Even if the senior discontinues the use of the home, if it is not done more than three years before death, the full value will still be included in the estate.

Finally, we have Larry and Karla, who have worked hard, perhaps put their children through college, and done their best to save for retirement. Their holdings are modest. Maybe a home valued at $150,000 and various other assets — perhaps two cars, a fishing boat, an individual retirement account or two, and some savings — worth $80,000. Although not extensive they would like to preserve those assets for themselves and their children if possible. Obviously, there will be no estate tax issues, but they can save money, and time, on probate by using some of the estate planning mechanisms previously discussed. Of primary importance to them, however, is planning for a future which may include the necessity of nursing home care. The potential costs of long-term health care are critically important in their estate planning. Unfortunately, even more than most estate planning areas, future projections are difficult and decisions need to be made earlier. For more information on this, and related issues see the chapter entitled *Medicare, Medicaid and Other Government Programs.*

Using Gifts to Reduce the Estate

Although creating a taxable gift will reduce the available estate tax exemption, it is still possible to use nontaxable gifts to reduce the estate without affecting the exemption amount. Basically, any time you give money or property — or the right to use money or property — to someone without being paid the full value in return, you are making a potentially taxable gift. However, there are several important exceptions to the rule, which should be utilized in appropriate circumstances.

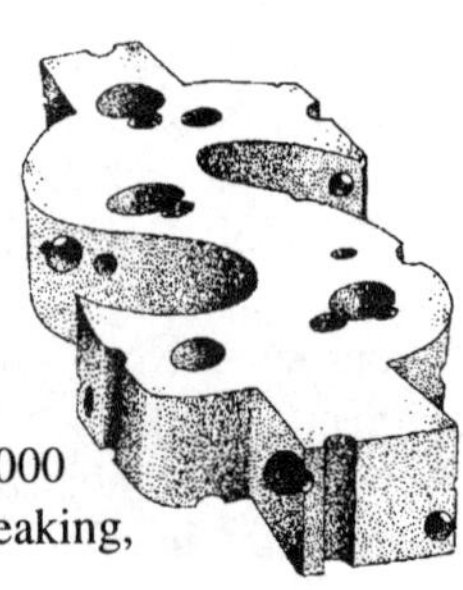

The first primary exception is the commonly known "annual exclusion." Up to $10,000 a year may be given to any number of individuals without paying gift taxes. If married, and your spouse consents, you may give up to $20,000 to each person tax free. So, if you have five children, each may receive up to $20,000 annually, for a total of $100,000 in gifts each year. Generally speaking, regardless of the total amount given, no gift tax return need be filed unless it is a joint gift with your spouse or any individual gift exceeds $10,000.

You may also pay any amount of tuition or medical expenses on behalf of someone else, give any amount to charities or political organizations, or give unlimited gifts to your spouse, all without incurring gift tax liability or creating the need to file a return.

It sounds simple enough but like most areas of the law, especially those dealing with taxes or governmental programs — each gift may impact Medicaid coverage even though it is not taxable — it can become quite a bit more complex. Within the context of this book, however, the primary concerns which create a recommendation to seek estate planning advice from a professional, are these. Engaging in estate planning, without considering long-term health care issues, is playing with fire. Furthermore, depleting an estate, through gifts or trusts may leave a senior without adequate resources to maintain his or her standard of living, but not doing so may subject your estate to oppressive taxation.

As may be apparent from the matters discussed above, the laws primarily pertaining to seniors leave them walking a knife edge of decision about so many related and conflicting issues that it is difficult to fully evaluate. Every choice made seems to affect every other matter; to further some goals and simultaneously retard others. Sometimes, it seems, no option or plan will provide absolute methods to accomplish all the things we may want to do. Do we care that our estates may be decimated by taxes or do we avoid those taxes in ways that shortchange ourselves? How can we preserve our estates for our children and at the same time insure that we retain enough for our own future needs and well being? These are the real issues that the estate planning community is concerned about. If you share those concerns as well, professional estate planning advice can maximize your ability to achieve your goals.

Medicare, Medicaid and other Government Programs

There are many programs, at all levels of government, which are designed to aid seniors financially, medically, and socially. In the Commonwealth of Virginia, the Department for the Aging is responsible for planning and coordinating senior oriented programs and projects which are funded through state and federal budgets. Locally, senior services are administered through one of twenty-five Area Agencies on Aging which also maintain detailed information about programs and services in their community provided by other public and private organizations. The Area Agencies provide or have access to many good programs, from transportation, meals and assistance with daily living activities; through legal, insurance and social services counseling; to educational, social and recreational programs. Since the availability of, and eligibility for, these services will vary, the second section of this book discusses many of these projects on an area by area basis.

SOCIAL SECURITY

Out of the Depression era, Congress created the Social Security system in an effort to provide supplemental income for senior Americans. It has never been intended to be the sole source of income for a senior, but to augment his personal savings and pension. Social Security is funded through the taxes that you have paid during your working years which is returned when you retire or become disabled and under certain circumstances to your spouse and children if you die.

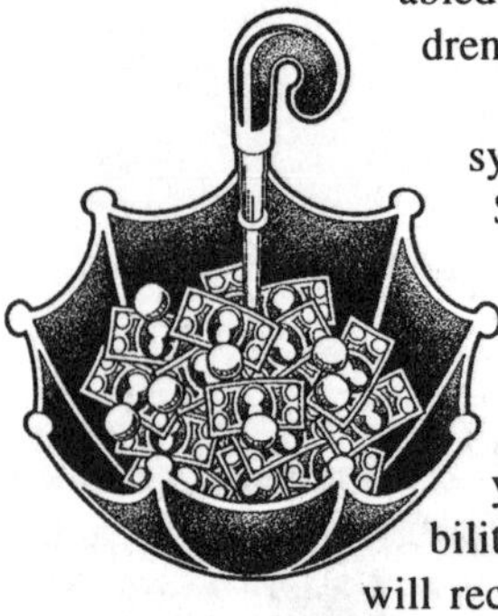

Eligibility for Social Security benefits is based on a credit system where you gain a Social Security credit for every $700 (in 1998) of income you receive annually. You can gain a maximum of four credits a year. To receive Social Security forty credits — ten years of work — will be needed, although fewer are required for people born before 1929. Credits will continue to accumulate throughout your working life and are used to determine not only eligibility for Social Security but also Medicare. The amount you will receive in Social Security benefits depends on the average of your income over the years you worked. Shortly prior to your fiftieth birthday, you should have, or shall, receive "Your Personal Earnings and Benefit Estimate Statement" from the Social Security Administration. That document provides information about Social Security and Medicare eligibility and benefits. If you did not receive or have misplaced your earnings and benefit statement, or merely wish to have an updated one, you may order it by telephone (800-537-7005).

You may apply for Social Security at age sixty-two, but the benefit amount will be reduced approximately twenty-five percent. Full retirement benefits are available at age sixty-five, but, under current legislation, that age will gradually increase to sixty-seven by the year 2027. If retirement is delayed your benefits will increase by a percentage each year beyond age sixty-five. Although direct deposit of benefits into a bank account is an option at the time this book goes to press, it will be mandatory after December 31, 1998.

Active seniors who continue to work and are not seeking Social Security benefits by sixty-five (and we are seeing more and more people in this category) should still sign up for Medicare. These seniors should see their Social Security office for more details. Other seniors may choose to receive Social Security benefits even though they are working. Between sixty-five and sixty-nine, there are limits on how much you can earn without losing some or all of your benefits. This earnings limitation changes each year. At seventy years of age full benefits will be paid by Social Security, regardless of the amount earned.

A spouse can also receive Social Security benefits based on the amount earned by the other partner. Traditionally this applied more to women, many of whom had not worked outside the home, or who worked in jobs which paid less than their husbands. With the changing social mores and career opportunities for women, more and more men are taking advantage of these provisions. When fifty percent of the benefits one partner is eligible to receive exceeds the amount the other person would be entitled to receive based on his or her own earnings, a spouse aged sixty-two or older (or those caring for a child sixteen years of age or younger, or a child who is disabled) would receive the higher amount.

For those who have been divorced there are special provisions. A former spouse age sixty-two or older and unmarried (provided the marriage lasted ten years or longer), would also be entitled to receive a fifty percent benefit based on the income of the former spouse. This provision will apply even if either spouse has remarried as long as the dependent spouse is no longer married at age sixty-two. It does not matter if the primary money earner is married at the time the former spouse turns sixty-two.

An unmarried child under eighteen (nineteen if still in high school), or a child over age eighteen if disabled before the age of twenty-two, would also be eligible for benefits through a senior. Widow(er)s — even if divorced, provided the marriage lasted ten years — may also be eligible.

If a senior is forced to retire before sixty-two, due to poor health, he may qualify for Social Security disability benefits. There are three essential requirements for eligibility. Initially, a minimum of twenty-eight credits — twenty of which were earned in the last ten years — are required (as of 1998). The disabling physical or mental condition must have lasted, or be expected to last for at least a year, and it must be severe enough to prevent work at any substantial employment. If there is any question, it is best to call the local Social Security office to get more information and, if necessary or appropriate, seek legal assistance. Fees in this area are limited by law and are paid out of any recovery obtained.

The future of Social Security has been the subject of much debate of late. Critics express the fear that the system will flounder and become bankrupt when Boomers reach the age to collect. Optimistic proponents, on the other hand, assert that the system is in good shape, as exhibited by its current reserves of some $650 billion, and as supported by our healthy economy. All agree that the system does need a tune up; the question is how much? At projected levels, the system will take in more than it pays out through the year 2018 and it will take another ten years before reserves are exhausted. Even then, say the economists, the system will still be able to pay out seventy-five percent of benefits. Whatever the ultimate answer, over the next ten or twenty years, there is bound to be a significant evolution in the system calculated to maintain the financial security of America's senior population.

MEDICARE

Medicare is a national health insurance program for persons sixty-five years of age and older, or certain younger, disabled people. It is divided into two parts designated Part A and Part B, both of which have limitations and deductibles. Commonly called "hospital insurance," Part A pays for care in a hospital or skilled nursing facility and home health or hospice care within certain parameters. Part B — the "medical insurance" — pays for doctors, outpatient hospital care and other medical services not covered by Part A, again within certain limitations.

Medicare is administered by the Health Care Financing Administration (HCFA) which is a federal agency in the Department of Health and Human Services. The Social Security Administration (SSA) helps HCFA by enrolling people in Medicare and by collecting Medicare premiums. In addition, various commercial insurance companies are under contract with HCFA to process and pay Medicare claims and groups of doctors and other health care professionals have contracts to monitor the quality of care delivered to Medicare beneficiaries.

Eligibility and Premiums — Medicare was established in 1965 and, like Social Security, was developed for people who have worked during their lifetime and who have earned credits. If a person — or his or her spouse — has worked for at least ten years in Medicare-covered employment, is over sixty-five years old, and a citizen or permanent resident of the United States, he is eligible for Medicare. Others not meeting those requirements may still be eligible although there may be a monthly premium ($309 in 1998), which changes every year, associated with their eligibility.

Enrollment in Medicare is automatic for those who have worked, are qualified and **are receiving Social Security**. Medicare cards are mailed about three months before the individual's sixty-fifth birthday. Both Part A and Part B are automatic but if a senior does not wish to be enrolled in Part B there are instructions which are provided on how to drop the coverage. **If you are not automatically enrolled you need to apply within a seven month initial enrollment period beginning three months before your sixty-fifth birthday.**

For most people there are no premiums for Part A benefits. However, everyone pays a premium of $43.80 per month for Part B coverage. If you are receiving Social Security the premium will be deducted from your benefits check. If you fail to enroll during the initial period you will have to wait until the next enrollment period to sign up. If you wait twelve or more months to enroll, your Part B premiums will be increased by ten percent for each year of delay. The increased amount must be paid for the rest of your life. If you have to pay a premium for Part A coverage that will increase as well. Enrollment periods are held from January 1st to March 31st of each year and Part B coverage starts the following July.

For seniors who are members of a group health insurance plan based on their own or their spouse's current employment or based on the current employment of any family member, there is an exception to the standard enrollment period. There is a choice of enrolling in Part B at any time while covered by the group health plan or enrolling in Part B during an eight month enrollment period that begins the month employment ends or the month when the senior is no longer covered under the employer plan, whichever comes first.

For seniors who continue to work after sixty-five, it is advisable to enroll in Part A no matter what the situation may be with group health coverage. There is no cost associated with Part A coverage, and it frequently pays for medical costs not covered by the group insurance. It may not be a good idea to sign up for Part B, however, since those benefits would be secondary to your existing health policy and you would start the running of your six month open enrollment period for the purposes of Medigap insurance. (See the Insurance chapter.)

Fee-for-Service or Managed Care — Medicare benefits may be received in one of two ways; **fee-for-service** or **managed care.** Regardless of the form of payment chosen, all Medicare benefits, protections and appeal rights are maintained.

With fee-for-service benefits, there is complete freedom to choose who or what doctors or other medical service providers may be used by the senior for any medical issue. When a medical bill is incurred, it is submitted by the doctor on behalf of the senior, and Medicare pays its share. The senior is responsible for paying the balance as well as paying for services not covered under Medicare. This balance may be paid by another insurance provider or out-of-pocket.

Under a fee-for-service approach, if the doctor you select accepts assignment from Medicare, you will not be charged more than the Medicare approved amount for the medical service rendered. Once your deductible for Part B is paid you must still pay the "coinsurance" amount of twenty percent (see below for further information on Medicare deductibles and coinsurance charges). If your doctor does not accept assignment he may charge up to fifteen percent more than the approved rate which would then require you to pay your coinsurance amount and the excess charged over the approved rate. Some doctors and medical suppliers only accept certain matters on assignment while others, called participating doctors and suppliers, will accept assignment of all Medicare claims. A list of participating doctors and suppliers may be obtained by calling the medicare service company for your area.

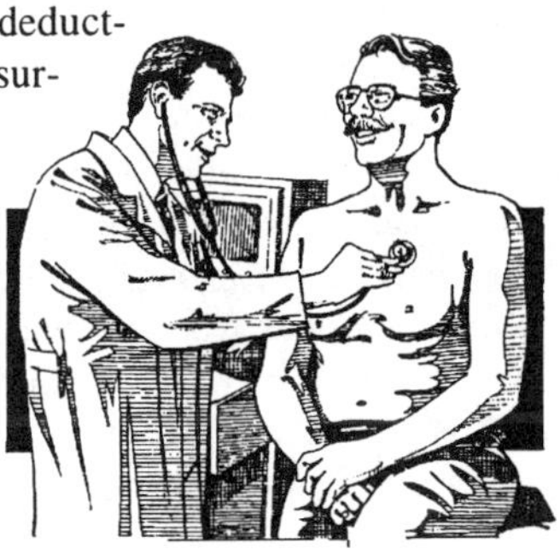

Managed care plans (commonly referred to as health maintenance organizations, or HMOs) contract with Medicare to provide all of Medicare's benefits to their members. They frequently offer additional benefits as well, such as help with prescription drugs, and preventative health care such as physicals, eye examinations, hearing aids, and inoculations not routinely covered by Medicare. There may be a small fee for those services but usually far less than what it would cost in a fee-for-service situation. Additionally, a member will not pay Medicare deductibles or coinsurance. He will, however, continue to pay his Medicare premiums and may have to pay a fixed monthly premium to the managed care plan as well as a small copayment each time a medical service is used. Although the use of a managed care plan does have its benefits it may also control some important health care decisions. Doctors and hospitals available for medical treatments, for example, may be limited to providers listed with the managed care plan and coverage may be denied if you wish to avail yourself of a different health care provider.

A network of doctors and hospitals, skilled nursing care and home health agencies service each plan . Some plans maintain a staff of primary care physicians, at one or several health facilities, while most contract with the services of hospitals and health care providers already operating in the area. Central facilities are less common in Virginia than in other states. Managed care is a relatively new trend in the Commonwealth, currently accounting for approximately sixteen percent of Medicare benefits. In some other states that figure is in excess of fifty percent.

Unlike some of the older managed care plans, all managed care plans currently allow the senior to select a primary care doctor from those who are members of the plan. If no selection is made, a primary care doctor is selected by the plan and assigned to the recipient. This doctor is then responsible for the case management of the recipient, including necessary hospital admissions and referrals to specialists. The primary care doctor may be changed at the request of the senior, but the replacement physician must come from the list of participating doctors. (See the Insurance chapter for further information about managed care plans.)

FOR A LIST OF PARTICIPATING DOCTORS OR SPECIFIC COVERAGE QUESTIONS

For the Counties of Arlington and Fairfax:
Xact Medicare Services
(800) 233-1124

For the rest of Virginia:
MetraHealth
(800) 552-3423

The National Medicare Hotline:
(800) 638-6833

Medicare Benefits — Within limitations, Medicare will cover a significant part of the medical needs of retired Americans. However, it is not designed to be the primary coverage in situations where another group health policy is in effect; nor will it be primary if there is no fault or liability auto insurance available for payment. In most cases worker's compensation coverage will be the primary source of medical payments for work related injuries. If you are eligible for veteran benefits as well as Medicare, you may choose which program will provide the necessary treatment.

While the broad categories of coverage extended through Medicare are fairly simple to state, the specifics of coverage are another matter. It seems Medicare coverage is in constant turmoil. Changes, sometimes substantial, occur at least annually relative to what is or is not covered. Additionally, there is a certain amount of flexibility and discretion held by the decision makers as to what will be covered in a particular case. Consequently, any questions of specific coverage should be directed to the appropriate Medicare carrier for your area, or to Medicare directly.

If you are seeking specific coverage but your request is denied there are remedies available. Typically, the medical provider will tell you that a certain procedure is not covered. If so request the treatment anyway and ask the provider to send in a claim in order to get an official determination from Medicare. If the decision is a denial there will be specific instructions on the back of the form describing how to appeal the decision. If you are part of a managed care plan, the first step is seeking a reconsideration by the plan, which may be done on an expedited basis if serious medical conditions warrant it. After the plan's reconsideration, the normal Medicare appeals process is then available if necessary.

Of course, in any of these matters, an ultimate denial after appeal will result in the charges being assessed against the person receiving the treatment. However, according to the HCFA, approximately seventy percent of all appeals taken result in at least some success. But, the appeals process is slow, often taking several months, if not years, to reach even the first level. As a result of the time and possible costs to the patient, it is extremely important that the treating physician support the treatment and the appeal. Medicare is bound by law to give a great deal of weight to the opinions of the patient's doctor.

Commonly, disputes arise regarding coverage of a hospital admission or the time of the discharge of a hospital or nursing home patient. Medicare provides payment for a variable number of recovery days for any given medical treatment subject to the discretion of the doctors and hospitals involved. If you feel that you are not well enough to be discharged you have a right to a review by the state's Peer Review Organization (PRO). During the review, if timely made, you may remain in the hospital at no charge and cannot be discharged until a decision has been reached. The rules of PRO review will vary depending upon whether you are in a managed care plan or fee-for-service. Make sure that you receive full details of your rights from the hospital or nursing home discharge planner and the PRO. Depending upon the magnitude of the problem, you may wish to have a personal representative acting on your behalf. An attorney versed in the minutiae of peer review will be able to cut through mounds of red tape and otherwise insure that your claim is appropriately handled. The time involved in a peer review, although short, may provide at least a couple of days toward the additional recovery period sought.

VIRGINIA'S PEER REVIEW ORGANIZATION

Virginia Health Quality Center
(800)545-3814

PROs are funded by the federal government and are charged with the obligation of monitoring the quality and extent of care provided to Medicare patients by hospitals, skilled nursing facilities, home health agencies, managed care plans, and ambulatory surgical centers. It is important to keep in mind, however, that the members of the PRO work daily with hospital and nursing home administrators and staff and may very well give their contentions more credence than your claims. It is important, therefore, that you clearly express your views to your physician and insist that the reviewer obtain and independently evaluate your medical record if your doctor concurs with your need for an extended recovery period or other complaint.

Medicare Part A coverage for hospitalization and skilled nursing care is allocated through the use of "benefit periods." There is a limit to the number of days Medicare will help pay for hospital or skilled nursing home care during any benefit period and once that limit is exceeded, the senior is responsible for all charges. A benefit period begins on the day of hospital admission and ends 60 days after discharge from the hospital or nursing home. Once a new benefit period has begun, the recipient is entitled to Medicare coverage on any new admission with the standard limitations. There is no limit to the number of benefit periods a recipient can use.

After a deductible payment of $764, Medicare pays all medically necessary charges (except for the first three pints of blood) associated with a hospital stay for sixty days and all but the coinsurance of $191 per day thereafter through the ninetieth day. A period of sixty "reserve days" is available at a coinsurance rate of $382 per day. The deductible is payable only once during any benefit period regardless of the number of hospitalizations, but once a new benefit period begins it must be paid again. A new benefit period also provides for an additional ninety days of hospital coverage, but used reserve days are not renewed.

Often continued nursing care or therapy is necessary after a hospital stay for further treatment of the medical condition. Medicare will provide coverage for nursing home care in a **skilled nursing facility** only and does not cover mere custodial care. Medicare will pay the full costs of the first twenty days and will pay all but the daily coinsurance of $95.50 for the next eighty days. The coverages will be renewed at the start of a new benefit period. Skilled nursing care coverage requires that there be at least a three day hospitalization for the condition being treated prior to the medically necessary nursing home admission and that the admission take place within thirty days of the hospital discharge.

There are also provisions for home health care which covers those who are confined to their homes and require skilled care for an injury or illness. Medicare pays the entire bill for covered services as long as they are medically reasonable and necessary. Prior hospitalization is not required, but confined to the home means exactly that. For example, a woman is not homebound if she can drive a car; goes to a daycare center or relative's home part of the time — even with help; leaves her home against doctor's orders; does shopping or business on a regular basis; or leaves home for any nonmedical reason. In essence, to be homebound it must be medically difficult and taxing for her to leave. She may go to the doctor if such medical care can only be obtained outside the home. For those who meet eligibility, Medicare covers part-time or intermittent skilled nursing services, home health aide service or physical, speech-language, and occupational therapy. They also cover the cost of some medical supplies when billed by the home health agency and 80% of the approved amount for durable medical equipment such as wheelchairs, hospital beds, oxygen supplies and walkers.

If a terminal illness has been diagnosed the patient may be eligible for "hospice care," which is intended to provide comfort and relief from pain as opposed to treatment of the underlying condition. Once hospice care is chosen by the patient, standard Medicare coverage **for that condition only** is discontinued. Hospice care takes place at home and includes many services not normally covered by Medicare such as pain relief medication and home maker services. All costs associated with hospice care are paid by Medicare except a token amount for prescriptions and inpatient respite care which is designed to provide some time off for the care giver. There are special benefit periods associated with hospice care consisting of two ninety day benefit periods, followed by a thirty day period, and then an indefinite extension as needed. The benefit periods may be used consecutively or at dif-

ferent times but if hospice care is cancelled during any of the periods the remaining time in that period is forever lost. If the care is cancelled by the patient during the last period, the hospice benefit cannot be used again.

Medicare Part B coverage — the "medical coverage" — costs $43.80 per month but helps to pays for a wide range of medical services and supplies including doctor bills. Essentially, most medical items are covered except routine physicals, dental work, routine foot care, hearing or vision examinations, glasses or hearing aids. Neither will it pay for most prescription drugs. Medically necessary services of a doctor are covered no matter where they are received, in a hospital, in a doctor's office, a clinic, a nursing home or at home. There are a number of changes taking place in Part B, including the extension of preventative examinations such as Pap smears and mammography. Flu and pneumonia shots are included as is a hepatitis B vaccine if you are at risk. There are limitations on the number of times some treatments or tests may be utilized in any given period (one, two, or three years).

After a $100 annual deductible, Part B will pay eighty percent of most covered charges except laboratory services which Medicare pays at one hundred percent and some outpatient mental health services which are covered at fifty percent. The twenty percent coinsurance you pay under Part B is twenty percent of what you are charged, not twenty percent of the Medicare rate. It is important that you determine, at the beginning, whether the anticipated charges will exceed the approved rate.

MEDICAID

Medicaid was created to assist people with little income and few assets. Although many would insist that Medicaid, therefore, is of no concern to them, there is **relevance to all but the very wealthy** or those with an adequate long-term care insurance policy. About forty-eight percent of the long-term nursing home costs in this country are paid through Medicaid. Approximately two percent is covered by long-term health insurance and Medicare. The balance is privately paid. So, if a senior requires institutional care there is almost a fifty percent probability that he will also need Medicaid assistance. But obtaining that help may be extremely costly in terms of the dissipation of assets and income. A Medicaid application requires you to count as a part of your assets transfers that occurred as much as five years earlier and eligibility requires you to "spend down" those transfers and your other assets, through medical expenditures, to a minimal level.

VIRGINIA'S DEPARTMENT OF SOCIAL SERVICES HOTLINE

800-552-3431

Medi**care** is designed to help older people from all income levels and is based upon work history rather than need. It could be considered, and in fact is, an insurance policy purchased over the years through payroll taxes. Medi**caid**, on the other hand, is designed to help low income Americans of all ages, regardless of their work history. Both programs are formulated to provide access to health care. While Medicare does not provide for "custodial nursing care," Medicaid does. Additionally, Medicare does not cover certain medical procedures, such as eye examinations, routine foot care, much home care or transportation for medical care, while Medicaid covers them all as well as the costs of prescription drugs.

Medicaid finances health care for more than 37 million people in the nation, including blind, disabled and elderly beneficiaries. Medicaid is a state-administered health care program jointly financed by federal and state monies according to a complex and often controversial formula. Unlike Medicare, therefore, the eligibility requirements and benefits of Medicaid will vary considerably from state to state. The extremely complicated rules, regulations, and formulae governing Medicaid are beyond the scope of this book in all but the most general way. Consequently, it is suggested that you request the free *Virginia Medicaid Handbook,* and the various eligibility criteria fact sheets from your local Social Services department. The state Department of Social Services hotline can provide you the location and telephone number of your local department. Obtaining and using that information long before you are in need will enable you to take steps to protect your assets, although it must be recognized that the system is undergoing massive changes on an ongoing basis and periodically updating your information is advisable.

Recently, more and more states have moved away from the traditional fee-for-service reimbursement system and toward the managed care model for Medicaid. Many states have completely turned over their Medicaid programs to managed care. In 1992 Virginia phased in a managed care program for Medicaid beneficiaries known as the Medallion plan. Under the plan, a primary care provider coordinates a client's medical needs. By July 1996, Medallion covered 200,000 people. It provided better case management and higher levels of care while reducing Medicaid costs for the populations served by five percent. It was considered so successful that a sister program, Medallion II, was begun in Hampton Roads.

To qualify for long-term care you must have no more than $2000 in **countable assets**. Those assets are determined through a listing of all your assets and subtracting assets you may keep, such as your home, a car, household furnishings, burial plots and savings for burial, and a small amount of life insurance. The balance, including bank and retirement accounts and other real estate and investments, are your countable assets. Generally, you must expend all but $2000 of your countable assets paying for long-term care prior to qualifying for Medicaid. Furthermore, virtually all income you receive will go toward the costs of long-term care. For example, assume you have $35,000 of countable assets and receive $1435 per month from your Social Security and a small pension. You require long-term care which costs $3600 per month. To receive Medicaid benefits you would first have to pay $1400 per month from your income ($1435 less your personal needs allowance of $35), and **spend down** your accumulated assets at a monthly rate of $2200. Doing so will reduce your countable assets to a total of $2000 in about fifteen months. Thereafter, you would pay $1400 per month and Medicaid would pay the balance.

If you are married you are deemed to have **all** assets held or controlled by your spouse subject to federal laws prohibiting "spousal impoverishment." Basically, excluded from countable assets is a minimum amount of $15,804, or fifty percent of all assets (after deduction of other excluded amounts), to a maximum of $79,020 which is allocated to the spouse remaining home.

For example, assume that a married couple have $250,000 in countable assets. They would have to spend down all but $79,020 and the $2000 countable asset base before Medicaid would begin paying. The $168,980 which the couple would have to pay could cover three to five years of nursing home care but would seriously deplete their assets unless they had an appropriate insurance policy in effect.

If the same couple decided to divorce, the property, including stocks or investments, could be split with half (or some other appropriate percentage), awarded to each partner under Virginia domestic relations law. In order for an ailing ex-husband to be eligible for Medicaid, he would only have title to the half of the assets which were awarded to him in the divorce and would therefore only have to deplete those assets before he would be eligible. Also, the assets awarded to the sick spouse could consist of primarily noncountable assets, such as the house, thereby decreasing the amount required to be depleted. The well spouse would have retained at least $125,000 in otherwise countable assets (and possibly a great deal more) rather than the maximum sum allowed by Medicaid.

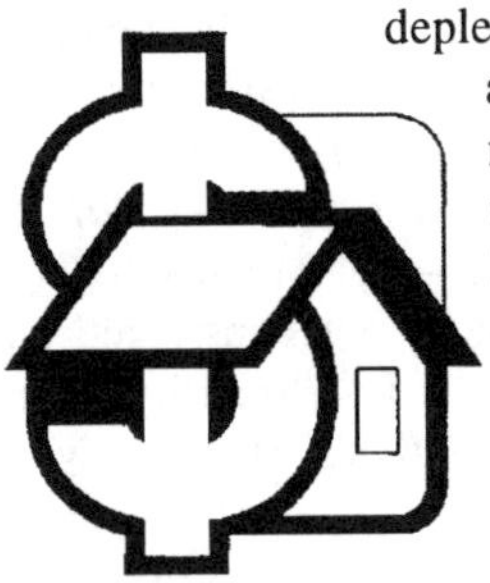

Marital income may also be protected to a certain extent. The spouse at home may retain the greater of his or her individual monthly income or an income allowance from the couple's total income. These figures are constrained by federal dictates that the minimum be at least $1295 and the maximum be no more than $1976 per month. The income allowance consists of the $1295 minimum and the amount by which the monthly rent or mortgage payment and utilities exceed $389.

If a couple each has a $1000 monthly pension for a total monthly income of $2000, and if the housing cost totals $789 per month, the at-home spouse will receive an income allowance of $1695 (the $1295 minimum plus $400 in housing costs). The institutionalized spouse would receive a $35 monthly personal allowance and the remainder of the $2000 ($280), would be given to the nursing home.

Suppose that the monthly income for the same couple consisted of $1600 in pension income and $400 in interest income from a $120,000 savings account paying four percent interest. Each spouse and the nursing home would receive identical amounts but the at-home spouse may be able, through a court proceeding, to retain the savings as part of the property transferred to him even though it exceeds the maximum allowable property retention of $79,020. If the money in the savings account were spent down for nursing home care, the reduction of income would put the at-home spouse below the minimum allowable income allowance of $1295 plus the $400 excess housing cost.

If a transfer of assets for less than fair market value is found to have occurred within thirty-six months (for some trusts within sixty months), prior to institutionalization or application for Medicaid, payments for nursing home care will be withheld for a certain time frame referred to as the **penalty period**. That period is determined by dividing the asset value by the average monthly private-pay rate for nursing home care. If an elderly woman decides to give her six grandchildren a gift of $10,000 each, and is then faced with the need for nursing home care within three years, the $60,000 will be deemed available. That sum, divided by an assumed $3000 per month nursing home cost, will result in a penalty period of twenty months. If the senior had no other liquid assets to pay for the nursing home, she would be in a great deal of trouble. If she had anticipated the problem and given, instead, a total of $30,000, she would have a penalty period of only ten months and the cash to pay for it.

After the death of a participant, Medicaid will generally seek reimbursement. A lien will be placed on a house and, if the house is sold or title is transferred, Medicaid will collect on that lien. If the participant is survived by a spouse, the claim will be postponed until the survivor passes away. Even though a house will not be included in countable assets for eligibility determination, it is fair game for Medicaid collection. If, however, the ownership of the house were deeded to the at-home spouse it could then be deeded, after three years, by the at-home spouse to another. If done prior to lien placement it may protect the asset from being taken or sold. If the house were transferred three years prior to Medicaid involvement, it would not be subject to collection at all. Since we are discussing transfers for less than full value there are gift and estate tax implications which should be considered.

There are a great number of exceptions to the transfer rules — not to mention a great deal of flexibility in the asset and income rules — of Medicaid. For example, a transfer to third party for the benefit of a spouse is not considered an improper transfer nor are transfers for a purpose other than Medicaid eligibility. But how can you know whether a contemplated transfer fits an exception? How can you position yourself to take advantage of increased asset retention? It would seem that legal and financial advice in the asset transfer area, and in evaluating your particular asset and income situation, would be extremely important, if not critical, in order to make informed choices about your future.

Unfortunately, recently enacted laws have had a significant chilling effect on the ability of a lawyer, accountant or financial planner to advise you. The Balanced Budget Act of 1997 created vast changes in Medicare and Medicaid law and continues a clear congressional effort toward the elimination of health care fraud and to financially shore up the faltering health care system. The 1996 Health Insurance Portability and Accountability Act (HIPAA), contained provisions to make it a federal crime, punishable by up to five years in prison and a $25,000 fine, to "knowingly and willfully dispose of assets (including any transfer in trust) in order for an individual to become eligible for medical assistance [through Medicaid]...if disposing of the assets results in the imposition of a [penalty period]." The implications of this law were so broad, and so much was written about making criminals of grandparents who gave money to their grandchildren to go to the movies, that the 1997 additions to the law imposed penalties only on professionals such as lawyers, accountants and financial planners who, for a fee, counseled others to make transfers to create eligibility for Medicaid. But what if there are other valid, legal reasons for making a transfer and Medicaid eligibility is just a by-product? Would, or should, an attorney risk his license and livelihood, not to mention incurring the possibility of going to jail, to help you with that transfer?

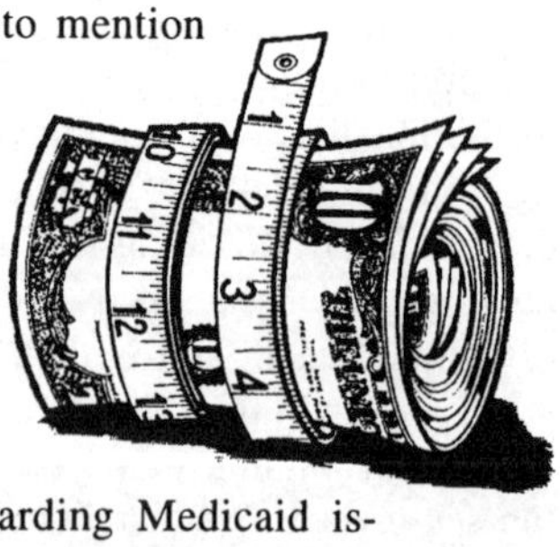

A spokesman for the American Bar Association, joining many elder law practitioners in questioning the law's viability, has criticized it as being unprecedented and unconstitutional. Advocates for the law believe it will resolve, at least in part, Medicaid fraud. But until settled out, this law will have a serious dampening effect on the planning and advice available regarding Medicaid issues. Since Medicaid staff are not allowed to answer substantive questions or respond to hypothetical situations, there may be no one for people to turn to for information and advice. For example, upon inquiry people are often told by Medicaid staff, only that they must spend down to the $2000 countable asset base to achieve eligibility. While true, it does not take into account the various marital considerations, nor explain perfectly legal and ethical asset transfer issues.

VETERANS BENEFITS

Qualified veterans may obtain from the federal government numerous benefits including medical and dental care. For service-connected pension benefits, the veteran must have a disability or disease incurred or aggravated during active service. If a veteran qualifies, medical care is also available on a priority basis.

For a veteran with a nonservice-connected disability to be eligible for pension benefits he or she must be permanently and totally disabled, have served at least one day during a period of war, and meet certain income and net worth limitations. If a different means test dealing with financial and insurance issues is met, the veteran may get medical care on a priority basis.

If a veteran is eligible a decision must be made as to whether to utilize Veterans benefits or Medicare. Various benefits are also offered to spouses and dependents of disabled veterans. To test your eligibility and apply for benefits contact the United States Department of Veterans Affairs at (800) 827-1000.

TAX REDUCTIONS

Most Virginia county and city governments offer senior property owners a reduction in their real estate taxes. Many also offer special personal property tax rates. The rate reduction amount and qualifications vary, but it is well worth a call to the tax assessor's office in your area to get the information.

Virginia provides an additional, personal income tax exemption for tax payers age sixty-five or older. There is also an age deduction of $6000 for individuals between sixty-two and sixty-four and $12,000 for those sixty-five or older (1996 figures). Further information is available from the Virginia Department of Taxation.

Insurance

Although the history of insurance can arguably be traced back to the Greeks and Romans who provided for the care and retirement of their leaders, the modern concept of insurance probably began in the 1600s. It was about that time that two French mathematicians, Blaise Pascal and Pierre de Fermat, developed the theory of probability which is now widely used to develop insurance rates. In 1695, in Paris, an Italian banker, Lorenzo Tonti developed a system — for investors to share the risks and benefits of all members — called a *tontine.* Upon the death of a member, all shares were divided among the survivors and so on until only one survivor remained who took control of all assets. A variety of this quickly developed with an expiration date and all surviving members divided the assets at the end of a given period of time.

The Great Fire of London in 1666 led a doctor named Nicholas Barbon to develop the first fire insurance office and Benjamin Franklin helped found the American colonies' first mutual fire insurance company in Philadelphia in 1752.

The practice of **underwriting** began about 1688 in the coffee house of Edward Lloyd. Shipowners and merchants met and developed a system of marine insurance. They recorded the ship's cargo on a piece of paper and it was read by the coffee house patrons. Those willing to share the risk of insuring the cargo signed their names under the statement and indicated the share of risk they would **underwrite** or guarantee. If the ship went down, the patrons paid. If it completed its voyage, they received a portion of the profit for their guarantee to pay in case of a disaster.

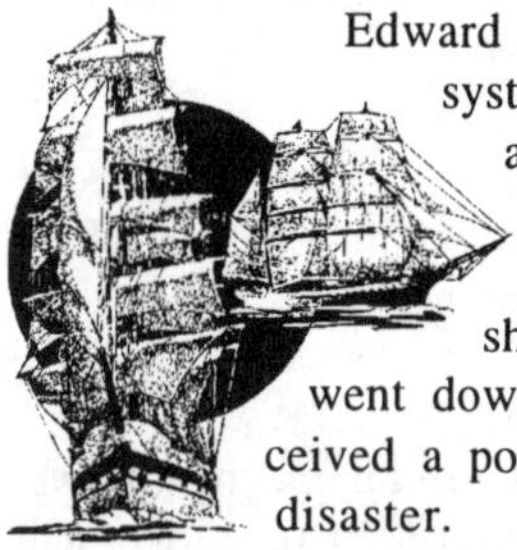

All insurance is based on the principle of sharing losses. It provides protection to those who experience a disaster by collecting from those who do not have the need to use the service. When a payment is made by the company, it is called a **benefit**. The greater the sum of money which must potentially be paid, the higher the cost of the insurance (**premiums**). The cost of the premium also depends on the statistical probability that the individual will collect and those who are more likely to collect will be charged more. Insurance works because policyholders are willing to trade a small, certain loss — the cost of the premium — for the guarantee that they will be paid (**indemnified**) in case of a larger loss. Insurance companies themselves expect to make a profit after paying benefits and meeting administrative costs. When more policyholders make claims, or when the claims paid exceed the amount collected in premiums, the rates, or cost of buying the guarantee, will increase.

With advancing technology, life has been prolonged. Penicillin was discovered in London in 1928 and ushered in the "Antibiotic Age." The first medical treatment using Penicillin did not come until 1941, when a British policeman suffering from bacterial blood poisoning received the drug. Because of the treatment's success demand rose yet the supply of the drug remained scarce. Fueled by the need for antibiotics during World War II, research pushed forward. In 1943 a high-yielding type of Penicillium mold was discovered and penicillin production increased greatly. Suddenly thousands of conditions which had previously been considered fatal, were not only controllable, but curable. The "Golden Age of Medical Science" emerged. New medical equipment and procedures were developed. The average life span of Americans went from sixty-three years in 1940 to seventy-six years in 1996 and continues to climb.

Today, new drugs and techniques are developing at an ever increasing rate and any number of major breakthroughs are controlling diseases and conditions which were considered terminal not many years ago. Not only are people living much longer than they once did, but rehabilitation is returning people to a normal life from conditions which a short time ago would have been debilitating or fatal.

Unfortunately, this type of care is expensive. A single prescription may be as much as several hundred dollars. Operations, even fairly simple procedures, may run $10,000-15,000 and complex procedures could readily exceed $100,000. A month in a nursing home will typically be $3,000 or more. Because of the tremendous expense associated with treatment, insurance has become a necessity rather than a luxury for our senior population.

The balance between controlling cost and providing for human need is one of the most urgent and growing problems faced by our health care system. Do we only provide health care for those who can afford expensive procedures? Do we provide care for everyone, even if they cannot pay? What about extreme or experimental treatments? Who will establish guidelines determining when extensive care is provided and when it is withheld because it is a waste of resources? When patients without insurance or the ability to pay are extended care, hospitals and doctors bear the cost of treatment in the form of uncollectible receivables. This raises the overall expense for insurance companies and private pay patients in obtaining medical care and continues the upward spiral of health care costs.

Many health care professionals believe that when Medicare became law in 1965, the whole medical establishment and its patients developed a "blank check" mentality under which the government and private insurers were expected to pay most or all of virtually any bill submitted. Fraudulent treatment and billing practices under traditional "fee-for-service" plans were engaged in by doctors and hospitals. Driven in part by increasing malpractice litigation and insurance premiums, unnecessary medical procedures were performed which were paid by the "system." In fact, abuse of Medicare and Medicaid was an accepted fact in the health care world until Congress put down its collective foot.

The result of all these factors was runaway inflation in the health care industry. In 1980, for example, Americans spent $247 billion on health care or 8.9% of the gross domestic product (GDP). By 1990 that figure had risen to $697 billion, which was 12.1% of the GDP. By the next century that figure is expected to rise to 16%. By comparison, Canada spends 9.6% of it's gross domestic product, while Japan spends only 7.2%, on health care.

With increasing health care costs the insurance industry responded with rising premiums and decreasing benefits. By the beginning of the '90s major corporations began to question if they were really getting healthier, happier workers for the amount they were spending on health coverage. Soon, they began to move employees into much less expensive managed care plans called HMOs (health maintenance organizations). Although the freedom of choice of medical providers was restricted, preventative care and screenings were often included in benefit packages and many medical problems were diagnosed sooner and became more treatable as a result.

The competition for managed care contracts and the controls placed on tests and procedures have made hospitals and doctors more cost conscious and more treatment conservative. The explosive growth of managed care in health policies, Medicare, and Medicaid compels continued respect for the cost of health care. However, not without social and political ramifications.

The controversy over the quality of care and freedom of choice provided under managed care programs continues unabated with vocal advocates on both sides. The fear of Medicaid fraud has caused the Congressional foot to stomp on the ability of people to make informed decisions by threatening criminal prosecution of their advisors. But it has also brought about modifications in managed care plans designed to alleviate or eliminate perceived problems. It has sanctioned legislation creating standardized Medigap health care policies enabling the senior population to evaluate medical coverage rationally and have freedom of choice under a fee-for-service system. And it has brought about the dialogue which will be necessary to enable the American populace to maintain confidence in the continued prospects of a healthy and secure system to maintain the well being and security of its senior citizens. Changes in all aspects of health care abound. The only thing which can unequivocally be stated is that the proportionate increase in the senior population, and the continued need for all people to avail themselves of ever more expensive health care, will continue to command refinements in the health care system and present challenges well into the next millennium.

At the present time seniors have several choices in medical insurance. Other than employment or organization based health coverage, most choices are founded on Medicare. A senior may **limit health insurance to Medicare**, may **purchase a Medigap policy** to supplement Medicare in a fee-for-service environment, or may **join a managed care plan** to extend Medicare coverage. For additional protection, **long term health insurance** is available.

Before buying any health insurance it is important to evaluate your anticipated needs and understand what insurance is already in place as well as what specific insurance product will be the best for you. Many seniors go through their work lives without paying a great deal of attention to the medical insurance plan provided by their employers. After all, each was likely a group policy sold to the employer with its terms and conditions well established by the insurance company. But when senior status is achieved and retirement contemplated, or in place, it is incumbent upon the senior to make affirmative choices about continued health insurance. With perhaps unfamiliar terminology, a large number of new issues to contend with, and a great deal of variety in the types of policies offered, the senior may find that choosing the right insurance is difficult.

For VICAP Services contact your local Area Agency on Aging or call

(800) 552-3402

The HCFA (Health Care Financing Administration) has funded the Virginia Department for the Aging and charged it with the responsibility of coordinating with state insurance officials to provide **free insurance counseling for people over sixty years old.** This service is called the Virginia Insurance Counseling and Assistance Program or VICAP. Whether the issue involves Medicare, Medicaid, Medigap, managed care, or long term coverage you can receive a confidential evaluation of your situation and information about your various options. The VICAP counselors are trained insurance specialists but they have no affiliation with any insurance company and are not licensed to sell insurance. Your local Area Agency on Aging can make a referral to a VICAP counselor or you may contact the Virginia Department for the Aging.

MEDIGAP INSURANCE

Medicare covers many health care costs, but you will still have to pay Medicare's coinsurance amounts and deductibles. And there are many medical services that Medicare does not cover which are referred to as "gaps." For that reason, many people buy a Medicare supplemental insurance policy, commonly referred to as "Medigap" insurance. Medigap insurance will enable you to stay in a fee-for-service environment, thereby maximizing your choices about medical providers and flexibility about medical treatments.

Medigap is private insurance which, in different forms, helps to pay Medicare coinsurance amounts and deductibles, adds other benefits and extends hospitalization coverage. There are ten standard Medigap policies, each offering a different combination of benefits. **It is important that decisions be made about Medigap enrollment within six months of your enrollment in Medicare Part B if you are age sixty-five or older.** For that period, called "open enrollment," seniors have a right to buy the Medigap policy of their choice. During open enrollment, by Federal law, a senior cannot be turned down or charged higher premiums because of poor health. (A company may refuse coverage for a preexisting condition for the first six months of the policy only.) Once the open enrollment period ends, there may be limits to the type of policy which can be purchased depending upon your health status. For those who are not yet sixty-five but who are currently enrolled in Medicare Part B, Virginia also has a limited Medigap open enrollment period.

There are specific federal laws governing the marketing and sale of Medigap policies which are policed by the state insurance department. All Medigap policies are guaranteed renewable unless there has been a misrepresentation on the application or the premiums are not paid. You may cancel a Medigap policy within thirty days of purchase and receive a full refund of all premiums. With a few exceptions all types of Medigap insurance are available in every state. Insurance companies which sell Medigap are required to sell a "core" package (Plan A). They are allowed to sell up to nine other options (designated Plans B through J) which include all the benefits of Plan A and add different combinations of other benefits to each.

The **Medicare gaps** and costs for Part A (hospitalization coverage) include for each benefit period: a $764 deductible; $191 per day for hospitalization for the third month, and $382 per day for the forth and fifth reserve months. After 150 days there is no further hospital coverage. There is a maximum of 100 days of skilled nursing home coverage, and days 21 through 100 require a $95.50 per day payment by the patient. Home health care is limited to two or three weeks and there is generally no coverage for medical care received outside the United States. Most Plan B services (doctors visits and other "medical" services) require a twenty percent payment by the patient after paying a $100 deductible. There is little or no coverage for prescription drugs, preventative care, or routine examinations.

Plan A of Medigap insurance — the core coverage — will pay for:

1. All of the coinsurance amounts of Medicare Part A for hospitalization ($191 per day for days sixty-one through ninety; $382 per day for the sixty reserve days);
2. A lifetime benefit of an extra 365 days of hospitalization;
3. Three pints of blood;

and, 4. All coinsurance amounts of Medicare Part B (twenty percent of most charges and fifty percent of mental health charges).

Plans B through J add to the core package payment of the hospitalization deductible of $764 per benefit period.

Plans C through J add coverage for the $95.50 per day skilled nursing care coinsurance and eighty percent coverage for emergency care in a foreign country after a $250 deductible. These plans also add various combinations of coverage for the $100 Part B deductible, any excess charges for medical services, provisions for "at home" care, prescription drug benefits and preventative care.

Although companies selling Medigap policies are required to have standard coverages, they do not charge the same amount. It is important to shop around and compare the premium costs between companies. Depending upon how strongly you feel about being in a fee-for-service system, you may also wish to compare pricing between Medigap policies and managed care, but keep in mind that coverage extended under managed care may not fall within well-defined groupings such as Medigap plans A through J. Therefore, any evaluation must take into account the differences in coverage as well.

MANAGED CARE PLANS

Generally speaking managed care provides a cost-effective way to deliver comprehensive health care at rates less than a fee-for-service system. Additionally, managed care is available to younger retirees and is not limited, as Medigap, to the sixty-five year old or older group. Complaints about managed care have tended to obscure the genuine gains that have occurred in the managed-care era. Now, employers can provide health benefits for their employees at a cost the employees (or the company) can afford. Seniors in managed care organizations receive affordable preventative care which is not provided through Medicare. Thanks to managed care, Americans probably have more money in their pockets and are healthier than they have been before.

The freedom of choice provided by any managed care plan is determined primarily by the contractual arrangement that company has with Medicare. There

are two basic types of managed care plans (the "risk" plans and the "cost" plans) and several organizational subcategories each with its own advantages and drawbacks. All types are required to provide all Medicare-covered services and will pay Medicare deductibles and coinsurance amounts and add many health care benefits. Most have restrictions regarding medical treatments obtained outside the plan. Generally, and not surprisingly, it may be said that the more restrictive the plan, the lower the cost and the higher the number of added benefits. Additionally, the more tightly-knit the organization the better the coordination of care but the least amount of consumer choice of medical providers.

A **risk plan** has "lock-in" requirements. This means that all normal services must be received through the plan or through referrals from the plan. Any services not authorized will not be paid by the plan, nor by Medicare, even though services might be those normally covered. An exception under some risk plans (see POS below) permit recipients to receive certain services from providers outside the plan's provider network but only a portion of the charges will be paid. The recipients will be required to pay at least twenty percent of the charge. Risk plans usually offer more in the way of added benefits than cost plans. Approximately seventy-five percent of all plans are the risk type and almost ninety percent of managed care enrollees belong to them.

Cost plans do not lock in the recipient. An enrollee may go to health care providers affiliated with the plan, or those outside the plan. If a health care provider is selected from outside those affiliated with the plan, the managed care company will not pay, but Medicare will pay its portion of approved charges. The senior receiving the treatment will be responsible for Medicare's coinsurance and deductible charges just as if he were under a fee-for-service system. Although usually not providing as many additional benefits as a risk plan, the cost plan is a good choice for those who travel extensively or live in another state part of the year but want to use a managed care plan when in the primary area. It is also useful for a person who wishes to have a managed care plan for most purposes but uses a nonaffiliated doctor for others.

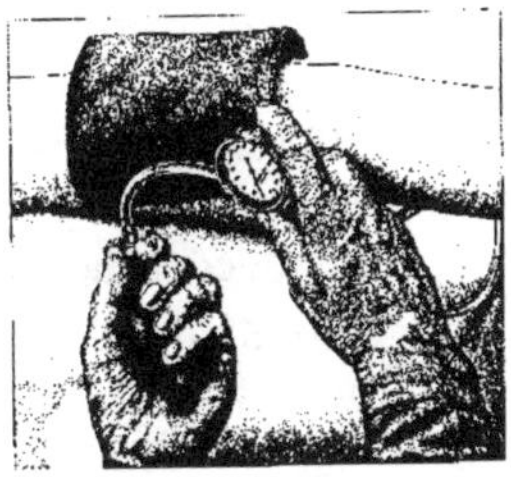

Emergency treatment when a senior is traveling is always covered under both risk and cost plans, as are services which are "urgently needed" when a senior is temporarily out of the plan's service area. A lost prescription might be an example of an "urgent needed " matter. However, active seniors who travel frequently, or who virtually live in two or three different parts of the country (sometimes visiting adult children or friends for extended periods of time) may find it difficult to use managed care. For that reason, some managed care companies are becoming multi-state providers with the capability of easily extending care throughout their jurisdictions.

Whether cost or risk, managed care plans are internally organized in many different forms. The two most prevalent being the Group or Staff Model Health Maintenance Organization (HMOs) and the Individual Practice Associations (IPAs). Other variations include Point of Service Plans (POS) and Preferred Provider Organizations (PPOs).

Staff Model Health Maintenance Organizations (HMOs) often have their own centralized medical centers where the majority of patient treatment occurs. Members choose their primary physician and all health care is coordinated through him. HMOs usually offer significant added benefits such as preventative care and prescription drugs with low copayments. However, they are the most restrictive type of managed care and few choices regarding the medical provider are extended to the consumer.

Individual Practice Associations (IPAs) are a less restrictive form of managed care. Individual practitioners agree to provide, from their own offices, services to members of the plan. Members choose their primary physician from a list of participating doctors who will refer them to another doctor from the list if special care is needed. This form usually provides many added benefits with low copayments. The vast majority of managed care members are enrolled in an IPA and it is the most common form in Virginia.

Point of Service Plans (POS) provide a greater choice in medical treatment options, but at a cost. Usually doctors within the plan must be used but some limited coverage may be provided for nonaffiliated doctors and the patient must pay the balance. Preventative care is often covered within the POS network.

Preferred Provider Organizations (PPOs) allow the patient a choice of using doctors within or without the network. Costs will be lower and some benefits will be added if PPO doctors are used. However, PPO premiums are higher and there is less coordination of care.

In an effort to resolve issues seen as adverse by the consumer, many managed care plans have revised their policies and procedures to the point where the lines between the organizational types have blurred. Some companies even have different options available, at varying premiums or increasing out-of-pocket costs, to provide the level of choice in selecting medical providers that you want.

Added benefits typically found in a managed care plan include dental, visual, hearing and physical examinations, and other preventative care. Also possibly included would be the cost of dental work, eyeglasses, hearing aids and prescriptions. Many managed care companies have different levels of care which provide different combinations of added benefits at, of course, different premiums. If you have Medicare Parts A and B, you can expect to pay around twenty dollars a month for a basic managed care policy. To have extensive coverage your premium will usually be ninety to one hundred dollars a month. Medicare deductibles and coinsurance charges are usually paid through the plan but if too much choice in medical providers is desired the plan may impose its own deductibles and coinsurance charges.

If, after you have evaluated your budget, your needs, and the services provided through a managed care plan, you decide to enroll, you may join during the open enrollment period of the company. Each plan must have an open enrollment of at least thirty days each year when Medicare recipients are accepted in the order of application. No Medicare approved plan may exclude you as a result of your health status unless you have been diagnosed with kidney failure or are terminally ill.

After joining, you are free to stay, change plans, or return to fee-for-service as you please. To terminate your membership in a plan send a signed request to your local Social Security office and you will be placed back on fee-for-service on the first of the following month. If you change plans, your new enrollment will automatically cancel the first plan.

The only potential trouble spot in either enrolling or leaving a managed care plan is the status of your Medigap insurance coverage. If you have a Medigap policy you may wish to cancel it since there will be overlapping coverages. On the other hand, if you do cancel it and then decide to go back to fee-for-service Medicare, you may be limited in the availability of Medigap insurance due to health and age issues. The better course is to maintain your Medigap policy until you have determined through use that the managed care plan will serve your needs.

Usually, the choices regarding managed care are not as difficult to evaluate as it may seem. In any given region, you may have only one managed care company operating and, at most, two or three. Since premiums and additional benefits can vary widely among plans, it is important to comparison shop if there are different plans operating in your area. Gathering the information readily available from the company or companies and discussing it with your local VICAP counselor will enable you to make the appropriate decision given your particular circumstances.

MEDICARE SELECT

Originally a fifteen state experimental program, Congress has now expanded Medicare SELECT to all fifty states. It is a hybrid Medigap/managed care insurance program which is offered by some insurance companies and managed care plans. The Virginia legislature has approved Medicare SELECT, but at the current time no companies have been approved to sell it. It will be available in the near future. Basically, it consists of one of the approved ten Medigap plans operating in a managed care (as opposed to fee-for-service) environment. Although providing identical coverage, these policies generally have lower premiums then standard Medigap policies because of this requirement.

LONG TERM CARE INSURANCE

Long term health care is not covered through Medicare, any Medigap policy, or within a managed care plan except in very limited ways. Long-term care insurance was introduced about twenty-five years ago to fill that need but even ten years ago it was still a very small part of the market. It has recently grown exponentially. It has also changed considerably. Early policies often had conditions which made them useless in any significant manner and home health coverage was offered in far fewer policies. Financial planners advise that the high cost of long-term health care is among one of the major threats to financial security which faces the retirement population.

Long-term care is any type of health care which involves an ongoing period of medical or custodial care. This may be simply care needed by those who can no longer perform some activities of daily living (ADL). (See the Assisted Living chapter.) It may also involve care in a facility which provides nursing care, or skilled nursing care. The average nursing home stay costs approximately $36,000 a year, but in major cities that figure can exceed $70,000, and home care may be almost as expensive! Depending on the study used, the average stay in a nursing home in a long term care context is thirty-two to forty months.

The 1996 Health Insurance Portability and Accountability Act (HIPAA) contains provisions that affect long-term health care insurance. The government has taken the position that the purchase of private, long-term health care insurance should be encouraged. To promote this position, HIPAA increased the tax deductibility for the cost of this insurance and provided for the benefits to be tax free. Among other "qualifications" the insurance is required to have no cash value nor can it be eligible to borrow against or be used as collateral. It must be guaranteed renewable and it must **only** cover long-term care and not provide benefits covered by government-funded programs.

Long-term insurance may be purchased on a group or individual basis. There are choices of benefits and policies are quoted and priced according to the level of daily benefits, which can vary from $50 to $300 or more. Some policies have a cap on total benefits, while others are open ended. A majority will cover home care. Many companies have dropped their exclusion of preexisting conditions while others still maintain them. Age, health, and family history are also factors used in determining the premium cost.

Different companies have variable waiting periods before coverage is effective and benefits are paid for long term care. Shorter waiting periods add to the cost of the plan. Some other things to look for are the types of care covered. Does it cover nursing care, skilled nursing care, custodial care and cognitive impairment needs? Is there a requirement to be hospitalized before collecting benefits? Are there limits to the type of facility used? For example, must a person needing ADL help, but not nursing care, reside in an adult care home (typically under fifteen or twenty residents and requiring only minimal licensing), or will it cover the more expensive assisted living facilities with enrichment programs and trained personnel?

When applying for long-term care insurance, expect to make an individual application and to provide medical records. There will probably be a telephone or face-to-face interview and in some cases a qualifying physical. Some policies have inflation riders which provide for future increases in the cost of health care. This provision protects the insured and is required in some states, but not in Virginia although many companies offer it voluntarily.

Studies indicate that a man has a one in ten chance of facing a long-term care bill of up to $225,000. Women face a one in seven chance, largely because women outlive men on an average. Many women will face this bill after the death of their husbands. At this time about fifty percent of all nursing home expenses are paid for by residents or their families. A smaller percentage is paid by Medicaid after all personal resources have been depleted. Only about 2% is paid by Medicare or private insurance.

Although the exact cost of premiums will vary considerably, the chart below will give some idea of how the premiums will increase with age.

Those not yet 40	$200 per year
40-50 years old	$375 per year
50-60 years old	$250-$1,500 per year
60-70 years old	$300-$2,600 per year
over 70 years	$1,100-$5,000 per year

Long-term care insurance is most advisable for those who have at least $75,000 in individual assets, not including a home, have an annual retirement income of over $30,000 per household per year, and can afford the premium payments comfortably, even with increases of as much as twenty to thirty percent. This group is the one most likely to lose the greatest economically should long term care be necessary. (See the Medicaid chapter.) If individuals ultimately needing long-term coverage wait too long, available policies may be expensive, subject to extensive conditions and exclusions, and may not provide the benefits that are really necessary in your situation. Prior to buying a long-term health care policy it is highly recommended that a full evaluation of the company, the policy, and your financial and medical situation be done.

Alternative Financial Resources

Frequently seniors have more financial resources than they appreciate, or at least more choices on how to use those resources. New programs are developing all the time to provide for the use of resources previously considered "tied up."

Home equity conversion and viatical settlements are two alternatives which have developed and grown in the last decade. These are valuable resource tools and may provide the financial relief possibly needed by seniors in an end-stage medical situation. Under other circumstances, they can enrich retirement years by providing funds to relieve financial pressure or engage in desired activities. Many of the procedures involve the potential of tax, long term care, and estate planning consequences so appropriate legal or financial assistance is recommended.

HOME EQUITY CONVERSIONS

A home equity conversion provides cash for seniors through a conversion of their equity — accumulated over years of making payments coupled with increased property value — into cash without having to sell the property and without having to make regular loan payments. There are several types of home equity conversion methods. The most common are reverse mortgages, sale leasebacks, deferred payment loans, and property tax deferrals.

Reverse Mortgages — Reverse mortgages take several different forms. Common among them is the fact that the amount you receive, and the accrued interest, does not need to be repaid until some future time which is usually when the last surviving borrower dies, sells, or moves from the home. Although rare, some newer products make monthly payments even if the senior moves out of the home. The money received may be a lump sum, may consist of monthly payments, may be available as a line of credit to be drawn against when you need the cash, or may be a combination of these methods of payment. The amount of the loan and the size of the payment made to you is determined by your age and the extent of your equity.

The terms and conditions of reverse mortgages vary widely from company to company, property to property, and area to area. They may be offered through federally insured lenders or in the private mortgage market. Many of these products have been only recently developed and the market is expanding and changing each year. In most cases, all owners must be borrowers and all borrowers must be over a minimum age, usually at least 62 though some programs are for those over 65.

> **Fraud Alert**
>
> Beware of companies that "offer" to find reverse mortgage lenders for a fee. Some of these "white collar muggers" charge as much as ten percent of the total amount borrowed for information that is free - call
>
> **HUD's Housing Counseling Clearinghouse** (888) 466-3487

Because a borrower is collecting money from the home equity each month and interest accrues during that time, the amount owed by the senior increases and, of course, equity diminishes. When the home is sold or transferred through probate its "cash value" may be significantly diminished. Also, since the loan will have to be repaid from an estate, it may require a sale of the home, although the amount owed can never exceed the property value at the time the loan is repaid.

Even though a lien is created against the property when a reverse mortgage is obtained, the home is still owned by the senior who may sell it at any time, pay off the loan, and pocket the balance of the equity value. As owners, they are also responsible for the payment of their property taxes and insurance and must continue to maintain the property. Failure of any of these responsibilities may make the loan due and payable in full.

Because of the wide disparity in costs, amounts, and other terms and conditions it is obviously important to fully understand all the rights and responsibilities associated with a reverse mortgage. As a result, one of the requirements for prospective borrowers prior to submitting their loan applications for a federally insured reverse mortgage is consumer counseling. Fortunately, confidential advice is available free or at a nominal cost. The American Association of Retired Persons (AARP) in conjunction with the Department of Housing and Urban Development (HUD) trains and operates a network of housing counseling agencies. These counselors can provide information about federally insured programs as well as alternative reverse mortgages lenders in your area. They can also offer advice and information on the financial implications and responsibilities associated with reverse mortgages.

The counseling agency nearest you may be located through your local Area Agency on Aging or contact the HUD Housing Counseling Clearinghouse. Because this information is free there is no need to pay for the "services" of companies or brokers — who charge as much as ten percent of the borrowed amount — to find a reverse mortgage lender or apply for a loan. In fact, legislation is under consideration which would prohibit such companies from doing business with the federal government. HUD Secretary Andrew Cuomo has called such excessive fees "...white-collar muggings of our parents and grandparents."

Sale Leasebacks — A sale leaseback is a method of receiving monthly payments for the purchase of your home while you continue to live in it. The buyer, normally a private investor — your adult child, perhaps — "rents" the property to you, usually for life, at the same time he buys it. The new owner/landlord takes over the costs associated with the home, such as taxes and insurance, and is typically obligated to repair and maintain the home as well.

The contractual arrangements may be formalized by an attorney versed in real estate. But there may be tax consequences and other "transfer" issues which should be investigated and resolved through a financial advisor or elder law attorney, if necessary, before finalizing the transaction.

Deferred Payment Loans — Such loans are used to repair or improve homes whose owners are not physically able to make the repairs themselves. Most carry charge little or no interest and they do not have to be repaid until the borrower dies or moves. Although they are not universally available, many communities and agencies have made provisions for them. To investigate the availability and the eligibility requirements of such loans in your area, contact your local Area Agency on Aging or the local housing authority.

Property Tax Deferral — Virginia is one of seventeen states which offers a program allowing seniors to defer paying their property taxes. Once approved, taxes will accumulate and will not be due and payable until the homeowner dies, sells or moves away.

Such tax deferral is especially important for the spouse of Medicaid patients. Under Virginia Medicaid guidelines the home may be exempted from assets which must be exhausted before Medicaid payments begin, but most other assets are not. This means that a spouse may be faced with trying to maintain a home but be without the means to pay taxes. The property tax deferral arrangement may be an important factor in allowing her (or him) to remain in the home.

VIATICAL SETTLEMENTS

The term "viatical" stems from the Latin *viaticum*, meaning preparation for a prolonged journey. Viatical settlement companies pay for the ownership and beneficial rights to life insurance policies from persons suffering a life-threatening or chronic illness. Established in the 1980s, this service has evolved and grown and was recently featured on CBS's *60 Minutes*. Today, most viatical settlement companies will buy virtually any type of life insurance policy including group, term, whole or universal life policies from any life insurance carrier.

Selling a life insurance policy provides access to immediate cash for the policy holder and once that is accomplished the viatical settlement company will pay all further insurance premiums regardless of the actual life span of the insured. Generally the settlement is in the form of a single large payment, but a structured payout providing payments over a specified time is also possible if desired. Although at one time the money received had to be allocated and spent for medical treatment, most companies now have no limits on the purposes for which the money may be used. And in many cases, the proceeds from the settlement are free of federal income taxation.

When a life-threatening or chronic illness strikes, the priorities of the affected person are likely to change dramatically. These changes may affect the entire family as well as the one who is stricken with the illness. For some, continuing to pay life insurance premiums in the face of mounting financial pressure may not seem to be the best use of available funds. The future income for beneficiaries from a life insurance policy may not look as important as the more immediate need for paying medical bills, buying medications not covered by health insurance, or obtaining the home health care and durable medical equipment perhaps necessitated by the condition. For others, the quality of life may suddenly become important. Visiting distant friends or family may become paramount. Or taking vacations to places never seen. Perhaps a desire to give gifts to family members, or quitting work to spend more time with them, may be a priority. Regardless of the motivation, a viatical settlement may enable the affected individual to achieve his or her purposes.

Any person, regardless of age, suffering a condition which shortens life expectancy is eligible for such a settlement. The Health Insurance Portability and Accountability Act (HIPAA) incorporates guidelines to establish when a viatical settlement would be tax free. Essentially, the individual must have been diagnosed with a terminal illness resulting in a life expectancy of twenty-four months or less, or be chronically ill as manifested by an inability, for at least ninety days, to perform at least two of the normal daily activities of living due to functional disability. A chronic illness also includes those suffering from severe cognitive impairment such that supervision for their health and well being is required. If the settlement otherwise qualifies as tax-free, the viatical settlement provider must be licensed in the State of Virginia to maintain that status.

A viatical settlement may be tax free under the HIPAA standard, but it may have an adverse effect on means-tested benefits such as Medicaid. If you are in doubt, consult a professional advisor such as an accountant, lawyer, financial planner or Medicaid specialist. Even if Medicaid qualification is not an issue, or if you do not meet the HIPAA tax benefit standard, it is best to consult a financial or tax specialist before the viatical settlement is finalized to be sure of the tax consequences and the advantages of using this financial resource.

Although the terminal illness provisions of HIPAA mandate less than a two year life expectancy for advantageous tax treatment, most companies will evaluate policies for people with a life expectancy of up to five years. Each company, of course, has different criteria in the application process, the length of time it takes, and the amount of the offered settlement. Generally, however, a confidential application is submitted, the company will review medical records, and perhaps discuss the situation with your doctor. Usually no application fee or physical examination is required and the processing will take one to two months from the initial application to the payout of money.

The National Association of Insurance Commissioners (NAIC) has published recommended minimum payment guidelines, although these guidelines are not binding. Some companies may make an offer which is higher than that recommended, while others may be lower. For anyone considering a viatical settlement, it is best to get offers from several companies and ask for a comparison with the NAIC guidelines for each.

Pursuant to the NAIC model regulations and model act, the original owner of the policy may change his or her mind within a fifteen day period after receipt of the funds and cancel the arrangement. Upon return of the funds, the company which has purchased the policy will convert ownership of the policy back to the original owner at no charge. It is important to determine if the company you are dealing with adheres voluntarily with the NAIC models since not all proposed regulations and statutes have been adopted by the state.

The settlement offered will be based upon the face amount of the policy adjusted for the insured's anticipated life expectancy and the costs of premium payments and the return on investment the company expects. Generally, the offer will fall within sixty to eighty-five percent of the face value of the policy and may go considerably higher if life expectancy is less than a year. This amount is negotiable and it may serve your best interests to approach the contemplated settlement with that in mind. But approach it also with the knowledge that the risks associated with the purchase of the policy will be borne by the company. If, for example, the insured lives longer than anticipated through advancing medical techniques or just plain strength of will, the company will be required to pay all future premiums while the policy holder has already received a significant portion of the policy's value.

Viatical settlement companies are dealing in a very sensitive area and, with that in mind, most of them deal with their customers with a high degree of respect and with a full understanding of the problems facing the insured. If you are not treated with appropriate dignity, do not deal with that company but find another.

OTHER LIFE INSURANCE BENEFITS

Accelerated Death Benefit — This benefit is created as the result of a rider attached to a whole life or universal life insurance policy which allows the policy owner to have access to a certain percentage of the face value of the policy for use during his or her lifetime. Typically, an accelerated death benefit is available only for people with a life expectancy of less than six months, although some may go up to one year. The amount paid will generally be from twenty-five to fifty percent of the face value of the policy. Administrative fees and interest charges will be deducted from the ultimate payment at the death of the insured. Such riders must generally be part of the life insurance policy at the time the policy was purchased and can seldom be added later.

Collateralizing a Life Policy — A whole life or universal life insurance policy may be used to obtain a loan. A perfectly healthy senior of any age might have enough cash value accumulated to borrow against the policy to finance the vacation of a lifetime — or for any other purpose.

The premiums are generally still paid by the policy owner unless other arrangements have been made. There are likely to be administrative charges and interest will be charged on the amount loaned until it is repaid. Usually the interest will accrue and be applied to the loan, although it is sometimes paid directly.

Ownership of the policy does not change. Such loans simply use the cash value as security for the loan, much like real property or other items of value might be used to secure a loan. If the loan is paid off within the lifetime of the insured, all liens against the policy will be removed and the total face value will be paid to the named beneficiaries at the insured's death. If the loan is still outstanding at that time, the amount of the loan and all accumulated fees and accrued interest, will be paid from the policy proceeds. The remaining balance of the policy's value will be paid out to the original beneficiaries.

Reverse Annuity Mortgages — This variation of the reverse mortgage consists of using the proceeds of a reverse mortgage to purchase an annuity which will pay the senior on a monthly basis for life. Like most reverse mortgages, the loan will have to be repaid when the borrower sells the house, moves, or dies. However, the annuity payments will continue for life regardless of the situation with the house. This is a risky venture since annuities are based on life expectancy. If the senior lives longer then anticipated the investment in the annuity can pay off handsomely. If not, the cost of the annuity may far outweigh any benefit.

Geriatric Care Managers

Today there are many options for seniors at all levels of function. Financial, physical, mental, and environmental factors all must be taken into account. Sometimes the choices become overwhelming. There are the needs of the elder person to consider. Sometimes there are the needs of the family, especially if one or more of them is acting as caregiver. And frequently there is disagreement between family members about what options would be best. Sometimes families live a long distance away and truly assessing the situation may be difficult for them. There may be disagreement about what is safe or what is "in the best interest" of the elder person.

When the elder person is unhappy, resisting change, or resentful of the decisions going on around them and the new role they have been relegated to fill, the situation is even harder.

A new professional specialty is emerging to help with problems of option evaluation. Some geriatric care managers work with state or local agencies, and some of them are connected to hospitals where families need to evaluate care of an older person who can be released from the hospital but who will continue to need care.

There are, too, a number of independent geriatric care consultants who run their own businesses. A professional organization, the National Association of Private Geriatric Care Managers, has established standards of quality and a code of ethics for their members. These standards are voluntary at this time, but they stipulate a professional degree in human services and at least two years of experience in the field of geriatric care.

Helping families understand and deal with problems in finding, evaluating, and setting up care for an older family member is the work done by geriatric care managers. Many of them have worked in the industry, in nursing homes, assisted living facilities, or with social service agencies before becoming geriatric care managers.

Usually a nurse, a physician, the hospital which has been involved in the case, or the family doctor will have made a complete work-up and assessment of the physical needs of the elder person. This includes health problems, physical limitations, and need for assistance in daily living. A social worker should have completed an evaluation of emotional state, current living situation, and mental clarity. Finally, an evaluation of the family and financial situation should be provided.

> A recent study from Cornell University found that when caregivers identified sources of stress, the most frequently mentioned was criticism from siblings. In most cases the criticism comes from siblings who are not on the scene or who have not participated in the care and responsibility for the elder parent in the past. Furthermore, it was noted that they were not likely to assume control and responsibility for care in the future, in spite of the fact that they were critical.

With all of this in mind, the geriatric care manager will meet with families and help them make decisions about options which will meet their needs. She will ask questions about family relationships, family structure, living situations, and previously expressed desires of the elder person. The geriatric care manager will identify and recommend community resources and private options which may be appropriate and try to give the family an honest evaluation of the ramifications of each option for the individual at hand.

Some public and non-profit agencies have a sliding scale of rates charged by their geriatric care managers. Private geriatric care managers will charge for their services, their fee usually being $30 - $150 an hour. This does not include the cost for any of the resources they recommend, but they are usually able to give family members fairly accurate figures of what those resources will cost and the probability of federal, state, or other financial assistance.

Their objective evaluation is frequently the best option, especially when emotions are running high with involved family members. Sometimes siblings cannot agree on the best option for an aging parent, and the intervention of a geriatric care counselor can go a long way to take pressure off a family member who is not able to assume responsibility for care but who may be pressured to do so by family members living further away. A professional, informed, and objective evaluation of options is valuable for everyone involved.

Sometimes the main job of the geriatric care manager is to find the right living option for an elder person. People who are not familiar with the field of long-term care are often unsure how to judge a facility and how to find the right one for their family member. Suddenly the decisions become overwhelming. With a careful evaluation of services needed and those offered, level of care, reputation of the facility, and personal preferences, the geriatric care consultant can help select the right facility for the patient and the family situation. Sometimes they will go with the family on visits for the purpose of assessing facilities, and they will ask questions of importance which the family member may not know enough to ask. They can also explain to family members what the answers mean in terms of their individual situation. This helps to insure that there is the best possible match between the facility and the resident.

Other times the geriatric care manager may be a facilitator. Imagine a situation where the elder person is living at home but lacks some of the assistance they need to maintain themselves. The geriatric care manager might put them in touch with a meals-on-wheels program which would help them meet their nutritional needs, a maintenance service which would help maintain the home in safe condition, recommend a trash service that was senior-friendly and would pick up the trash at the door rather than at the curb. The geriatric care manager might help the senior evaluate financial assistance programs which would apply and help them apply for reimbursement.

In other cases a geriatric care manager might help an active older couple evaluate the feasibility of remaining in their home or entering a continuing care community. This could be done by investigating finances, the home itself, emotional attachments, and housing options as well as the current physical and emotional needs of the couple.

If an older couple decided to remain in their family home, an on-site inspection of the house might be appropriate. The geriatric care manager would do a safety check and recommend features which might make the home more senior-friendly. The geriatric care manager might also recommend a construction company that specializes in senior remodelling.

Finally, a geriatric care manager might become involved with the individual case on a continuing basis. For a family which is far away, a geriatric care manager might become the ears and eyes for a senior who is living alone or even in a facility. They would help manage the personal checkbook and keep in touch with the family about concerns for the welfare of the elderly family member.

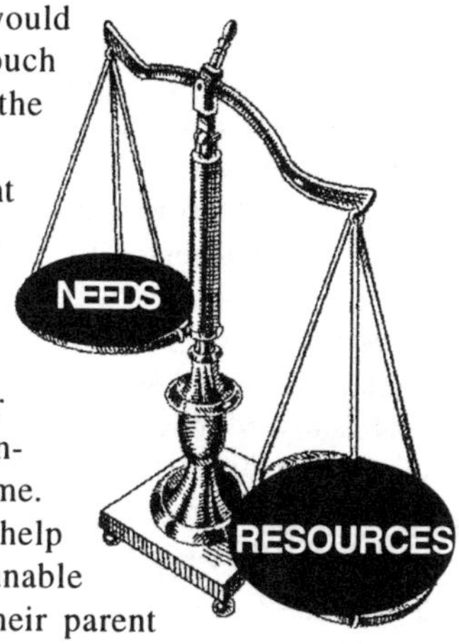

In other cases the geriatric care manager might help define the need for help. A live-in companion, for example, might be the best solution for a senior or a couple desiring to stay at home, but too dependent to be completely self-sufficient. Adult children living in the area might not have the time or emotional energy to cope with seniors who need constant care and support in order to remain in their home. But there are many times when the senior refuses help from outside and the adult children feel trapped, unable to cope with the stress and demand of caring for their parent or parents, but also unable to simply refuse without an alternative. As a neutral and objective professional, the geriatric care counselor is often able to negotiate a solution. They will take time with the senior to write a job description for the companion and to help interview prospective applicants. They will help manage problems which arise between the companion and the senior, keeping the family from being drawn into the emotional turmoil. In some cases the geriatric care counselor would even do the paperwork necessary for the employee such as filing withholding taxes.

The geriatric care manager is someone who is familiar with resources in the community and available alternatives yet who is emotionally objective. This helps the elderly and those who are responsible for them reach important decisions on a wide range of problems. A geriatric care manager may make long-term plans, do friendly visits, help with relocating a senior, advise on safety adaptions for the home, set goals for physical, emotional, or financial needs, arrange transportation and services, help with bill paying, arrange for home repair, or screen and hire caregivers. Their expertise can make the process of aging and decisions which are associated with it much easier.

Senior-Oriented Service Providers

There is a rapidly growing industry which revolves around seniors and their needs. With seniors expected to make up such an important part of the America economy in the next century, it is not surprising that more and more companies are turning their attention to seniors. Marketing campaigns which show companies as elder-friendly are beginning to take their place in the media.

But what is even more interesting is the growing number of businesses which have been appearing to serve the needs of seniors. Some of these need training, experience, or certification while others simply need the desire to serve seniors and the ability to market the service. This growing community of senior-oriented service providers are putting a new twist on some old fields and adding services and businesses to meet the new market in innovative and original ways.

Daily Money Managers — Helping seniors cope with daily money problems has become a field in itself. There is a national association, the American Association of Daily Money Managers, which is a newly formed organization committed to promoting high standards for persons working in this field. The job of daily money manager is rapidly evolving. At this point no federal or state regulations or licensing has been established.

> So common is it for seniors to simply forget to pay monthly bills that the Virginia Power company has instituted a program whereby seniors designate someone to be notified, if the bill is not paid, before service is discontinued. This notice gives the responsible person time to find out what the problem is and pay the bill so that seniors will have uninterrupted service.

Daily money managers come from a wide variety of backgrounds and in some cases the job they do reflects their area of specialty. Social service needs that help an elder person cope with daily living chores have merged with financial needs and the complex paperwork that accompanies some all-important aspects of senior living.

In some ways a daily money manager resembles a geriatric care manager, but the role is much more that of a facilitator than an advisor. They do not evaluate, nor do they analyze evaluations done by other professionals. They organize, schedule, and oversee without orchestrating the outcome.

In some ways the daily money manager functions much like the old version of a private secretary. They offer assistance with a broad range of paperwork problems, home budgets and simple money management. They may maintain a daily schedule, make doctor's appointments, make sure medications are renewed on time and delivered, and arrange transportation when it is needed. They can arrange for companies to provide home health services, home repair, house keeping, or other services which elder residents might no longer be able to handle themselves. For younger, active seniors, they can plan trips and make sure that bills are paid while a senior is away.

They can advise a senior about a budget which will fit his or her needs and resources and help them decide what is doable in terms of expense — home repair, hiring a service, or what might be better postponed. With long-range planning they can help make decisions about financial outlays such as renovation or planning a trip to visit far-off family. If they have a strong financial background they may also help evaluate options such as the best program for buying a new car.

Or they can function as a support service by providing assistance when the elderly person becomes too forgetful to handle daily chores of money management. They will pay monthly bills and insure that utility service is not interrupted. Frequently elderly people forget to make monthly payments because they lose track of time or because they make out the check but neglect to mail it or cannot find a stamp. Seniors may also forget to deposit checks which are not directly deposited into their accounts. It is not uncommon to find income checks sitting unattended on a desk along with unpaid bills.

One elder man, who was functioning well in a number of ways, reached a point where he would go to the bank on a daily basis and move money from one account to another. The problem was that he did not keep track of checks which had already been written. The result was, although there was more than enough money to meet his needs, that checks frequently were returned for lack of funds because those funds had been moved to another account. The daily money manager streamlined his banking, closed unnecessary accounts, and assumed the responsibility for paying bills.

A daily money manager will take care of such simple bookkeeping problems. If they are working with a senior living independently they can help hire, do payroll and file withholding taxes for an employee such as a live-in companion.

In some ways daily money managers are advocates. They will take care of bills which are in dispute. They review bank statements, balance checkbooks, and review such things as VISA/MC bills. If there is a dispute they will contact the company and do the paperwork which is necessary to get the problem straightened out. Sometimes seniors become very alarmed about an error on billing and the daily money manager eliminates the stress of coping with the problem. Or they may deal with insurance needs. They may file insurance claims, Medicare and Medicaid billing, and review both medical bills and coverage to be sure that the senior gets the maximum from his or her policies.

One of the most obvious things about daily money managers is that they are not restricted to serving the elderly. Like personal shopping services, they may also serve middle-aged adults with busy work schedules. When careers and family demands leave no time for the chores of handling financial matters, the daily money manager can eliminate stress and handle problems before they begin. Many daily money managers specialize in working with seniors, and most of them are elder-friendly, but the field has developed from a long history of service for busy people. Retired persons may have the time, but limited vision, arthritis, confusion, loss of a perception of time, and early dementia may all contribute to the need to depend on someone else to help with planning and following through with simple tasks.

Frequently the adult child will seek the assistance of a daily money manager because they do not have the time or they live too far away to take care of their parents' financial affairs. In other cases siblings may be happier with a neutral person looking after finances and advising the family when major decisions must be made.

A daily money manager does not replace a lawyer, investment counselor, or business manager if there is a considerable amount of money involved or if there is complex accounting and several income sources. They do not evaluate the physical or mental needs of a senior. The daily money manager helps identify needs and may seek the help of other professionals when it appears there is a need. When necessary, their clear and concise maintenance of daily accounts can give an accurate picture of the financial resources if the family is evaluating options. They may provide information for an accountant preparing a tax return. After the tax return has been prepared by a professional qualified in the field, they can be sure the forms are signed correctly and get them mailed into the IRS on time, with a check for any required amount.

Sometimes a daily money manager will help a senior make the move to some type of senior housing. They may help make arrangements for the move, help coordinate efforts by the realtor, a packing and/or moving company, and the family.

In most cases, a daily money manager does not sign the checks. They prepare checks, post accounts, and present them to the senior in a concise manner which can easily be understood. Theirs is work of organization rather than control. Their work, however, is very personal and strictly confidential. Finding a daily money manger whose service everyone has confidence in and whose personality blends with the senior is very important. When a daily money manager is hired it is not the same as a guardianship. The seniors do not loose control of their lives and their finances; they have simply sought help in managing the daily details, much as very busy or famous people would hire a private secretary. For many, a monthly, bimonthly, or weekly visit by a daily money manager will help the senior maintain independence and avoid pressure to appoint a guardian or legal representative. The daily money manager helps keep track of financial obligation and avoid errors which may raise the concern of loved ones.

Especially if there is a large estate involved, or a large family which is not on the best of terms, the daily money manager assures everyone that the senior's affairs are in order. They are the first to know if money is being moved irresponsibly, if the senior can no longer understand what his responsibilities and obligations are, and if the senior is able to make rational choices. Frequently their presence keeps family members from fighting about the need for a guardian. And if the senior is no longer able to handle his or her own affairs, the daily money manager is a neutral party who is in a position to be the first to know when a guardian is needed.

> A recent study suggests that at least 12 percent of the people over 85 years of age need help with daily financial chores. This may be everything from remembering to pay bills and make deposits, to balancing the checkbook, and even making sure the senior does not become a victim of a growing number of confidence rackets which prey on seniors by phone contact or in person.

Referrals are probably the best way to find a daily money manager. Be sure to ask if they are bonded or insured. Are they affiliated with any local or national organizations? Ask for, and check on references provided. Ask about how they handled problems or conflicts on behalf of their clients and how they handled or resolved problems or complaints between themselves and their clients. Take a good look at the scope of the work the daily money manager feels comfortable handling. Look at the scope of the work which is required. Do they match? Does the daily money manager have the experience and training to handle the client's needs? Is there a free primary consultation? Is the daily money manager willing to work with lawyers, accountants, or others who are already working on behalf of the senior client? How will billing be handled and what are the charges? Will there be full access to records for those who have an interest?

Charges will generally be at least $25 an hour and may run as high as $60. The charge depends upon the area of the country, the training and experience of the daily money manager, and the needs of the client. Reports to a number of people may be extra, especially if there is likely to be conflict between family members over details. Daily money managers who are required to negotiate conflicts between family members may not only need training in the social service areas, but they may also feel justified in charging for the extra efforts. They will also charge for travel expenses, mailing, and phone expenses incurred on behalf of the client.

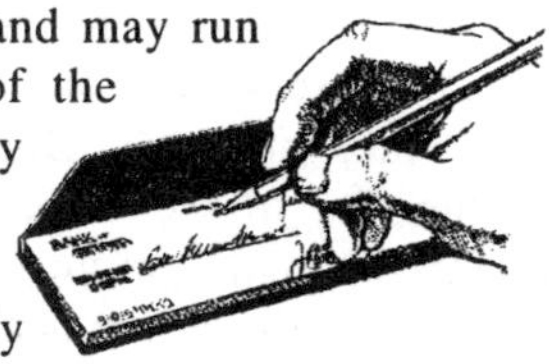

As the population continues to age the daily money manager may well become a popular and necessary elder service profession.

Visitation Services are one of the most interesting new services. Designed and developed for people who live away from aging family members, visitation may be part of the geriatric care manager's or daily money manager's domain, but it can also be done by a specialized company. Studies have shown that 60% of the population live at least an hour away from senior family members. Many live across the country. One of the fears of both elders and their families is the feeling of abandonment when an elder person moves into a senior property.

A visitation service contracts to send a visitor once a week, twice a week, or at whatever frequency desired. They may visit the senior at home, in an assisted living facility, or in a nursing home. They report to the family on the condition of the senior and follow up on problems which may arise. For example, suppose Mrs. Brown in Virginia calls her daughter in Oregon and talks about her red robe which has been lost. Her daughter is concerned that this is something which is truly bothering her mother. She calls the visitor, who will look into the problem to see if the facility has located the robe and will see if the robe is mentioned on the next visit. Perhaps it was simply mislaid but was on Mrs. Brown's mind at the time she talked with her daughter. Now she does not remember her comment. Perhaps it has been many years since she has had a red robe, and she is confused, remembering the past. Perhaps it was simply in the laundry. The visitor can look into the situation with discretion and make sure it is not something to cause real concern.

Visitors can also talk to the nursing home or assisted living staff and monitor how Mrs. Brown is doing and if there is anything which should be mentioned to the daughter. And Mrs. Brown receives an interested visitor each week who brings news of the family and who is interested in what she is doing and what is going on in her life.

Sometimes a visitor will call if the adult child has a job which requires extensive traveling. In that way the family member can visit when in town, but there is someone to visit and see to the senior when business travel makes regular visits from the family member impossible.

Visitation services can also visit a senior who is living independently. Sometimes, such as companion services, they combine other tasks with visitation such as cleaning, shopping, or light maintenance during these visits.

Companion Services will provide much the same type of services as visitation services. However they serve seniors who remain in their homes and live independently. Because isolation is always a problem and because many seniors get to the point that they need someone to check on them and to help them with daily activities, companion services make a lot of sense.

While a companion service may provide full-time companions, many of them will offer companions on a part-time basis. This is much more economical and works out well if there is not a place for a live-in companion or if the senior places particular importance on privacy. Part-time companions may come in one, two, or three times a week, every morning, or every evening, depending on the schedule which fits best. They may fix meals, leaving them in the refrigerator ready for reheating. They may do light cleaning, provide transportation, handle maintenance problems, or help with bathing and laundry. They may check for safety precautions and report on the physical condition of the home and the senior resident.

As with visitation services, they are wonderful for seniors whose families live some distance or for times when families must be away on business or vacation. When the caregiving family members will be unable to provide care for the senior for a while, the companion service will either increase their already scheduled visits or initiate the service. They can keep family far away advised about what is going on with the senior through objective and professional evaluations.

Real Estate has developed rapidly around the senior market. Today there are a number of specialists in the field of senior housing. These realtors handle property which have amenities appealing to the senior market. Frequently these are homes which have been converted to allow seniors to age in place. When it comes time for their owners to move to a long-term care facility such senior renovations need not be considered valueless. Especially if the home is located in an area with appeal to seniors, the home would have an increase in value to the right market, and that is a market which is growing. Realtors who list and find these properties can make maximum profit for the seller, and they can save the buyer money by finding a home which already has the features to make senior living easier.

Some realtors have developed consulting companies. These consultants know their market and the needs of seniors. They go into a home, evaluate what needs to be done to make it elder-friendly, advise the owner about the approximate cost involved, and even help locate companies which can do the remodeling. If the location or general floorplan will not make the home appealing to the senior market, even with the renovations, the consultant would advise the elder owner to sell before making changes, maximizing his profit from the home without the costly senior remodeling. The larger profit can then be invested in property which has been developed as a senior property. In this way the elder owner can make an informed decision before undertaking remodeling. When senior renovations must be reversed before the house can be sold, or when the renovations will only lower the eventual sale price, it is usually better to sell.

Finally, these consultants can advise seniors who wish to sell about what small things they can do — frequently without investing a lot of money — that would make the house more salable or even increase the market price.

Contractors and Renovation Companies are also obvious fields for specialization in the senior market. Renovation may be small changes such as better lighting, handrails in the bathroom and bathtub, and lever knobs on faucets and doors. More extensive projects would make wider doors and hallways, larger bathrooms, and kitchens with workspace at counters for sitting instead of standing.

In addition, new home contractors are developing floorplans which appeal to seniors, such as those with first-floor master bedroom suites, entrances at ground level, wide-open floorplans, and accessible plugs and switches at eye level.

Medical Alarm Companies are a natural outgrowth of home security alarm companies. These companies monitor seniors in the same way they once monitored homes for burglary and robbery. If equipment is already in place to receive signals from home security systems, it is a simple matter for these companies to change their receiving stations and, in some cases, their own response teams to respond in an appropriate way when a senior needs medical help instead of when the home is being entered by an intruder. Many of these companies have already expanded their services to monitor for fire or other problems which can prey on the peace of mind of the homeowner. Senior alarm systems can work instead of, or in conjunction with, other monitoring systems.

Such systems can be set up in a number of different ways. One system is designed for elder persons with Alzheimer's or other forms of dementia. Sometimes these alarms will sound when the wearer breaks the beam installed in exterior doors. Other systems have a tracking device to locate an elder person who has wandered away. Nursing homes will frequently use these alarms to insure the safety of certain patients.

Another type of alarm is worn by the senior, especially those who live alone or with other elder people. When the senior activates it, a signal is sent to a central monitor. Sometimes this is a special response team which reports to the home to give aid. Sometimes a family member or neighbor is alerted. Sometimes a medical unit such as the paramedics or an ambulance can be summoned. This type of alarm was made famous several years ago by a company whose television commercial showed a frail old woman plaintively calling, "Help, I've fallen and I can't get up!"

Many new systems are being developed to help seniors living alone. Every year, more than three million Americans over age 65 are hospitalized due to failure to take prescription medication correctly. At least one company has developed a system which automatically dispenses medication up to four times a day, seven days a week. When connected with a phone or alarm system, the medication dispenser automatically contacts the company when the senior fails to take the medication in a timely manner. An attendant phones the senior to remind him or her to take their medication. If there is no response, a personal visit will be made to insure that the senior is all right.

Pharmacy Delivery has been added by many pharmacies. This is actually a reversion to an old service, popular in the 1950's when many families had only one car. With delivery, the pharmacy can bring medication when it is needed, even if transportation is difficult for the senior to arrange. They can also deliver medical supplies for daily management of a wide variety of problems from incontinence to diabetes. Some larger health care providers are incorporating prescription delivery service into their home health care packages, but even independent local pharmacies may have delivery programs. Sometimes these are limited to a certain time of day, when prescriptions for several people accumulate for one trip, or even to certain days of the week.

Shopping Services are very useful for seniors who have mobility problems. During Christmas these services are especially active, serving seniors who live at home as well as those who live in various senior housing residences. Some senior housing facilities have staff who serve this purpose, though there is usually an extra cost associated with the service, especially if the shopping is extensive. Other facilities have staff members who make frequent shopping trips for groceries, prescriptions, and other personal care needs, but who do not do gift or personal shopping.

A shopping service may do everything from helping decide on the gift or item to be purchased, to taking the list, getting the items, accounting for the money, and making any returns which are required. For seniors living at home such services may make regular grocery shopping trips and sometimes unpack the items and put them away, saving the senior from dealing with parcels and bags.

Home Packers are among the newest services, and their popularity seems to be growing. Reducing clutter and eliminating unnecessary home furnishings is an important part of making senior housing more hospitable. Since this kind of sorting and packing may be necessary for seniors who are moving to senior housing, these services are well worth their cost. Home packers will go through the home with the residents and advise what can be eliminated and how. Since they are not emotionally involved and are not judgmental, they can often accomplish much more than a family member. A daughter may ask her mother why she needs to keep something. She may feel free to make comments about the worth of something, or she simply may not have time to invest in the undertaking. Any of these approaches may cause hurt feelings between the generations.

Home packers, however, will ask what is important to the client without making comments or asking questions. It is their job to accommodate and accomplish whatever the client has in mind. These companies know their area and the outlets within it. Many of them are well advised about value and what shops, sales, or methods are best for realizing profit from unwanted items. In some cases they arrange estate sales, which are particularly popular and well attended in Virginia.

This kind of sensible reduction of "things" acquired over a lifetime can be invaluable and saves the family from trying to do it under emergency conditions when a move has been forced. And it certainly saves many problems in the event of death.

If a client is moving from the family home to a new home, either in a senior community or simply another house or apartment in a different location, the packing company can make things easier. Packing companies will evaluate the home or the destination home and determine how much can fit comfortably into the surroundings and still leave room for the elder person to get around safely. Then they determine which pieces and things should remain. Items which are important to the elder person are carefully packed and stored, in an attic, in a garage, in a storage area, or the home of a friend or family member. Items which will eventually be part of a will or that are designated for a specific person may be passed along to them if appropriate, and if the piece is not something which

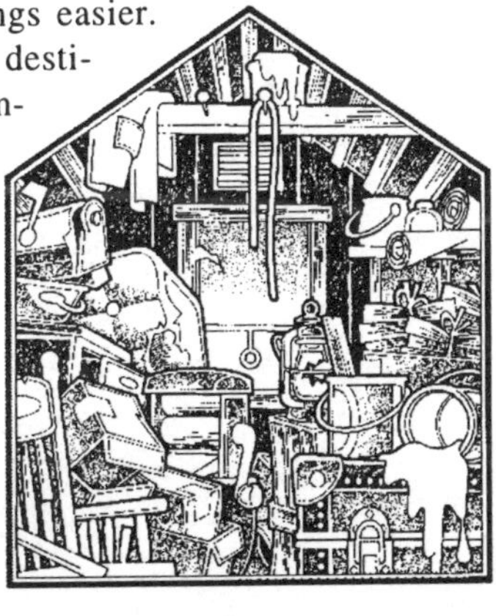

the senior wishes to keep. Finally, those items which are not important enough to be part of the estate, not cherished enough to be kept, nor part of the living environment can be sold, put out on consignment, or given away to charity. Packing companies have contacts for all of these methods and will take care of the lifting, packing, and distribution.

One company said that people very seldom end up paying for their services. Usually there are enough items which can be sold to pay for the cost of their service, leaving the home in much better condition as far as safety, comfort and ease of moving are concerned.

Home packers can also help if no move is planned. As people get older they tend to accumulate things. Not all of it is important or personal. Simply the accumulation of furniture and clutter can fill up a house and make it difficult to move around. A good cleaning and sorting can do a lot to give a new look and a new life to both seniors and their home.

When Seniors Move

Whether the move is across town or across the country, moving is never easy for anyone. Because of emotional attachments or physical limitations a move may be even more stressful to seniors.

Surprisingly, seniors move more often than we would think. Seniors of all ages may move because they wish to retire in an area away from where they currently live, but sometimes a senior will have such a desire to age in place that the decision to move is very difficult, even when it becomes necessary. Many of the services we mention in this section can help an elder person remain in place as long as possible. For others, the decision to move is made with a positive attitude and the desire to enter a freer and less structured phase of life.

Traditionally, when we think of moving to retire, we think of those who go south from northern climates, trying to get away from long winters, cold temperatures, high power bills, and snow-removal problems. But sometimes those who move south miss friends and family and move back. Sometimes high crime rates may make a senior consider a different part of the country. In Virginia there is a growing number of "half-backs." These are seniors who moved from the north to Florida for warmer climates and to be with other seniors. But rising crime rates or a desire to be closer to family still in the north have brought them "half-back" to North Carolina or Virginia.

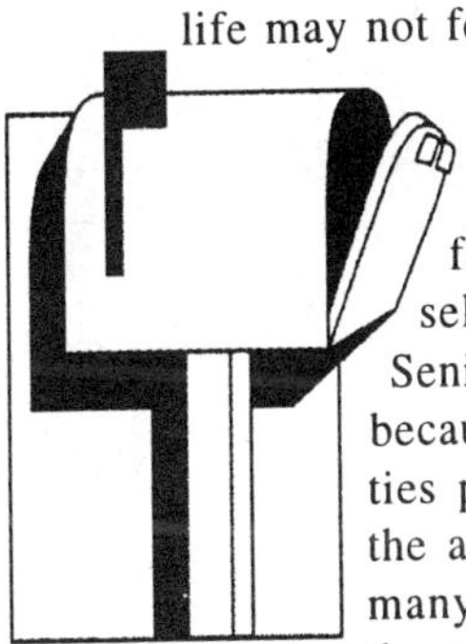

People who have moved frequently during their working life may not feel like any place is truly "home." If the children and other family are scattered, these people may well simply pick a place they like and move to it. They may wish to go back to somewhere they lived in the past but moved away from because of career pressures. Younger seniors frequently select college towns such as Charlottesville or Blacksburg. Seniors move to college towns where they went to school or because they simply like the small town feeling with the amenities provided by the college, the relatively safe community, and the activity around the campus. Some of them take classes, but many of them just enjoy the feeling of energy and newness these towns provide.

For active seniors, relocating in a "lock-and-leave" residence will give them more freedom to travel and pursue other interests. They intend to travel and visit friends and family and are not tied to one location in order to keep in touch with family. Affluent seniors who enjoy traveling and recreation may be drawn by resort areas which offer golf, tennis, swimming, or travel groups and other recreation. They want to enjoy the resort setting, the freedom, and the activities. Frequently the desire to down-size to a smaller house with less cleaning and maintenance will give the senior more time to pursue interests he or she may have put off for years. Or they may simply move to what is perceived as a safer environment or to be nearer doctors and other services.

Even elder seniors move. With scattered families, seniors may stay in their homes until many of their friends have left or passed away, then decide to move closer to adult children. Frequently adult children move parents when it is finally necessary for them to be in assisted living or nursing homes. Once the home is left behind, adult children may wish their parents to be closer so they can visit and oversee their care. And older seniors may move to spend their final years close to family which has relocated to another state.

While it is true that, like everyone, seniors are prone to postpone a decision to move indefinitely, changes in their lives often make those decisions easier. Such changes are very likely to occur. The last child moving away from home, retirement from a job, a change in health, or even an incident in the neighborhood which frightens them or causes them to perceive the neighborhood as dangerous or unfriendly may precipitate a move. Whether the move is made voluntarily or from necessity, frequently the decision to move is the easiest part.

Calling on experts makes moving much easier. A problem for many seniors, especially those of sound minds and bodies which may be slowing but are still far from feeble, is that adult children are just that — children. This is especially true when disagreements about details or egos arise. Experts are safe referees. For example, an adult child may feel that the market value of the home may be one price while the senior who lives in the home may have a figure in mind which is much higher. Any real estate agent will appreciate how frequently sellers of any age have an inflated idea of how much their home is worth. Seniors are no exception. A good real estate agent is valuable even at the decision-making stage. They will help guide the sale of the property, and there is less likelihood that their opinion will be challenged. Professional services throughout the move help keep the decision moving forward in a timely manner and prevent procrastination and continuous re-thinking once the decision has been made. A good realtor can also refer a company which can help put the home in the best possible condition for sale.

A packing company (as mentioned in the previous chapter) or a moving service company (sometimes called moving coordinators) will be a big help in reducing the amount of furnishings which must be moved. Anything which can be disposed of, sold, given away, thrown away, or packed and stored before the move will make the move easier and far less expensive. Careful evaluation of the new space is important. How much storage space is there? What are the measurements of the rooms? Some movers or packing companies will help the senior lay out a floorplan and decide what furniture will fit into the new space. There is no point in paying to move a ten-foot sofa if the longest wall in the new living room is only eight feet long! If there is room for only two armchairs there is no point in moving four. Moving services that help make these kinds of decisions can help make a move much easier. The cost of their service can well be made up by the savings in the actual cost of moving the smaller amount of household goods. Unlike traditional moving companies, moving services help plan the process and facilitate the transition.

Moving service companies will also make a timeline to give seniors a reminder of when things need to be done. Changing power bills — on both ends — change of address, and other details of moving will be included on a checklist or sometimes handled by the moving service. A complete inventory of possessions and a floorplan of where they will fit in the new location may also be helpful. When the movers arrive at the other end, all the decisions about where things belong have already been made. In addition, the floorplan eliminates the need for the senior resident to hurry from room to room directing the unpacking.

Moving is physically demanding. Even with a moving company which handles everything there are a lot of things that need taking care of when the move is complete. Unpacking boxes, finding linens and making beds, hanging shower curtains, mini-blinds, curtains, and moving furniture can be very demanding. Companies which specialize in moving seniors are well aware of the difficulty of crawling around on the floor to plug in lamps and lay out extension cords where they will not be tripped over in the future. Trash from the move must be removed. And, of course, kitchens, bathrooms, and bedrooms must be unpacked and put into new spaces. A packing service company may be on the scene to help here, too, especially if the moving company which is doing the actual move is not willing to supply such services.

Moving service companies are familiar with elder moving and can provide emotional support as well as advice and service. They understand where seniors will need help and can provide that help while preserving dignity.

Adult Day Care and Respite Care

As the American working population moved into the last third of this century, families with two working partners became more common. Along with an increased need for child care came an enhanced need to provide care for elderly family members. Because of the increased cost of long-term care, and the desire of some families to care for the elder generation at home, adult day care began to emerge. With the use of adult day care facilities, family care may be feasible for working adult children. If family members or caregivers are available for the nighttime hours, an adult day program may be appropriate and more affordable than assisted living or a nursing home.

To keep pace with mushrooming demand for home and community-based care, the number of day care centers has doubled since 1989. To get an idea of their growth, there were just 300 such centers nationwide in 1978. By 1989 that number had jumped to 2,100, and by 1997 there were more than 4,000. Today they are regarded as "the best kept secret in health care." Not only do they present a cost-effective way to help older people stay at home, they give needed relief for a caregiver, helping to reduce emotional stress and allowing the caregiver to remain at work which reduces worry over money. Finally, adult care centers are a positive step in preventing social isolation and the mental deterioration that often accompanies such isolation. Planned individual programs encourage maximum participation by each person. Maintenance of independence and dignity is facilitated by providing a step between home and a full-time care facility.

These centers are often viewed as community-based alternatives to skilled nursing facilities. They typically provide health and therapeutic services, social activities, and supervision for people with functional or cognitive impairments. In some cases adult day programs and nursing homes can both serve people with the same profiles and the same set of needs, but for different periods of time. While nursing homes provide 24-hour a day care, an adult day program will provide eight to ten hours of care a day. When the patient becomes more critical, they may eventually move into a 24-hour facility, sometimes into the same facility where they already feel comfortable and know nurses and staff through day care participation.

A recent survey indicated that approximately 80% of these centers were nonprofit, 10% were for-profit, and 10% were public. Fees range from $25 to $70 per day, with an average cost of about $50. Most facilities provide transportation and 50% provide transportation at no charge. For facilities which do charge it is usually on a per-mile basis. Most sites offer full-time nursing services. There are a growing number of facilities which offer day care programs in conjunction with nursing home or assisted living facilities. Most adult care is not covered by Medicare, but, in Virginia, Medicaid will cover some or all of the cost under several programs and conditions.

VIRGINIA TRIVIA

Famous Virginia natives include actor George C. Scott, writer Willa Cather, U.S. Supreme Court Justice John Marshall and Dr. Walter Reed.

Some day care centers have respite care attached to them. Respite care is a place where seniors who need attendance can come to spend the night. This gives the caregiver a break, a chance to go on vacation, or even go out for a needed party.

A typical new center might have full-time nursing home facilities, day care, and a certain number of beds set aside for respite care. One center we talked with has eight private bed overnight units, each with a toilet and sink, TV, and call system. The unit is staffed by state certified nurses' aides with medication certification. There is a supervisor on call. Overnight respite guests participate in the adult day care program during the day and return to the overnight unit in the evening. There are three hot meals served each day and they can accommodate special dietary needs. Adult day care participants congregate in the great room for group activities and can join smaller groups in the four breakout rooms for music, exercise, arts and crafts, or TV watching. There is an Alzheimer's suite, designed to meet the needs of the cognitively impaired. A garden is accessible from all the units, the great room, and the Alzheimer's unit. The cost of an overnight respite stay for this facility is $105 per day. Seniors can stay from one to fourteen nights.

Respite care programs are becoming popular enough for facilities to begin advertising in the media. Richmond, Northern Virginia, the Tidewater, and the Charlottesville areas have print, radio, and TV advertising for respite care over the holidays. Some facilities increase their staff to accommodate more senior guests, allowing caregivers a chance to travel or attend holiday parties or New Year's Eve celebrations.

There are several functions which adult day care provides. As mentioned previously, isolation, frustration, boredom, and depression are always a danger with seniors who lose contact with the outside world. Having nothing to focus on besides their deteriorating physical and sometimes mental condition, seniors who are at home alone suffer worse than those who remain as active as possible and in social contact with others. Day care centers have a lot to offer. The participation, friendship, protection, and care offered by these facilities can do wonders for both the senior and the caregiver.

Seniors have access to activities which can help them stay interested in life, make new friends, and relax while they have a change of surroundings. Memory stimulation through discussion of current events is one example of positive programs usually offered. Music and arts, both in the surroundings and through participation in group singing and craft classes, keep seniors enjoying life. Guest speakers frequently present topics of interest. Games, field trips, activities, and visitation programs provide seniors with variety in the daily routine. Therapy through gardening and plants, pets and social interaction supplement speech, occupational, and physical therapies which may also be available. Rest periods are offered, along with nutritious snacks and a noon meal. Exercise classes tailored for seniors help tone and maintain the body.

Centers are designed to provide a warm, comfortable, safe place for those who need supervision. Almost all centers have staff trained in CPR and First

Aid. There are two primary types of centers focusing on social or medical needs.

Social centers attempt to alleviate feelings of loneliness and isolation among older adults while fostering socialization and feelings of belonging. Even seniors who live independently or semi-independently but who need assistance with daily activities benefit from adult care center activities. These people need social activities, but they need more help and care than can be provided through attendance at ordinary senior center programs. These centers focus on recreational and social activities.

Some centers are medically oriented. They provide health and rehabilitation services in additional to recreational services. These centers are staffed with health care professionals and may provide therapy and rehabilitation services which allow an older person to regain lost functions. After hip or knee surgery, for example, a senior may use an adult center to promote recovery through exercise and therapy. In such a case, when a full recovery is made, the senior may decide to discontinue the day care service or to move to a social center. These medically oriented centers also provide care for seniors who need constant acute care but who have family members who are willing and able to assume that care at night. They cater to individuals who need physical assistance or structured environments.

Caregivers experience tremendous changes in their lives when they become primary caregivers for an adult who needs constant supervision. Sometimes new skills must be learned by the caregiver in order to assist the senior family member. Living patterns must be changed. Sometimes even new living habits must be mastered. Steps to insure the safety of the infirm elder person may include removing such normal everyday things as scatter rugs and resetting hot water heaters to lower temperatures. Time becomes part of a set schedule to include treatment or medication. Physical changes may have to be made to the home to accommodate the elder person.

Stress related problems affect nearly all of the caregivers as indicated by a recent survey. While more than half worried about money and expenses, 81% reported that care of a dependent adult was emotionally taxing. Three-quarters reported feeling occasionally depressed, while 35% reported being frequently or almost always depressed. Caregivers tend to be women in their mid-50's, earning about $35,000 a year. Many make sacrifices in their careers. More than one-third reported that they had cut back on the number of hours they work, while one in five stopped working altogether. Adult care helps caregivers maintain their working schedules, which reduces stress over money, and gives them needed time off from the pressure of providing 24-hour support and care for a loved one.

The stimulating programs provided by adult day care centers also help eliminate the guilt a caregiver may feel about the quality of care they can provide. Social workers who work with the elderly caution that caregivers are often so taxed that they provide care without stimulation. Since there are no regulations or certification for providing home care to an elderly family member, people sometimes take on the responsibility without knowing all of the needs a senior may have. Reading, sharing an activity, going over old photos or keepsakes, taking a walk, or talking about something besides the health of the elderly person are all suggestions.

As part of their community service orientation, many centers offer support groups, education, and counseling for the caregivers. Support groups and education help caregivers maintain perspective, have realistic expectations, and process the resentment they may occasionally feel toward the senior.

If you are considering adult day care, visit the facility and talk openly with the staff. State regulations, building codes, fire and health codes, and licensing regulations will ensure that the facility is safe and meets certain criteria. What you need to concentrate on is how well the individual center fits the needs of your family and your senior.

If there is transportation, what are the times, type of vehicle, driver, and how long is the drive?

Is the center attractive to you and will it be attractive to the individual who will spend time there?

Are the activities going to be of interest to your senior? **How strongly is activity and participation encouraged and how is it encouraged? Is your senior willing to participate?** Evaluate the life-style of your senior and see how well it fits the programs offered.

Do the needs of the senior match the services of the center?

Does the environment promote a maximum level of independence?

Watch for a while without talking to a staff member. Does the staff seem happy? Do they treat the seniors with dignity? Does the staff interact with the seniors? Do the seniors in the center seem happy?

Simply sniff the air. Does it smell clean and pleasant?

Look around. Is the room bright? Does it seem to be what your senior family member needs (active, quiet, peaceful, busy, colorful). For this you must not only be able to evaluate what you see and hear, but you must know your senior's individual needs and wants. A place which is wonderful for one person may be very stressful for another. How successful the use of an adult day care center is often depends simply on how well it fits your situation and the disposition of your senior.

Once a center has been selected keep the channels of communication open. Talk frequently with the staff, and, if possible, with your senior. Get to know the staff and show an interest in what is going on at the center. Request and read the weekly or monthly activity schedule.

Take time to show interest in it and talk about it with your senior. For a senior with memory deficiency, try to interact without asking questions which require memory skills.

Home Health Care Services

Home health care bridges the gap between independent living and assisted living or nursing home facilities. The wide variety of services provided depend on both the care providing company and the needs of the individual. An individual living independently at home might use such a service to hire a live-in companion or an assistant to come in during the day to help with anything from medication management to bathing and dressing. The home health care might service a 24-hour emergency hotline and a call system to keep the senior in touch with help when it is needed. Or they might supply services which the senior is no longer able to handle such as shoveling snow.

Home health care also provides help and support for families who have aging parents living with them. They will supply skilled care services the family caregiver might not be able to provide, someone to stay when the family is away, or rehabilitation services such as physical therapy or speech therapy.

The average lifespan for Virginians is 73. Virginia ranks 24th in states for the number of dentists per 100,000 population, 34th for nurses, but 16th for the number of doctors.

And recently home health care companies are working in partnership with senior independent living housing to allow the senior to age in place through the assisted living phase of his or her life. By contracting with independent apartments or housing developments for seniors, those seniors living in the community pay only for the care they need, but they may pay at a lower rate than they would if they lived outside the senior community and hired the home health care service on an individual basis.

Such services are often seen as alternatives for nursing homes and hospitals. Originally home health services were developed for short-term recovery programs. Those recovering from a hospital stay, recovering from an injury, or in need of postoperative care used home health services. Today such recovery may also be served by a temporary stay in a nursing home or an assisted living facility offering skilled or specialized care. In turn, home health care has taken over some of the long-term care previously reserved to nursing homes. Today only about one-third of all people using home health care fall into the historical category of short-term care after a hospital stay — frequently called post-acute care.

Home health care services may be provided by individuals who specialize in a single or limited service and usually find their clients through referrals. They might be nurses or companions, either licensed or not, depending on the needs of the patient. Or these individuals may band together with others from complementary fields to form a company. Large private companies may provide a complete line of services from skilled care to homemaker services and from equipment to emergency call systems. Public agencies may provide some or all of these services according to need.

Although Medicare and Medicaid have been slow to recognize these companies, more and more such services are being picked up and paid for, and home health services are currently the fastest growing part of Medicare. Home health services are also increasingly paid for by various other insurance policies. Like many doctors and private individuals, the state is trying to determine if home health care services can supplement family care or independent living and maintain the individual for a lower *per diem* cost than can a nursing home. There is still controversy about the ultimate cost, potential for fraud or abuse, and the quality of service provided by institutions as opposed to care at home supplemented by home health care.

Home health care services do allow people to come out of high-cost hospitals and return home sooner than they would be able to do if there were no way to continue skilled care at home. Several factors support the growth of home health services. There are currently increased efforts by health care professionals, and the concern of society, to prevent unnecessary institutionalization. Strict enforcement of limits on Medicare-covered hospital stays mean that frequently patients go home faster — and sicker — than they have in the past. And the overall increase in the elder population is driving the reliance on a growing variety of alternative services of all kinds for seniors. This, too, is promoting growth and diversification in the field.

Services Provided by Home Health Care

Skilled care services are prescribed by a doctor and must be provided by those who are licensed in the field. Wound care specialists, registered nurses, and licensed practical nurses provide care and teach the individual and/or family members who act as caregivers how to handle specific procedures which may be required on a regular basis. The need for catheters, injections, wound care, IV maintenance, and postoperative care are some examples of services which may be temporary. The home health care service can provide that care until the condition has improved. In more chronic cases, the home health care service may only provide the service until the individual or caregiver can learn and become comfortable with the procedure. Or the home health service may provide care on a permanent basis, either as a supervisor or as a primary, daily caregiver.

On a social level these services help with counseling, making referrals to community resources, and handling the stress of illness. They minimize the effects of the illness or injury on the person's ability to cope with daily life, without being forced into an institutional setting. Financial and emotional issues may slow recovery or create an intolerable situation. Such counseling helps handle the stress which is natural when individuals and families try to cope with illness, injury, or disability.

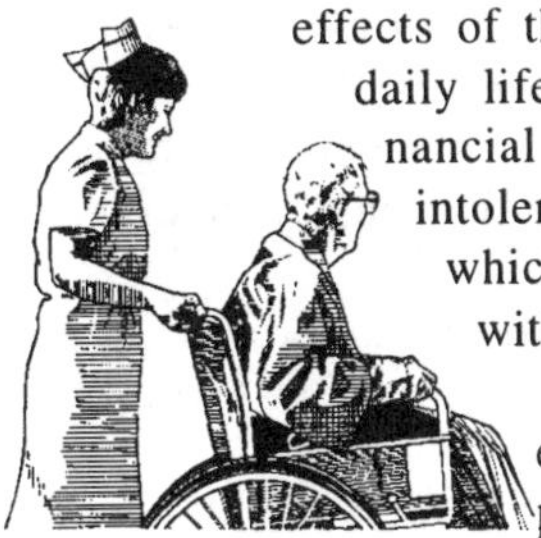

Specialized therapies promote recovery at all levels. Trained and licensed physical therapists, speech therapists, occupational therapists, and even respiratory therapists will come to the home on a regular schedule to provide services so important to improvement of life quality.

Some companies rent medical equipment as it is needed so that a wider range of patients than ever before can remain at home. Lifting and transferring equipment, or the staff to help with daily routines in personal care which require lifting and transferring, are being added to the more typical services provided by large companies.

Support services are much like those provided by other types of senior-oriented services. They may help with bathing and dressing, or they may prepare or bring in meals for basic nutritional requirements or special diets. Light housekeeping, laundry, shopping, and basic home repair may be provided. For families who care for dementia patients, a "sitter" service provides time away from the responsibility of care without jeopardizing the safety of the affected family member.

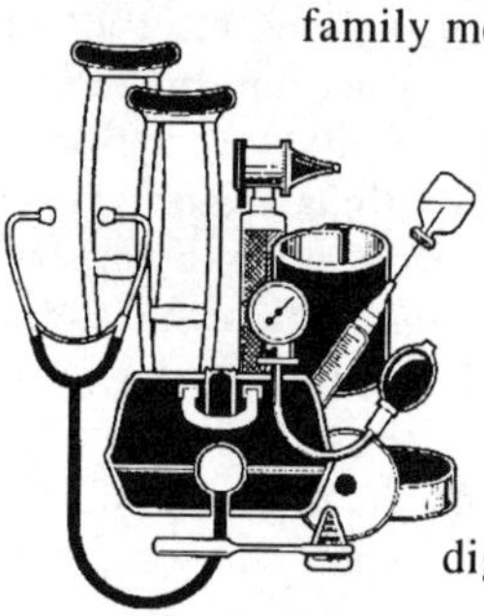

The aim of such services is to restore, promote, and maintain health in a non-institutional setting. They make life more enjoyable, easier, and safer for older people who wish to remain in their own homes or live with family members rather than move to an institution on a temporary or permanent basis.

Finally, a home health care service might provide skilled hospice care, allowing a terminally ill patient to die with dignity at home.

What To Consider When Looking for a Home Health Care Service

When hiring a home health care provider it is important to fully evaluate the care needed as well as the company. Can they provide all of the services needed? Is it important to have a single provider for everything from shopping to skilled nursing care, from meals to emergency response? Can some of these services be provided by family or other agencies which may be less expensive? Will they be doing chores and services which are critical? How much supervision will they have both within their agency and from family, friends, and the individual who needs care?

What is their reputation in the community? Be sure to call references and ask around in the health care community. Chances are that someone has heard of them and can give you an opinion of their competency. Are they licensed if that is needed and are they bonded? What experience does the agency or company have and does it match the needs of the patient?

How do they screen and train their employees and what is the recourse if there is a problem? A large agency may be able to provide an alternative employee if someone does not work out because of personalities. If it is a large agency, how fast do they turn over employees? It is important to have a continuing caregiver, one who knows the patient and the home situation. A fast turnover or a different nurse every day or week can be very upsetting to the patient and family.

What kinds of responsibility does the service accept and what kind of records to they keep? Do they help with insurance or Medicare billing? Do they have accurate and secure records which are still accessible to the family and caregivers who need to review them? Will they work with the family physician? Are there any systems in place to ensure arrival and departure times and what will happen if a storm or personal problems prevent the scheduled caregiver from arriving? Do they have the ability to dispatch a replacement person with the required qualifications in a timely manner? Do they have a 24-hour number where someone can be reached in case of an emergency? Does their system alert a physician in case of a patient emergency and is there an emergency procedure which has been planned in advance? Is it a procedure the patient and family are comfortable with?

Even more than a nursing home, the relationship between a patient or elder person, the caregiving family, and the home health service is a working partnership. Because the agency comes into the home they must work with whatever conditions exist there rather than being able to create the environment they are most comfortable working in. The relationship with the people and personalities must work and is as important as the care given. They are an extension of the home and family and work best when they extend and supplement the care of the family in meeting the needs of the individual. When they are successful they can help people remain in a non-institutional setting and allow them to age in place.

Adapting the Home for Seniors

Many seniors, especially those who are still in reasonably good health, want to remain in their homes. Sometimes it is because they like the neighborhood, know the neighbors, and feel comfortable there. Sometimes it is because their families have grown up there and they have a lifetime of memories collected. Sometimes it is because they feel they will lose independence if they move. And sometimes it is because they fear making a change. Whatever the reason, making changes in the home will make it easier for them to live safely and comfortably.

With the growing number of seniors, many consulting firms have grown up to help seniors make choices about their homes. One realtor we talked to specializes in advising people about whether renovating their home for their convenience will in fact lower its value. In that case they may be better off to sell the home and invest in another property which would be better suited to their needs. In other cases, she might advise them to use the money they would put into adapting the home for their needs into fixing the home to maximize the market value — again with the idea that they should sell at the top price possible and invest in another home. Finally, she can advise them as to the approximate cost of renovating their home for senior needs. If the property is located in the right area the renovations would be appealing to other seniors who are looking to buy. Since there are a growing number of seniors in the country, elder-friendly homes have more and more market appeal, especially if they are in the right location to attract other seniors.

Construction companies are taking a look at senior needs and tailoring renovation packages to them. Sometimes the changes can be fairly simple, but they can make a big difference in the ease of living for the elder residents. These remodeling companies help create accessible environments. To evaluate its worth contractors often compare the cost of renovations against the cost of an accident.

A new way of thinking about housing is beginning to take shape. The belief is that designs which are easy for the least-able user will accommodate everyone and inconvenience no one. A home which can accommodate a rolling walker because it has no doorsills can also accommodate a stroller or baby walker. And it is a blessing for someone temporarily disabled in an accident. As long as the renovation is not unsightly, it will not detract from the value of the home. These contractors promote quality renovations which blend visually with the home.

For those who want to age in place, it is very necessary to take a good look at the home and evaluate whether it will allow room for aging.

First, is the home in basic good repair? For those who are planning on aging in place, it is important to keep the home in as good a condition as possible for as long as possible. Older residents find it increasingly difficult to cope with daily repairs and must incur the expense of having work done. But if the home is in good condition repairs will be necessary less frequently. Preventive maintenance from the beginning is the best way to make sure the home and its occupants will age well.

Next, look at the basic design of the home. If there are no bathrooms on the first floor or no bedroom which can be used if getting up and down stairs becomes a problem, if the doors are narrow, the rooms chopped and overcluttered, if there is no easy access to the car, poor lighting, uneven flooring, or other problems which might impede easy movement the home might be considered "non-aging-friendly." Homes with tall front porches will need ramps when the resident is no longer able to climb the steps. In some neighborhoods ramps are a sure tip-off that the resident inside is easy prey. There should be easy, level access to the door, the outside, the garden.

Those who know they wish to age in place, and who have considered options and needs of the home, may begin to make changes gradually. In this way, by looking ahead, every time normal home repair needs to be done, it can be done in a way that is elder-friendly. Just as people consider it reasonable to plan ahead for financial security, physical security may be planned before it is needed. Even for people who are only in their forties it may be time to consider future needs if they plan to live in the home and age in place. When a major renovation is planned, think about the future. Put the extra square-footage in the bathroom so that, later, handrails can be added. Make the staircase wider, so a lift-chair can be added. Remove sills from doorways, make doors wider, and make the traffic pattern flow easily with few barriers. Planning and decisions are best and modifications produce the best results when they are made without the stress of an emergency.

Other things which are appropriate for elder residents are increased lighting, electric garage doors, convenient location of electrical plugs and switches, and clear floors. Throw rugs can be dangerous and should be eliminated. Heaters and heat vents should be shielded to make sure someone with poor balance will not be burned reaching for support. Shelves may be lowered so they can be reached easily, and multiple-height work spaces allow a resident to sit to prepare a meal. A lift-chair can make stairs not just easier but fun. Faucets can be changed from small knobs which must be grasped to levers which can be pulled. Similarly, door knobs can easily be replaced with attractive lever-style door handles. A good call system or medical alarm is necessary for seniors who live alone.

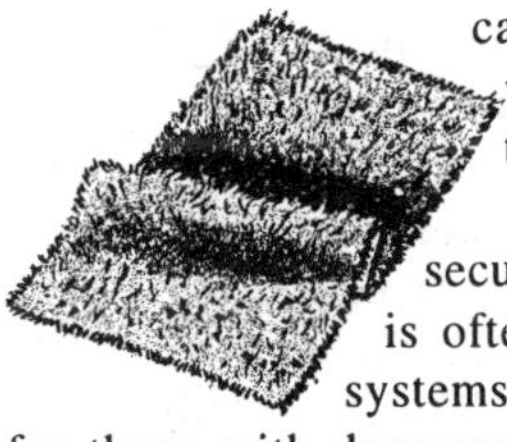

One of the hardest things for seniors to cope with are security systems or bars and locks. While increased security is often needed for those who are more vulnerable, the security systems and locks are themselves difficult to cope with for those with decreased mobility and flexibility. Difficulty in entering or leaving the home because of stairs or security systems discourages seniors from leaving the home. This contributes to isolation and decreases activity. In such cases, aging in place becomes a detriment to the senior rather than an asset.

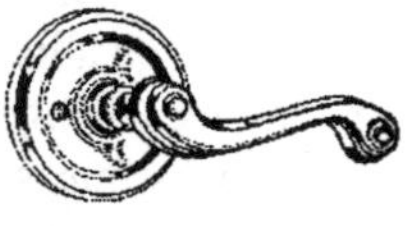

For seniors who are already finding that they are having trouble with some areas of everyday life, it is sometimes simply a matter of stopping to take a look at what needs to be done and finding another way to do it. Growing older sometimes means finding a different way to interact with your environment. Improved safety and comfort does not always mean structural changes. Sometimes simply taking the time to evaluate what is still needed and removing, selling, donating, or bequeathing items can make a home much more livable by reducing the sheer volume of items in it. Removing excess furniture, clutter, knick-knacks, and throw rugs can free up traffic patterns and make it easier to move about the house. There could even be a nice surprise in the money which can be realized by selling unnecessary items.

Now there are consulting companies which specialize in coming into the home, helping seniors evaluate what they want to keep and what can be passed on. They pack away and store what is too precious to be eliminated. And they arrange for sale or dispersal of items which are no longer needed. One consultant we talked to explained that they were often more valuable than family members in assisting with this process. "A daughter will often say something like 'Mom, what are you keeping this old thing for. It's junk!' We will simply accept that is it important. If the person wants to talk, we listen to the reason the item is important. We are safe and non-judgmental, and I think that is important for those who are reducing the size of their household."

Medicare will frequently pay for a physical therapist or an occupational therapist consultant to analyze the home and make suggestions about equipment and minor changes in routine ways of doing things which can make life easier. These one-time safety assessments can be very useful in evaluating what can be done in the specific environment and can help elder residents begin to think in new patterns about everyday routines. In some areas home health care agencies

or local hospital rehabilitation departments are also able to do environmental assessments.

Sometimes cooperation from service people is only a matter of asking. The garbage collector in some areas will come up to the house instead of insisting that the garbage be put out at the curb. A newspaper may be delivered in a tote bag hung on the door instead of thrown on the porch. This eliminates the need to bend over and pick it up.

For those who are elderly, a wide range of household items are on the market. These items of assistive technology are specially designed to make daily activities easier. Scissors, silverware, tooth brushes, can openers, and other items which are designed to conform more easily to arthritic hands are available and more are being designed all the time. Touch-control can easily be installed on lamps to eliminate the need to grab and turn small knobs. Reaching devices extend the reach of those who no longer have the ability to stretch or the balance to climb. Rolling carts make carrying easier. In fact, they are appearing on the market to the point that they have been featured on the NBC nightly news. Happily, most of this technology is inexpensive.

Continuing Care Retirement Communities

The philosophy of continuing care (often called life-care), is very different from other types of facilities where residents may live for a short time. There is a permanence here, and it attracts a very different type of resident.

A Continuing Care Retirement Community (CCRC) is a retirement system that has been available for half a century or more. But the greatest growth has come since 1960, especially since 1980. Today there are almost 1,000 such communities across the country. And they are changing in nature, reflecting a more independent resident who does not want to give up the amenities they are used to. Older units are frequently being remodeled to reflect the new attitudes. Remodeling often includes more square-footage, more closet space, patios, and skylights.

They are part housing complex, part activity center, part health care system. They are all of these things, but not exactly like any one of them. Their distinction is that they provide a continuum of housing, services, and health care that is centrally planned, located, and administered. The written agreement between resident and CCRC is intended to last the resident's lifetime. Emphasis is placed upon quality of services and quality of life for each resident.

Facilities in this category operate on all levels of adult care. Retirees are usually required to be in good health at the time of entrance, and they move into individual units which may be anything from condo or apartment units to cottages. The units are usually purchased and a contract for monthly fees is signed, though there is a lot of variety among companies and sites. The entrance fee for the community may be a large sum, sometimes representing the sale of the family home or life savings of the retiree. There may be an opportunity for a refund of the entrance fee within an option period, usually a year or two, while in other cases there may not be. The refund is usually a portion of this fee, often based on how far into the option period the resident has stayed. Generally seniors may not move into the community at the assisted living or nursing home level if they are new to the community. Those levels of care are very much a part of the system, but they serve the residents who have been living in the independent units which are part of the community. Because moving out of the community at those levels involves the loss of the original entrance fee, seniors who move into the community usually remain there for the rest of their lives.

Unlike assisted living or nursing homes, whose residents may move there out of need, residents of continuing care communities move into the community because they have planned to do so. They have taken time to plan and investigate their move since it will last them for the rest of their lifetimes. They are young in comparison to nursing home or assisted living residents,

and they are active. Most of them have reached their decision without the aid of children and they have very high expectations. They are making a life choice which is sometimes the result of years of investigation and thought. Typical continuing care residents are planners. They are independent and want to get the most out of life, and they are typically very responsible and wish to secure their future.

Seniors often think in terms of what they will lose if they leave the family home. Those in continuing care communities have usually planned and evaluated the move for some time before making their decision and they focus on what they will gain. These residents are looking into their retirement years early enough to have a choice instead of waiting until they need another level of care.

Typically the longer seniors wait to make decisions about living and care issues, the more limited their options may be. Throughout this book, the emphasis is on the need to look ahead and make decisions before they are needed. This pro-active approach to aging insures that the "Third Age" of life will be fulfilling until the end and will reflect the desires, preferences, and attitudes of the senior individual.

One of the main characteristics of the Continuing Care Retirement Community is stability. Because of the investment seniors do not often move. The population is very consistent and friends made there will stay for life. Sometimes retirees will choose a continuing care community which is near their family residence. Friends for years, those with the same church affiliation, or people they knew from work may also be living in the community.

During the years when a family is being raised, housekeeping, yard work, gardening, and even home repair may be an enjoyable part of life. The feeling of accomplishment a husband, wife, mother, or father may derive from doing the work needed to keep the family residence safe and pleasant is part of the natural nesting instinct which keeps life going from generation to generation. But when the family moves out on their own, those same activities of daily home care may not be as rewarding. They may become more a burden than a source of pride. Many seniors would like to use their time doing other things. In a continuing care community maintenance of the unit is included in the monthly fee so residents are free of day-to-day problems associated with a house. If the plumbing leaks, they call maintenance. Yard work is done and even housekeeping is available. The area is secure, so leaving for a week, or even a month, is never a problem. One phone call to the main office assures that the unit will be kept up and secure during their absence.

In these communities seniors are very active. Social groups may book tours and cruises. Volunteer groups keep seniors active in the community at large and keep them learning new things. Short courses may cover subjects from books to crafts. There may be a community woodworking shop, there are community holiday celebrations, and frequently there is a place for a small garden. Community dining, even on a once-a-week basis, allows for social interaction, and meetings of various interest groups are frequent. Plays, concerts, and local festivals are frequently part of a monthly schedule open to all residents. One administrator commented that she finds entering residents more concerned with the view from their unit, the availability of closet space and storage, and the floorplan than they are in the nursing care and assisted living.

Because all levels of health care are available, yearly checkups and other medical care is part of the contract. Doctors and nurses are employed by the community and get to know the residents on a personal level. If there is an illness such as a severe bout of flu which might necessitate a short hospital stay, the resident may move to the nursing area and then back to the independent living unit when he or she has recovered. This easy mobility between levels of care helps eliminate the anxiety which often accompanies the move to a health care facility such as assisted living or a nursing home. By the time a resident of a continuing care property moves to the next level they are known and among friends, both on the staff and among the other residents.

Couples who have been married for many years do not have to experience the trauma of separation when one must move to a different level of care. The active member may remain active with a strong support group and still easily visit the one who has moved to the next level of care without worrying about driving. A simple short walk within the community is all that is needed. Many of the couples who now live in these communities come from a generation for which long marriages were more of a norm than today and when two family careers were uncommon. Frequently they have never been apart for any length of time. Moving one partner to another level of care is much easier if they are still easily accessible to the other partner for visiting and comfort.

Sometimes there is an urgency in entering the continuing care community. When a new community opens units may sell rapidly, necessitating a fast decision on the part of the senior. Because resale units are available on an irregular basis, the decision to enter the community may have to be made when the unit becomes available, or there will be a further wait until something opens up. This is especially true if there is a variety of floorplans offered and the senior is interested in a particular one.

Shopping for the right continuing care community requires time and patience to select the best life-style, health, and financial plan. There are many different types with new alternatives being added every day. One administrator commented that these facilities are like sunsets, each distinct in its own way. Each CCRC has its own particular mission, philosophy, and personality that reflects the sponsor, board of trustees, residents, and staff. Also influencing the way a community feels and functions are the location, facilities, available services, and amenities.

Prospective Residents Can Now Choose From a Wide Variety of Options:

Location — city, suburban, rural, or even resort properties

Building type — garden style, mid-rise, high-rise

Living unit type — apartment, cottage, townhome, single family home

Sponsored by — not-for-profit religious, fraternal or community sponsors, for-profit hotel chains and developers

Size — few or many residents. Some of these communities are almost the size of small cities.

A wide variety of payment plans, health care services and coverage, and a range of services and amenities are part of the package or may be contracted through the community on an individual need basis.

Health care services are at the heart of the continuing care concept. The availability of a wide range of health-related services, which can be used as needed, can contribute a great deal to peace of mind. Health-related services may include an emergency response system, resident health clinic, wellness programs, gym and exercise programs, health education, hospice services, nursing advice, physician services (both primary and specialty), podiatry services, dental services, therapies (physical, occupational, speech), and pharmacy. There is a strong emphasis on preventive medicine and in maintaining a healthy life-style through nutrition and exercise programs.

All of these services work together because they are all part of the same system. For example, a person might have a medical condition which could be improved with a special diet. That resident could select meals from the dining room which would suit these dietary needs. He or she could also get help from support staff in planning meals to cook in the kitchen of the independent living accommodation which would be easy, appealing, and still meet the dietary needs. The benefit of the diet would be monitored by the health care professional at the regular checkup in the clinic. Special exercise programs which might also help the condition could be set up through the gym. Adjustments to the program could be made easily because of the integration between services.

Communities may also offer shops, stores, beauty or barber shops, recreation facilities, a swimming pool, an auditorium which may offer movies, common areas for specialized activities such as crafts, woodworking, painting or sculpture, and even a library. There are frequently a chapel, chaplain, and religious services which are appropriate for the community. There are usually a game room, post office, and guest accommodations. Many properties have hiking or walking trails. Larger communities may have banks, golf courses or putting greens, greenhouses, saunas and whirlpools, and coffee shops and restaurants in addition to the main dining room.

Continuing Care Agreements

Continuing care retirement communities offer residents an agreement for services. It will include at least independent living and nursing care and cover more than one year, usually the lifetime of the resident. It will cover monthly fees, health care coverage, cancellations and refunds, services, insurance requirements, conditions for transfer within the community to other levels of care or living accommodations, transfer out of the community, and the CCRC's responsibility should you become unable to pay the fees. There are many types of CCRC agreements, but they differ in two major ways: *the amount of health care included* and *how payment is made.*

The three most common types of health care coverage are **extensive, modified,** and **fee-for-service agreements.** In the extensive agreement (known as lifecare) medical expenses are prepaid similar to an insurance arrangement. This allows residents to plan future health care expenditures. Although not all agreements are alike, most of them involve pre-payment for short- or long-term nursing care. These agreements provide not only housing with services and amenities but also unlimited specific health-related services with little or no substantial increase in monthly payments except for normal operating

cost and inflation adjustments. Extensive agreements allow residents to plan future health care expenditures.

For example, a couple might pay an entrance fee to a community of $130,000, perhaps obtained from the sale of their family home. Monthly expenses of $1,245 would need to be paid, but this would probably not represent much change from their monthly budget outside the community because this payment includes maintenance of a home, house payments or rent, sometimes basic utilities, some health costs, and health insurance payments. That fee might also include some meals. The closeness of the community and services provided might even allow a couple to eliminate a second car. All of this would offset the cost of the monthly fees. Under an extensive plan, should either of them need temporary or permanent nursing care, this would be included in their monthly fees which would not increase even though the level of care increased. A plan might allow for additional charges, such as for three meals a day or other miscellaneous expenses such as medical supplies. These additional charges would be added to the monthly billing.

A modified agreement includes housing, residential services, and a specified amount of long-term nursing care with no substantial increase in monthly payments. For example 30 or 60 days of nursing care might be included each year without further charges. After that period of time was up a resident would pay a daily rate for nursing care which might be lower than those paid by residents of nursing homes outside the community. Entrance fees in this kind of agreement are usually less than those with extensive agreements, as are monthly fees.

For example, a couple might pay $60,000 to move into an apartment under a modified agreement plan, with a $1,000 monthly fee. They would expect to pay for meals in addition to these costs. If one of them moved to nursing care, the one-person fee for the person remaining in the apartment would be reduced to $770, with the cost of meals for just one person — say $175. But the person in nursing care would pay, perhaps, 85% of the standard daily costs (for example, if the standard rate for a semi-private room in nursing care is $70, the resident would pay $59.50). Adding the nursing care to the reduced monthly fee paid by the partner remaining in the independent living apartment, the monthly fee would jump to $2,730 after the initial 30 or 60 day period.

A fee-for-service agreement has the lowest entry fee. In proportion to the examples we have given above, a fee-for-service agreement might have an entrance fee of only $40,000. The monthly fees would also be lower, perhaps around $650. There may be a meals charge in addition to the monthly fee. In some communities, a minimum number of meals is required in the dining room. This allows the facility to maintain its kitchen staff and plan a menu. Services such as laundry, cleaning, and transportation are available for modest fees as the resident needs them. When more care is needed, the monthly fee will increase. This fee will be less than what the going rate is for assisted living or nursing care at an independent facility, but more than would be paid under an extensive care or modified agreement.

Comparing different properties may be confusing because of the wide range of choices and variety of agreements. And, to make it more confusing, many communities now offer a choice of plans. One administrator tells us that his community offers a choice of seven different plans! Before making a choice it is important to take a good look at individual financial, health, and life goals.

The second way continuing care agreements differ from each other is in payment and fee arrangements and the types of rights to the property. There may be an entry fee and monthly fee for an ownership interest, or a monthly fee only under a rental agreement.

Monthly-fee-only, or rental, has no lump-sum entry fee. The costs of the living unit, services, and care are covered solely by the monthly fee. Sometimes a small, up-front fee or deposit is charged. As compared to other types of arrangements, the monthly-fee-only is likely to be higher than the monthly fees paid in the more traditional agreement, but since there is no entry fee it may be years before the costs balance.

The entry fee and monthly charge agreement provides for a living unit, services, and care as specified in the resident's agreement. This is the most common type of fee arrangement offered by not-for-profit CCRC's. The entry fee may not be refundable and this should be made clear and understood before any agreement is signed. Ownership or equity agreements may involve membership only or the actual purchase of real estate. The latter are the least common type but are growing in popularity. One reason is that retirement property, especially in some desirable communities, is increasing in value as there is a growing demand. This kind of arrangement allows residents to benefit from the increased market value much as timeshare owners, or the owners of regular townhome or condominium properties, do. There will be an agreement that the unit can only be sold to a party who qualifies under the original guidelines for financial requirements, health, and age. Sometimes these units are sold on the open market but usually they are sold through the association which governs and runs the community. The service and health care package transactions generally are separate from the purchase transaction. There is sometimes a fee charged for transfer of ownership and service packages.

Another variable involves the entry fee. In new properties, or where there is not an immediate vacancy, a reservation fee (usually 10%) is required to reserve a place. Some communities will allow a refund if a vacancy does not become available within a certain period of time. New properties frequently have a large push for sales, accompanied by a lot of advertising and a sales force. They are looking for people who will make a serious commitment, and they will set their budget and plan their services based on occupancy. For that reason there is often a penalty for withdrawing from the project, even if the withdrawal is before the completion and move-in date for the facility. These penalties are usually not enforced, however, if a person is unable to enter the community because of an illness. Sometimes CCRC's charge fees to defray costs of processing an application. These fees are usually not refundable.

For most up and going properties, entry fees are nonrefundable after an adjustment period. The initial agreement will specify the period of time after which the entry fee is nonrefundable, even if the resident wishes to move out of the community altogether. Some entry fees are refundable on a declining scale. For example, if an entry fee refund declines at the rate of 1% per month, then 92% would be refundable after eight months. Sometimes a fixed amount is deducted

before the declining rate is applied. Thus, if there was an entry fee of $130,000, with a fixed amount of $10,000 and a 1% per month penalty, and a resident wished a refund at the end of one year, they would receive 88% of $120,000 (which is the original fee less $10,000 as the fixed amount), or $105,600.

In a partially refundable agreement, the agreement will specify the amount of refund available, perhaps 50% to 75%, and the time period during which the refund will be available.

Under some conditions and time periods a full refund may be available. In some states the law entitles a person to the right to cancel with a full refund for a certain period of time, usually somewhere between three and thirty days. Or an agreement may be written to allow a refund pending the sale of a family home. The agreement should specify the type of refund available and the conditions of the refund. Be sure to inquire about refunds when considering a property.

Entry requirements are usually based on health and financial resources. Residents must show that they are in good health (as determined by the individual community) and have the financial resources to cover monthly fees throughout their lifetimes. Some CCRC's provide financial assistance. In addition, some CCRC's may not have facilities and services to care for some conditions. CCRC's with extensive and modified agreements have underwriting criteria similar to those which are used by insurance companies. Some require that residents have maximum Medicare coverage. These may cover some of the health care services provided by the community. CCRC's will often manage the paperwork and file the insurance claims on behalf of the resident. While some CCRC's provide insurance-like coverage, others require commercial coverage. It is important to evaluate coverage which may be offered by the community and compare it to other insurance coverage to ensure that gaps are covered without duplication.

Continuing care retirement communities often grew from not-for-profit organizations which wanted to provide their members with a place to retire. Consequently a large number of them have been historically and philosophically affiliated with sponsoring organizations such as churches or fraternal organizations.

Today for-profit corporations, partnerships, and investment syndicates are entering the market. It is important to determine the financial security and experience of the governing body before entering into an agreement. Day-to-day management is very important and responsibility for personnel and planning should be well established and to the satisfaction of the resident before a move is considered. And as with schools, insurance companies, or other major investments prospective residents should look at objective evaluations of performance and credibility. There are several agencies which accredit CCRC's, including The Continuing Care Accreditation Commission based in Washington, D.C.

Independent Living

The difference between independent living and seniors who are living independently is that the latter applies to seniors who are living without assistance in the general population, while the former applies to seniors who are living without assistance in a community providing certain services for seniors and generally limited to seniors. These communities attract active older adults who want a life-style which is free from many of the concerns of home ownership. They are at a point in their lives where they enjoy traveling, volunteering, social activities, and hobbies instead of focusing on care and problems associated with home ownership.

Independent living communities cover a wide variety of patterns. Some of them are federally subsidized or part are of the state's low-income housing projects. These are aimed at low-income elders. Frequently one of the problems for seniors is a lack of income. Especially if they have not set up a pension fund, been covered by a retirement plan, if they have been self-employed, or changed jobs frequently they may have very limited resources. Single women make up a disproportionately large number of seniors who fall into this group. Subsidized housing provides them with housing which meets their needs for a price they can afford. Frequently this kind of housing option has a sliding scale of monthly rent, depending on the income of the individual.

At the other end of the scale are communities, often developed by private contractors, investment groups, or for-profit corporations who have developed communities catering to seniors. These may be high-rise apartments in a desirable location, a resort community, or a community developed around a golf course. Tennis, a community swimming pool, jacuzzi, activity rooms, and meeting rooms are usually part of these properties. Stables may be available. A country club with a restaurant, sometimes shops or small stores, may have been planned into the community. In all cases they cater to seniors and senior interests. In these kinds of developments the property is usually purchased and may be sold at any price at any time the same as any other real estate. There is usually an association which maintains the community area and services, like homeowner associations in many communities around the country. Association fees are part of ownership and not part of the purchase price. Association regulations in these communities usually require that the home be owned and/or occupied by people over a certain age. Resale of the property would be subject to the same requirements as the original purchase. Typically these communities provide security, social interactions, organized activities, and designs which are appealing to seniors and which provide amenities to help seniors maintain their independence.

Some of the common design features are first-floor master bedroom suites to eliminate the need to climb stairs. Good overhead lighting and lights in hallways and at doorways may be features. Simple floorplans keep traffic patterns open in case there is a need for a walker or a cane, and doorways which are at least 30" help insure access between rooms. Plenty of storage area which is easy to get to is very appealing for those who have collected a lifetime of possessions. Large bonus or playrooms are not especially desirable, although a small study or separate TV room may be included if the floorplan is large enough. Laundry facilities and other amenities of daily living are also included on the first floor with easy access.

For the first time, properties are being developed, in fact, entire communities are being designed, with seniors in mind. These living quarters, from high-rise apartments, to townhomes, to separate homes, are being designed and developed around the needs and desires of seniors. Firms and individuals now specialize in building for an older audience. They are aware that light is a necessary feature for seniors. Patios which open off a living area bring the outdoors inside, but things like garden windows — which look wonderful but may be very hard to access — are avoided.

Sometimes it is simple things that make a difference. Designing a laundry room next to a kitchen, or even as part of the kitchen, makes the flow of housework easier. A younger family might want the laundry close to bedrooms and bathrooms. For those families the main concern is a large quantity of family laundry and the need to eliminate carrying clothes very far from where they are used. Seniors who are living alone, or with a single other partner, typically have a much smaller volume of laundry and they typically do it more frequently because their schedules are not as crowded with family needs and work. But an older person may move slowly. For them, it is not as important that the laundry be located near where it is used as it is that they can do laundry — which is an intermittent activity — at the same time as they cook — which is also an intermittent activity. A close location between kitchen and laundry allows them to put in a load of clothes, move to the kitchen, put something on the stove, go back to the laundry to move clothes from the washer to the dryer, go back to the kitchen, and so on. For a person who moves slowly the location of the laundry close to the kitchen allows them to get more done and feel better about their accomplishments at the end of the day without being worn out.

Other typical features of independent living communities are the availability of services. The community itself may contract for housekeeping, landscaping, and general maintenance. This allows the senior to conveniently handle the problems of home ownership. An independent homeowner who wants help around the house must locate someone to provide the service, then hope that they are reliable and reasonable. It is frequently time-consuming. Seniors often worry about being vulnerable to people who come into their homes. And they are concerned about the price and recourse they may have if the job is not done properly.

When homeowner associations or management companies contract for services they have buying power to contract at the lowest rate; they frequently have a contract with the service provider which has provisions for problems if the resident is not satisfied. Even though the homeowner will pay for the services he or she needs, the contract with the community represents enough business to make them an attractive client. While a private individual client might not cause much concern, the chance of losing the contact with the larger community usually encourages the service provider to try a little harder to be sure the homeowner is satisfied. And when a service provider arrives at the community they will usually have several jobs to do instead of traveling for a single homeowner. This also cuts costs and makes the contract with the community more attractive to the service provider.

Just as other categories of senior living options are extending their services and overlapping into other traditional categories, some communities are extending into assisted living by contracting for services such as speech therapy, physical therapy, nursing care, or daily supervision.

Take, for example, one new location in Charlottesville. This high-rise apartment complex has a pool, exercise room, meeting rooms, and a community dining room which is similar to a restaurant. Owners have purchased their apartments, which are one-, two-, or three-bedroom units. They pay a monthly fee, which is like a homeowners fee. It includes a certain number of meals, depending on their own needs. They pay for no services which they do not specifically wish to use. When they want housekeeping, laundry service, or shopping service they call or go down to the management service desk and request the service, for which they will be billed in their next monthly billing. They may remain in their units even when they need more care by arranging for therapy, nursing care, or other health services as they are needed. Thus the independent living apartment extends to assisted living.

Although an independent contractor developed and built the property, and a real estate team sold the units, once they were sold out the contractor and real estate team no longer had any interest in the property. The management association (homeowners association) supports a full-time manager and staff. When someone wishes or needs to move from the property they can list their unit with local realtors, who can deal with the management association. New owners must meet the criteria of age and financial qualifications of the original buyers but the price is market value, allowing unit owners to make a profit as the value increases.

Seniors in independent living communities where property is purchased take advantage of their equity. However, they must qualify to buy the unit or home just the same as any other homeowner. They must show financial resources to meet monthly fees. Some insurance plans may pay for services provided by the community which fall under health needs.

Other services typical of senior independent living communities are security such as gates, controlled parking, and frequently medical alert monitoring. When the homeowner travels, security is taken care of by the community. If the

> **VIRGINIA TRIVIA**
>
> Virginia is the 12th largest state in the union in terms of population. 11% of the population is over 65 years of age, ranking it 43rd against the other states. However, the percentage increase among the elderly from 1990-1994 was 9.1%, ranking it 12th in states in terms of increasing elderly population.

homeowner will be away maintenance of the home or unit may also be provided by the community, or through them, with the homeowner being billed directly for the service. Most communities offer some kind of meal plan, but provide for residents to prepare their own meals in their living units. Beauty shops are frequently part of the community as well as small convenience stores. Many communities, even HUD and low-income housing, provide or make available transportation and shopping trips.

All low-income housing, and many senior apartments, rent on a month-to-month basis rather than a lease. This allows an elder person who is suddenly in need of more care to move to another level of care without being encumbered by the large financial obligation of the remainder of a lease.

Social activities and interaction with others who enjoy the same lifestyle is another reason why seniors move to such properties. There is freedom from the noise and clutter of children. Cultural outings are organized by the association or volunteer leaders. Parties, travel groups, holiday celebrations, and other activities such as lectures, meetings, workshops, and classes are usually on the monthly calendar. Exercise areas are often available and classes may be available for groups who are interested. This kind of living situation makes staying active easier than it may be for those who live in mixed neighborhoods.

The main concern for seniors who seek this living option is future health care. Some independent living communities are affiliated with health care providers. In others, independent insurance plans are necessary.

Assisted Living

Depending on the state and the individual residence, an assisted living facility may be termed a residential care facility, an adult congregate living facility, a personal care home, a catered living facility, a retirement home, a home for adults, or a community residence. These are communities for people who need some help with daily living tasks but who do not need the skilled nursing care provided by a nursing home.

ALFA, the Assisted Living Federation of America, defines an assisted living residence as a "special combination of housing, personalized supportive services, and health care designed to meet the needs — both scheduled and unscheduled — of those who require help with activities of daily living." This includes residences which are not licensed as nursing homes which provide care and support services for people who need help as a result of physical or cognitive disabilities. Sometimes these assisted living residences are part of nursing homes or continuing care communities. In a growing number, they may offer adult day care or respite care programs.

Assisted living is generally considered to be consumer friendly. It does not have to contend with some of the negative stereotypes of nursing homes, and has been able to maintain its image as many expand into areas of service traditionally served by nursing homes, such as skilled or specialty care. Assisted living emphasizes resident autonomy and customer service.

Assisted living residences may be high-rise apartments or a converted Victorian home. They may be renovated schools or buildings specially designed and built to accommodate seniors. But, whatever the structure looks like, there are more than a million Americans living in an estimated 30,000 assisted living communities across the country, and the number of residents and residences are growing every year. In fact, assisted living is the fastest growing type of senior housing today. It is now a $12-15 billion per year industry, and that number is expected to reach $30 billion by the end of the century. That will continue to grow until people over 85 will number about 7 million by 2030.

Building of senior housing is increasing tre-

ALFA members subscribe to a 10-point philosophy of care:

* Offering cost-effective quality care that is personalized for individual needs
* Fostering independence for each resident
* Treating each resident with dignity and respect
* Promoting the individuality of each resident
* Allowing each resident choice of care and lifestyle
* Protecting each resident's right to privacy
* Nurturing the spirit of each resident
* Involving family and friends, as appropriate, in care planning and implementation
* Providing a safe, residential environment
* Making the assisted living residence a valuable community asset.

mendously. In June of 1997, 435 senior housing residences were reported under construction. Two-thirds of all new properties being built were assisted living facilities. One reason is that aging parents are either unable or unwilling to live with their children and their children's families. Many want to be near their families, but they wish to maintain independence and a feeling of self-determination. Assisted living properties serve this purpose.

The building boom in assisted living facilities has a benefit for the consumer. Although many facilities are full, we found that few had long waiting lists. With more companies and properties in the marketplace, there is more chance to shop for a facility which really fits the prospective resident. Even residents covered by managed care or other insurance carriers have more chance to shop, compare, and make a choice than ever before. As competition between properties and companies increases the consumer has more voice in the types of facility and service he or she wants.

Another factor contributing to assisted living development is the increased number of people who can afford assisted living. Over 53% of people 80 years or older will have incomes topping $15,000, and nearly 35% will have incomes of at least $25,000. This growing number of seniors who are living above the poverty level has led to increased investments by corporations and investment groups in assisted living housing. The assisted living industry remains largely financed by private funds. About 90% of all assisted living services are paid for with private funds. Supplemental Security Income, Older Americans Act, and Social Services grant programs have begun to pay for some assisted living services. Medicaid funds will be paying more for assisted living in the future as modifications in regulations take place. In fact, 42% of assisted living residences have at least some residents whose care is supported by a state program, with Medicaid being the most common.

The emergence of managed care and integrated delivery health care systems have helped make health care more affordable. Assisted living stands out as a less costly alternative to nursing homes or to home health care. The average *per diem* rate for assisted living in a private room is $71, compared to $111 for skilled nursing home care and $83 per visit for a home health nurse. According to ALFA, daily basic fees range from as low as $15.33 to as high as $215. Depending on the nature of an individual's health insurance program or long-term care insurance policy, costs for assisted living may be reimbursed. Assisted living combines independence with personal care in a warm, dignified community setting.

The average age of residents is 82. The likelihood that a person will live alone increases with age. Women outlive men and therefore outnumber men as residents of assisted living facilities. Social factors such as the divorce rate, people choosing not to marry, and mobility of children contribute to the number of people living alone. Assisted living is an especially helpful alternative. It gives them access to services, help with daily living, social interaction, and challenging activities. One recent study indicated that people are increasingly interested in seeking housing options which are appropriate to their needs.

There is a wide variety between residences. Some charge one price for all services, while others segment costs. Some charge monthly rates, while others have rates which vary according to the predicted length of stay. Some have long-term rental commitments, while others are on a month-to-month rental. Flexibility seems to be the key word in this part of the senior housing industry. The average length of stay is 2.8 years; 44% of those residents who left went to nursing homes, 13% went to hospitals and 15% returned to their homes.

Services provided usually include meals which are served in a common dining area. These meals meet special dietary needs as required. They are nutritious as well as appealing visually and to the appetite. One of the biggest problems for seniors living alone is cooking. Because there is only one person, they often rely on quick meals, snacks, or other alternatives which may not provide nutritional balance and are almost never recommended for special dietary needs. Because seniors may not take the time and energy to plan and prepare food so that it is appealing, they frequently suffer from dietary deficiencies and skipping meals can be common. Malnutrition is all too common among seniors, especially those living alone.

Housekeeping services, 24-hour security, and transportation for shopping and other necessary trips are also usually part of what is provided by the residence. Assistance with eating, bathing, dressing, toileting, and walking are available as needed. Personal laundry services and an emergency call system for each resident's unit are usually provided.

Medication management is frequently another problem for seniors who may not understand or be able to remember complicated drug schedules. The assisted living residence maintains records, administers medication, and monitors reactions or side-effects of medications. They maintain information about dosages and watch for drugs which may be in conflict. Many facilities now have licensed nurses on staff, which is especially important as some residents move into the area of more critical care.

Finally, assisted living facilities provide social and recreational activities. They promote health and exercise. Many of them have activity directors who plan a wide range of interesting choices aimed at keeping seniors active and interested in life around them.

Although assisted living is not traditionally designed to provide skilled nursing care, it does provide help with activities of daily living. The needs of each resident are different, and the assisted living community is designed to respond to those individual needs. Independence is encouraged, as is interaction with a resident's family, neighbors, and friends. Some facilities have a range of payment plans which are determined by the services needed.

Choosing an Assisted Living Facility

The best way to choose an assisted living facility is to make several visits to the properties being considered. The first impression of the approach to and the outside of the building is important. The facility will become the legal domicile of the resident and will serve as a home, hopefully for some years. It should be appealing. There should be a place to entertain visitors, with an attractive decor. Everyone wants to be proud of their home and enjoy a pleasant environment. Assisted living facilities are no different. They should have the feeling of a home, not an institution, and should promote a feeling of comfort. Every individual will have personal tastes and finding a home which appeals to the resident is important to mental well-being.

We're right where
you want to be.

Does the staff and the administrator greet residents by name? Is there warm interaction? Do the residents socialize with each other and do they seem proud of their home and happy to be there? Talk with several people and see what kind of people live and interact at the facility. Does the staff seem concerned that the residents are involved? What is the staff-to-resident ratio on each shift? Do the staff members seem competent and professional and can they answer questions without hesitation? Who gives direct care and what training do they have? Is there is an Alzheimer's or dementia unit and, if so, does the staff have special training to deal with the residents?

Is the layout of the building easy to follow? Are the corridors and doorways wide enough to accommodate wheelchairs or walkers. If it is more than one story, is there an elevator? Are there handrails to aid walking if necessary? Is the floor a non-skid surface and is the carpet firmly in place to avoid sliding? Is the lighting throughout the entire building good? There should be plenty of natural light and windows, but is there also adequate artificial light? Are the recreation areas appealing and are there a wide variety of activities? Is the facility clean and free from odors and does it have good heating and cooling systems?

Be sure there is a written plan for the care of each resident. Although residential care plans are required by many states and under most licensing programs, not all states require such plans for assisted living residents largely because not all states regulate assisted living residences, and those that do have a wide range of requirements and regulations. But a good assisted living residence will take time to develop a care plan that reflects the needs of the individual resident while still promoting independence and personal dignity. Development of the individual plan should include input from the resident, their family, friends when appropriate, facility staff, and the resident's physician. The process for assessing the resident's needs for service should be clear from the beginning and should allow for periodic review and modification.

Take a good look at the contract. When can it be terminated and what are the refund policies? What deposits are required and what do they cover? The cost of services should be clear, as well as specification of what those services include. Are additional services available if needed, and, if so, what are the costs? Are there different contracts for different types of services or combination of needs? Does it include accommodations, personal care, health care, and supportive services? How is the billing handled and what spe-

> This year, for the first time, ALFA (Assisted Living Federation of America) sponsored " Hero Awards." These are designed to recognize outstanding administrators, caregivers, staff members and volunteers in assisted living residences nationwide. The criteria for selection are indicative of where the industry places importance and the goals they work to achieve.
>
> The criteria are: ✓ Offering cost-effective quality care that is personalized for the individual's needs ✓ Fostering independence for each resident ✓ Treating each resident with dignity and respect in care planning and implementation ✓ Promoting the individuality of each resident ✓ Allowing each resident choice of care and lifestyle ✓ Protecting each resident's right to privacy ✓ Nurturing the spirit of each resident ✓ Inviting family and friends ✓ Providing a safe, residential environment ✓ Making the assisted living residence a valuable community asset.

cial financial arrangements may be available? May residents handle their own finances with staff assistance if able or should a family member or outside party be designated to do so? Are residents required to purchase renter's insurance for personal property in their units? What types of personal property can accompany the resident? If something happens to property — of the resident or of the facility — who is responsible for cleaning, repairing, or replacing lost or damaged property?

Health care concerns are very important when evaluating a residence. Most states require that medications be stored and administered according to specific procedures. Be sure that the staff can explain these procedures and can provide assurance that all provisions for medication are available. If appropriate, check to see if self-administration of medication is allowed and be sure the staff is comfortable that it is appropriate for the individual resident. Is there coordination of care visits from a nurse, physical therapist, occupational therapist, or other specialists if needed? There should be a designated staff person who can answer questions about scheduling and coordination of these visits. Does a physician or nurse visit the resident regularly to provide medical checkups? Is there a clearly established procedure for responding to a resident's medical emergencies? Is there a licensed nurse on staff and during what hours?

Assisted living communities provide ADLs (activities of daily living) which should include 24-hour help with dressing, eating, mobility, hygiene, grooming, bathing, toileting and incontinence, using the telephone, shopping, and laundry. Can a resident arrange for transportation on fairly short notice and what is the cost? Is there transportation for shopping, to the doctor's office, the hairdresser, or pharmacy? Is there housekeeping for each unit and what form does it take? What services does it include? Is there is laundry service and, if so, is it included in the price or is it extra?

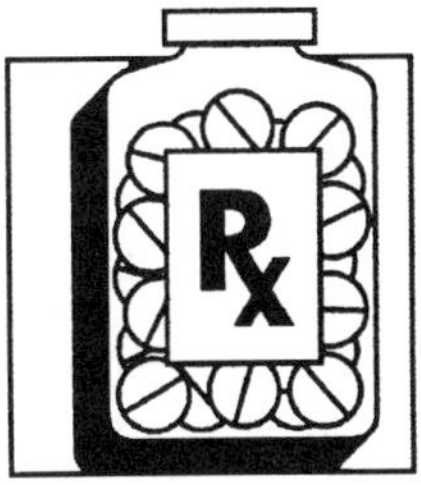

What types of units are available? Are there different sizes? Are units for single and double occupancy available? Are roommates assigned and if so, on what basis? Most facilities in Virginia reported that there were 24-hour emergency response systems in each unit. Are the bathrooms private and equipped with handrails and can they accommodate wheelchairs and walkers if necessary? Do all units have telephones and cable TV and how is the billing handled? One of the assisted living companies in Virginia is taking steps to include personal computers in each unit and provide instruction for each resident on their use. Is there a kitchen in the unit and are residents allowed to keep food in their units? Is there a place for the resident to cook if they so desire? May residents smoke in their units? In public spaces?

Are there organized activities and are they of a variety which will appeal to the resident considering the facility? Are they clearly posted and are daily schedules and events laid out well in advance? Are the activities appropriate for the individual's level of function? There should be reading material available, visitors and speakers scheduled. Is there access to community events and programs and are residents encouraged to get out of the building and into the neighborhood? Are there volunteer programs for residents to participate in and are there members of the community who are encouraged to come into the facility? Are residents encouraged to participate in a wide variety of programs? Does the residence create a sense of community and how are residents encouraged to participate? Is there a director who keeps track of participation and can the family of residents stay informed about participation and changes in levels of participation? Are residents required to do simple chores? Are resident's pets allowed and who is responsible for their care? Does the facility have pets in the building and what are their areas of access? Is there a nice outdoor area, a place to walk and/or a garden? Is there a way for the residents to participate in gardening activities?

Is the security good? There should be a fire emergency plan available, an emergency generator or alternative power source available, and some kind of security for protecting personal property. What kind of security locks are on the windows? Are the call bells and smoke alarms in each room checked on a regular basis to be sure they are in good working order? Are the exit doors alarmed?

Is the menu varied and does the food look, smell, and taste appealing? Are snacks available and under what circumstances? What kinds of snacks are served? What are the meal times and does a staff member make sure the resident gets to meals?

Other considerations are the location and convenience for friends and family to visit. Will this be a temporary or a long-term stay? In many cases assisted living facilities act as halfway houses, aiding in recovery and rehabilitation for temporary conditions. Who will assess the needs and what provisions are there if recovery does not take place in the time frame predicted?

One of the interesting things about assisted living, in the changing field of senior housing, is the wide variety of assisted living options which are now available. Many facilities are taking on skilled care units which were previously considered to be part of the nursing home specialty. These units, sometimes serving specialized needs, make the range of services wider. For some residents this means that they will be able to age in place longer, drawing from additional services as they are needed. These specialized care units must blend in with the staff and the residence to be successful. Sometimes an assisted living community will expand a skilled care unit and find it does not comfortably fit into the facility. After evaluation, such services may be discontinued.

The feeling of an assisted living home is very important. It should provide the feeling of a home, a residence, rather than a hospital. At one time Alzheimer's units were frequently found in nursing homes. In recent years, more and more of these units have been moved to assisted living facilities as studies have found that many Alzheimer's patients do better in a more informal and homelike atmosphere.

Activity directors are key staff members for assisted living residences. It is important that they keep abreast of their field, developing activities for their residents which reflect the needs and attitudes of those in their care. Today's seniors are remarkably determined to keep the spark of life alive. Many are interested in the world around them, enjoy lively discussions of current events, and participate in exercise programs which are appropriate for their abilities. Improved strength, flexibility, and mobility from regular exercise programs is a reward in itself for residents. Many activity directors make special plans to include people with physical limitations in excursions outside the residence. It is especially important to continue to offer challenges to those who have become confined.

Recently there has been an emergence of assisted living facilities specifically designed to maximize function for seniors. Special designs and development teams are creating residences with an innovative approach, sensitive to increasing consumer demand for individuality, choice, and personalized care programs. These flexible and adaptable designs focus on independence. They produce responsive solutions for reduced mobility, combine new needs with familiar elements of past life-styles, and physical spaces that encourage social interaction and personal growth within the daily life patterns of residents. The goal is to evoke a high quality life-style with emphasis on dignity, safety, security, comfort, privacy, and a feeling of home and hearth.

Negotiated Risk

Negotiated risk is a term often used in assisted living. It means that the facility acknowledges that it cannot guarantee to provide for every need of every prospective resident. The problem lies in maintaining independence. The balance between autonomy and risk is a delicate one which is different for each

The average assisted living resident is an 82 year old female, ambulatory, and needing help with one or two activities of daily living. She is likely to have moved to the assisted living residence from home and will move to a nursing facility or hospital when her medical needs become too serious for an assisted living environment.

Twenty-five percent of residents need help with early-stage dementia, while six percent need assistance with late-stage dementia. Seventeen percent need help dealing with incontinence.

The average length of stay in assisted living is 2.8 years for facilities which are part of a nursing facility, but 3.3 years for those without such connections.

resident. When independence is promoted, the facility must relinquish some oversight, which increases risk. The concept of dignity has shared risk inherent in it. For example, suppose one resident monitors her own medicine, while another resident does not. When they are together talking, the first resident offers the second medication which causes a life-threatening condition. What happens if residents are able to determine when and what they will eat, but then they repeatedly do not show up for meals? Who is responsible for making sure they eat?

A complete physical and psychological evaluation at the time of admission is very important to determine limits to individual independence and accountability. Where the residents need help and where they are capable of doing for themselves must be defined as well as possible.

Services should then be designed to establish physical care and supervisory needs. Reevaluation should take place on a regular basis, based on staff acuity, to revise the care level or to make the decision on when it is time to move the resident to another facility with increased levels of care.

It is also important that the risks involved are agreed upon by the family members, the resident, and the facility staff. A balance between safety and risk should be determined and enumerated as clearly as possible, although it is impossible for any contract or care plan to provide for every contingency. Regular communication with residents and families is important. The key to evaluating changes in assisted living needs are "triggers" or signals of a change in the resident's routine, behavior, or safety. When changes take place it may be time to reevaluate the care plan.

Emerging Assisted Living Roles

The role of assisted living is still taking shape. Some states have limited the types of services which can be provided to residents of an assisted living facility. Consumer advocates frequently mention the desirability of "aging in place," meaning the ability of a facility to continue to care for a resident as the level of care increases. Many believe this is a desirable goal and leads to more secure feelings for the elderly. With this in mind, assisted living companies have begun to add subacute care to some residences. A backlash from residents who do not wish to share a residence, dining areas, or recreational areas with those who need acute care has sometimes driven companies to reverse their decisions. Another problem is how to maintain the residential environment as health care levels are intensified. Many consider this residential atmosphere to be the industry's hallmark.

Today about one third of all assisted living facilities offer nursing care. Some provide this care with on-staff personnel while others have contracted with outside agencies. Some feel that providing nursing care betrays the fundamental mandate of assisted living and detracts from the primary goal of maintaining interest and independence in the senior residents. These divergent needs and opinions will continue to shape this rapidly expanding field of senior housing. The balance between aging in place and limiting the services of assisted living should be considered before an assisted living residence is selected. Residents with strong feelings one way or the other should seek a facility which matches their philosophy.

Nursing Care
(Nursing Homes)

Nursing homes, post-acute care, long-term care facilities — whatever they are called — provide care on a regular basis for people who need nursing care but do not need to be hospitalized. Many of these people would have been hospitalized a decade or two ago. With the expansion of nursing homes, or long-term care facilities, these people are now able to move to facilities that are much more personal and far less formal and forbidding than a hospital. Within a long-term care facility the patient's needs are administered by skilled nursing professionals under the direction of a physician. All facilities operate under state and federal regulations and are required to have the appropriate licenses.

Although these facilities have grown out of the traditional need to care for those who cannot care for themselves and have no place to go, advances in medical technology have developed them into places for people who need skilled care which can not be provided by the family in a home situation. Today they may also provide interim care, rehabilitation, recovery, and post-operative care in a setting which promotes and encourages regaining the level of function lost by accident or disease. Now, people do go home from nursing homes, or move to assisted living facilities, and resume more normal life.

> *Men are like wine. Some turn to vinegar, but the best improve with age.*
> Pope John XXIII

Names have changed for many facilities in the industry as the years and perceptions have passed. One home in Cincinnati for example was once called "Beechwood, the Home for Incurables." As their administrator says, "...it's 1997 and we couldn't be The Home for Incurables any longer." The name was changed some years ago to Beechwood Home, and this year it is being changed simply to Beechwood.

Nursing homes have often been the target of negative perceptions by consumers. Sensational reports on exceptional homes where abuse or neglect has taken place have frequently given the impression that this is the norm rather than the exception. Reports of deficient surveys and closure of homes in Virginia has added to that perception. For most long-term care facilities whose concern is for the dignity and well being of the patient it is a decidedly unfair assumption.

Nursing homes were the first long-term care facilities to be licensed. Their establishment and rules of conduct and procedure are well regulated by each state. Though the terms used to describe these properties may differ from state to state and requirements may be different, they fall within general guidelines and promote the same level of care for their patients. They are controlled under Health Services, rather than Social Services which regulate assisted living and other senior residences in many states, and therefore they are much more closely regulated and policed.

In recent years they have come to be an extension of hospitals. Many have developed specialized care units, offering additional services. Specialized care units provide for ventilator patients, dialysis care, or specialize in quadriplegic or comatose patients. Some have specialized in certain specific diseases, regardless of the age of the patient. One facility in Lynchburg, Virginia, for example, specializes in Lou Gehrig's disease. When many patients are gathered, each suffering from the same relatively uncommon disease, there are several advantages. Families can get support from other families and from realizing that they are not alone. Care can be developed which is distinctive for the needs of those patients, and patterns of treatment, reaction, and progression of the disease can be monitored and noted, adding to the knowledge and treatment available for these patients.

With the high cost of hospital stays, skilled long-term care facilities can provide the care and treatment needed by patients who would otherwise take up a bed in a hospital facility. This extension of skilled care helps relieve some of the strain on hospitals. Traditionally long-term care facilities also offer a more home-like atmosphere in a smaller, more comfortable setting than large hospitals can provide. One administrator says, "That's why we are called 'homes.'"

The emergence and growth of managed care has also promoted diversification. Facilities are beginning to form networks of services. Contracts from managed care providers seeking care for specialized patients have become an important part of the nursing home business. Expanded services, an aggressive approach to marketing and public image instead of a wait-and-see attitude, which was often prevalent in the past, and an increased sensitivity to the consumer, are now typical of nursing homes. No longer are they a need-driven industry. Managed care contracts, increased consumer awareness, and increased competition have promoted many changes which are beneficial to the consumer and reflect more concern for consumer satisfaction.

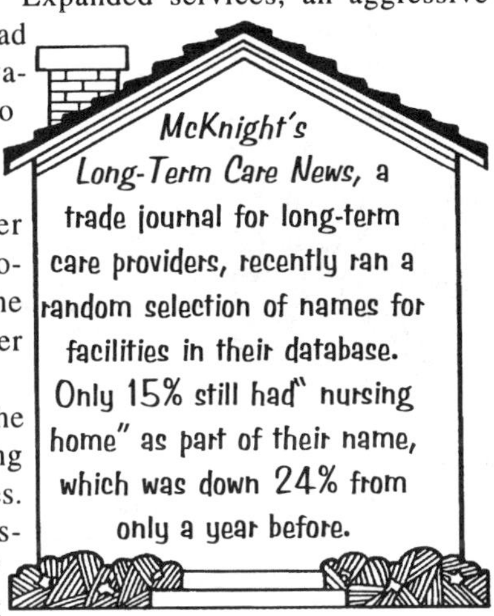

What with facilities diversifying and the stigma sometimes attached to the term "nursing home," many facilities have changed their names. Although the title seemed to capture the essence of the industry for years, "nursing home" may no longer reflect all that is being done at the facility. The new names may reflect the services offered and the fact that they are part of a system.

When Laurel Crest Manor, a county-owned facility in Ebensburg, Pennsylvania, for example, renovated and developed an Alzheimer's unit, a ventilator care unit, and hemodialysis services, the name was changed to "Laurel Crest — Rehabilitation and Special Care Center." Like most changes in the industry, rural areas are slower to change than those in larger population areas where there are more patients but also more competition. In small communities, the facility is known by the name it has had for many years and is often an established part of the community. People in the area are aware of the services provided and a change in name, or restructuring of services, is more likely to be looked on with apprehension.

At one time concern for consumer perception and what the consumer wanted didn't make much difference. The patient was a person, usually of low income, who had nowhere else to go. Today higher income seniors are seeking more amenities and more attractive surroundings. Families with two working partners mean that there may not be anyone in the family available to care for an aging parent. Advances in medical technology mean that lives can be extended, but the care required may be beyond the capabilities of family members. But these people are still very actively interested in the care and conditions in which their parents reside. Nursing homes are spending more and more time with families, holding family meetings on a regular basis, sending newsletters, and keeping lines of communication open.

Not All Long-Term Care Facilities Are Alike

There truly are differences among facilities. Not only do services offered vary considerably, but there are differences in attitudes of the staff and owners. There are differences in mission statements. The physical building can make a big difference in the way a facility operates. The makeup of the residents makes a difference. The location within the state makes a difference.

The variety is not a bad element. It simply means that people need to take time to investigate both the facility and the desires of the resident. Not everyone feels comfortable in the same environment, with the same people, or on the same schedules. For example, with the development of rehabilitation and expanded services for skilled care, some homes now take children or young adults. These younger people may be mixed in with the general population of residents, or may be in a special area or wing. This care for the chronically ill, post-operative, or young people in need of rehabilitation has mixed reactions. Elderly residents are frequently happy to have younger people around. But some seniors do not like children or young adults in residence, feeling that it is depressing to see young people in poor health or need of care. Others do not feel comfortable with the mixture of ages, preferring a homogeneous age group where they feel compatible.

Progressive attitudes on the part of the owners, administrators, and staff are reflected in the programs offered and the perceptions of the residents. A positive demeanor, appreciation of the individual, and a focus on the quality of life will in turn be reflected by the level of function and successful recovery of patients living at the facility.

Nowhere is this position more obvious than in the emphasis on promoting positive mental attitudes which has been taken by the state. Survey teams now evaluate activities and social interaction offered and promoted for each resident, just as they do for health care and record keeping. Several homes have been cited for lack of a qualified activities director or substandard activities programs, and — in at least one instance — this has been a contributing factor for freezing admissions to a facility. This was unheard-of a decade ago.

The state of Virginia and a number of facilities have begun to develop some interesting programs. Therapy dogs can be found in many facilities. Companion dogs and cats are also found much more frequently than they were a decade ago. Research has found repeatedly that there is benefit from the presence of animals. Their quiet companionship, love and ability to accept love, the interaction between human and animal, and the warmth and tactile stimulation of the animal have a positive therapeutic affect. Rabbits and birds may also be a regular part of the staff. Once these animals were limited to a lounge or a single area but now they frequently make their rounds among patients who appreciate their presence in the room.

Individual window gardens or boxes which can be moved to a bedstand allow residents to putter and plant when the central garden is inaccessible. Music, crafts, and reading programs are part of innovative therapies which improve the feeling of self-worth and stimulate the mind. Both of these actually promote physical well-being. Research in all fields has proven that a positive mental attitude extends life and promotes recovery. Nursing homes are implementing these techniques as important parts of maintaining and maximizing function for each individual.

Nursing homes today have extended their concept of care to recovery and rehabilitation. Goals and plans for returning their residents to a more active level of function is documented by resident assessment plans and measured not only in lack of decline, but in improvement. Such resident-assessment provisions were part of the OBRA '87 legislation program which so decidedly changed senior care throughout the United States. Physical functions, activities of daily living, cognitive performance, and social engagement may all be part of the assessment as well as mental attitudes such as anxiety or depression. A reduction in rate of decline and an increase in rate of improvement are both analyzed. Skilled and trained professionals deal with the whole person instead of the single ailment or condition.

Pro-Active Involvement

Pro-active involvement of residents is based on the assessment that nearly all nursing home residents can judge nursing home quality. Even residents with cognitive difficulties can render meaningful responses to quality-of-life questions, according to the findings of an eleven state study done by the American Association of Homes and Services for the Aging in Washington, D.C. Resident satisfaction is tracked over time. The initial study found a surprisingly low correlation between family and resident responses to identical questions, indicating again the need to allow the resident to make choices before those choices are made for them by family members.

When residents feel that they have input to programs, policies, and factors which affect their quality of life, they are much more satisfied with their environment. Residents do perceive a distinction between facilities with low and high qualities of life. Improvement of the facilities perceived as providing a low quality of life can often be achieved by involving residents in setting goals and objectives for those improvements. Involvement is in itself a key factor to satisfaction because it promotes feelings of self-worth and control over one's own life.

Has all of this been successful? According to several studies appearing in the August 1997 *Journal of the American Geriatrics Society* there has been a 28% drop in the rate of hospitalization of the frailest nursing home residents, with no increase in their death rate. There has also been significantly less decline in daily living function, cognitive performance, and social engagement. Researchers have also found that nursing homes are using fewer catheters and restraints. Fewer residents had ulcers or experienced dehydration in 1993 than in 1990. And fewer residents had vision problems or suffered from malnutrition.

When residents at one facility indicated on customer surveys that bath time would be more pleasant if it were less chilly, an enthusiastic team of nurse assistants went to work devising ways to warm things up. Heated soaps, heat lamps, warm towels, and relaxation music are now part of the bathing routine, and the latest survey indicates that the new program is very much a success. This is an example of the new pro-active role of patients in long-term care facilities.

After HCFA implemented the national Resident Assessment Instrument, the care in nursing homes changed and improved and more accurate information about the patients was collected and available. This allows facilities and the industry to develop care programs that address each resident's problems. The conclusion has been that facilities and staff, together with families, should think through the care of the resident. The overwhelming findings are that there are things that can be done to help the patient stay healthier longer.

Nursing homes are also branching into other services beside specialized and subacute care. Respite care provides a place for at-home caregivers to leave their family member. The elder member may welcome the change of scenery and chance to interact with new people, and the caregiver gets some time off for a vacation or simply a few stress-free days of rest. Other facilities are incorporating adult day care centers for those who need medical rather than simply social attention and care.

Who Pays for Nursing Home Care?

About 10% of Americans older than 65 enter nursing homes every year according to federal statistics. About a fifth will spend more than five years in a nursing home. Medicare and Medicaid have long been the major sources of payment for nursing home care. Rates are set by the state and reimbursement is according to regulations dealing with treatments and length of stay. Because much of the cost of nursing homes is covered by Medicaid, many states have limited or put a moratorium on building for nursing homes or adding new beds. Virginia had such an embargo on new beds for several years, but it has recently been lifted to meet the growing demand. Even now the number of new beds is regulated. One factor which will work to fill nursing home beds to overflowing within the next few years is the approach of an over-85 age group boom. There will be tremendous growth in this population within the next ten years. The average age of people entering nursing homes has increased over the past few years. This is partly because of medical advances which are helping to keep people active and living longer and partly because people are eating better, exercising more, and staying more active, all of which increases their active life-span and pushes their need for skilled long-term care further into the future.

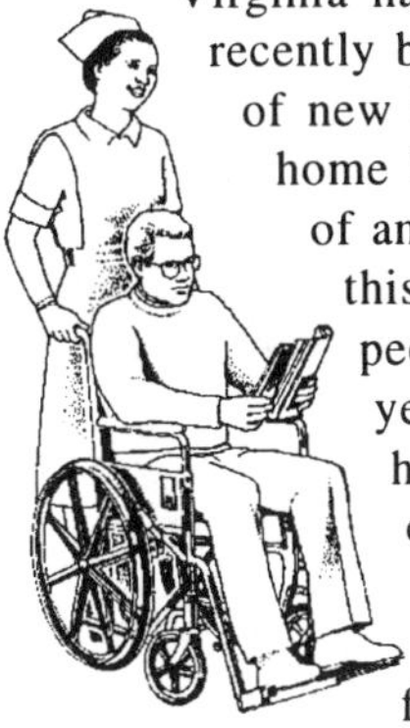

Managed care providers (HMOs) and private insurance have recently become a major source of income for many facilities and the number of patients who fall into this category is growing.

Personal assets are used to pay for services if the patient is able to provide for his or her own care. These patients are referred to as "Private Pay" and they are part of a growing group of semi-affluent or affluent seniors who are beginning to emerge. There is no predetermined rate or number of days allowed for this group.

Choosing a Facility

When choosing a facility, either for future use or for a family member, a physical inspection is just as important as references and public records. Simple lists can often be misleading. Although a facility lists that it offers a certain amenity, it may not fit well into the pattern or physical layout of the facility. A listing of the number of times a facility has been assessed with a deficiency is almost useless. As discussed in the chapter on regulations and surveys, any home can be cited for ***something*** because of the number and complexity of regulations. And there is room for interpretation on the part of both administrators and inspectors. Every year homes all over the country are cited and fined for deficiencies which are appealed by the facility. Many of these are overturned upon further inspection and deeper investigation. If a person is not familiar with regulations, it can be quite confusing. A citation for the way an approach was stated on a care plan is probably not as much of a concern for most people as a citation for failing to have adequate staff to meet the overall needs of the residents. Yet both are things that a facility could be cited for and both would simply show up as a code or number in the records. Past records of evaluations are available, though they may not be as easy to access. Without further investigation the simple fact that the home has been cited does not necessarily reflect on the quality of care for the patient.

Call the facility and talk to several people, from the person who initially answers the phone to the director of admissions and the administrator. Remember that there is some latitude in choosing a facility, even if the resident is part of a managed care program. Frequently there are several alternatives, especially in populated and competitive areas. If you or your family member has taken the time to investigate, has good reasons for the choice, and has made the choice known before any medical emergency, the consumer often has much more input into the final decision, regardless of the source of payment, than might be evident at the outset.

Contact the Ombudsman program and the Area Agency on Aging in the area and see what kinds of complaints might have been lodged. Request any information they might have on the facilities under consideration. Be sure to make this only one part of your consideration. The passing of a loved one often triggers a negative reaction with the family, so almost all facilities have complaints against them from time to time. Try to find out what the complaint was and how it was resolved.

Visit the facility and see if it is pleasing to the potential resident. Each individual will have different things which appeal or put them off. Sometimes it is the little things which make a difference. Visit at different times of the day if possible, and talk with the residents and staff. Are the answers satisfying and is there a comfortable match between the facility and prospective resident?

Look at the facility. Does it look clean? Is it pleasing to the eye? Take a look at the rooms. Are they what you expected? Ask about personal affects, where are they stored, and whether there are limits to the size, value, or type of property which can accompany the resident?

Does the facility smell clean? Pay attention to smells which may leave an institutional feeling, the so called "hospital smell." A surprising number of people are sensitive to that smell and may have negative reactions to it. Be sure that the facility does not smell like urine.

Listen to the sounds of the facility. Is there music? Do people seem quiet and well-adjusted or is there screaming and unrest?

Document your feelings. While you may not have a right to reject the facility because of the color or because the drive is further than you would like it to be, you certainly will have a voice if you cite that the facility smelled like urine and that there was a stack of soiled towels by the door to one of the rooms.

Look for facilities which are progressive and seem to care about their image. ***That attention to consumer awareness and satisfaction is the single most obvious measuring stick for the attitude and basic philosophy of the facility.*** It is simply a matter of who is most important, the facility's opinion of itself and impressing you about how long their waiting list is and why they don't need to make changes, or their willingness to put the resident's care and individual dignity first. Is it important to them that you are happy and satisfied with their image? If they have this kind of progressive attitude about the resident, the family and the consumer in general, they probably also have adopted the new attitudes which are changing and improving senior care and quality of life. This is a rapidly changing industry and those facilities which have the attitude that it is an exciting and challenging time to be working in the field will have staff with the same positive attitude. This translates directly to better quality care for the resident and a higher level of function for a longer period of time.

Special Care

Since 1980 nursing facilities have marketed special care units as a way to provide focused care for residents with special needs. By 1992, 14% of Medicare/Medicaid-certified facilities had at least one special care unit. By 1996, nearly one-quarter of all nursing homes had a special care unit. By 2000, 42% of all facilities will be operating with at least one such unit.

Part of this growth is due to the emerging network of nursing homes operating together to provide specialized care for a wide variety of illnesses and disabilities. These units within nursing homes are a natural extension of services and are a continuing part of the specialization which has been taking place since the middle of the nineteenth century. The function of specialized facilities allows focus on particular ailments and needs, and they help develop new methods of treatment.

Aside from the economic benefits for the homes there are some obvious benefits for the patients. When managing patients who have the same care needs in one location, nursing staff can develop an expertise and awareness of patients suffering from the ailment. By comparing cases, they learn symptoms of changes and developing problems and are more sensitive to progression of the illness. This sensitivity and expertise will sometimes allow them to spot early warning signals and alert doctors. They can also develop better ways of handling a crisis when it occurs and are alert to small shifts in response. A lot can be learned in these units which can be applied to other cases, and new treatments can be evaluated sooner than from isolated patients spread out across several facilities.

Special care units also allow families to form support groups and to realize that they are not the only people whose families have been touched in such a way. Staff also develop sensitivity to family needs in relation to some diseases or disabilities.

There are actually three different types of specialized facilities. The most common, as mentioned above, is a unit, operating within a nursing home, sometimes within an assisted care facility, devoted to serving patients with one particular need.

A second type of special care unit is the home model, which serves a particular population, often for a variety of levels of care. These provide an atmosphere where patients can feel comfortable and interact with each other because they share a bond of some kind. Veterans' homes are an example. Certain church or fraternal facilities are another example. Sometimes women will prefer a home which serves only women, and sometimes it is even more specific, serving women who have been teachers or who have taught at a university. These facilities are specialized horizontally rather than vertically, often serving their specialized population through a number of different levels of care. Cave Creek, for instance, provides three levels of care — residential, assisted, and intensive assisted living — for veterans with various mental disabilities who may or may not also have medical problems. Their fifty-five residents, all men, receive respectful personal care and assistance. As a group they feel comfortable with each other by virtue of their common bond of military service. Although some are elderly and in frail health, others are fairly independent and active but in need of supervision.

Finally, there are specialized free-standing units. These facilities may also provide a variety of levels of care, but they will serve only one type of patient. Such facilities might be completely devoted for example, to caring for dementia patients. These freestanding residences provide all levels of care for dementia sufferers, with the building divided into pods which insure the best possible care for patients at each level of care needed. As the patient's condition deteriorates and more care is needed there is no disruption or move to another location. The patient simply moves to another pod for all or part of the day. The surroundings remain constant, as does the medical staff. This continuity is very comforting for many patients, especially those suffering from dementia where learning a new environment can be traumatic if not impossible.

Alzheimer's Disease

The most common type of specialized unit is for Alzheimer's patients. Although there are other kinds of dementia (reduced cognitive ability) Alzheimer's is the most common. High-quality dementia care is a continually evolving process according to the Alzheimer's Association. On-going staff education and training is part of most facilities which have dementia units.

There is certainly not a single approach which works best for all patients or all facilities. Flexibility seems to be a key, both in developing facilities and in working with patients and their families. Dementia care settings should encourage open communication and seek feedback from staff, families and residents.

Assisted living facilities have begun to enter the field, developing homelike settings for patients. And there is a growing number of free standing facilities which are specially designed to care only for Alzheimer patients. Such facilities often allow more time for special treatment and have a staff which is trained in the field. Special training programs for the staff keep caregivers abreast of the latest innovations in treatment.

Dementia care priorities

- Encourage maximum independence
- Support dignity
- Provide safety and security
- Minimize discomfort
- Manage medical conditions
- Promote the health of skin, feet, teeth and gums, perineal area, and bowels
- Provide nutrition and hydration
- Offer physical conditioning and fresh air
- Provide appropriate stimulation
- Promote continence
- Keep families involved, satisfied
- Rigorously evaluate and diagnose treatable causes of increased confusion and other dementias
- When presenting an activity, direct and inform rather than ask questions
- Personalize the resident's room entry to make it more relevant and understandable to the resident

For Alzheimer's patients, whether they are living at home, with family, or in a facility, one of the dangers is wandering. It is important to allow these people as much freedom from restraint as possible so they continue to be stimulated and active, but there is a danger that they will wander. Most facilities equip patients with monitors. Perimeter doors, or doorways which enter into parts of the building which should not be accessible to these patients (such as the kitchen), are equipped with sensor devices. When the patient crosses the sensor threshold, an alarm is sounded. This insures the patients safety while allowing for independent movement. Creating freedom and stimulation are important in the treatment of Alzheimer's, especially in the early stages.

Needs of dementia patients are very diverse and with new treatments and new drugs, that diversity is becoming even more obvious. Some treatments have been shown to be very effective in reducing the level of deterioration. Especially in early stages, a patient might be quite cognizant in some ways, while they show impairment in others. It is important that programs are designed which stimulate the areas of memory not yet impaired to keep them active and functioning.

Finally, specialized care units, especially for dementia, may be part of Continuing Care Retirement Communities. Depending on the size of the community and provisions made for their residents, these special units provide for different levels of need. In the case of dementia, the special unit allows for a continuation not only at the same place, but with the same staff and medical personnel they have had for the years that they have been at the community. Friends and family members are readily available for visits which provide stimulation, and the surroundings are familiar when they exercise or walk the facility grounds.

Other Types of Specialized Care Units

Often conditions require special care which is quite complicated. At one

Developments in Alzheimer's Disease

1907 Alois Alzheimer is first to describe Alzheimer's Disease.

1976 Researchers show acetylcholine is depleted in brains of people with Alzheimer's Disease. Too little acetylcholine means messages can't travel between brain cells.

1984 Structure revealed for beta-amyloid protein, the sticky substance that clumps to form plaques in the brain that are characteristics of Alzheimer's Disease.

1987 Gene responsible for amyloid precursor protein (APP) is sequenced. APP is broken down to form the beta-amyloid protein of Alzheimer's plaques.

1990 About 10% of all nursing homes with at least 30 beds have Alzheimer's special care units.

1991 Tau protein identified as main component of neurofibrillary tangles.

1993 The Alzheimer's Association, Chicago, releases the first national guidelines for special dementia care.

1993 Gene responsible for apolipoprotein E is sequenced. People with the gene have a higher risk for Alzheimer's Disease.

1993 Tacrine, a cholinesterase inhibitor, is first drug approved by FDA for Alzheimer's.

1994 The National Institute on Aging funds a five-year study to screen for potential toxic effects of new Alzheimer's drugs.

1994 The Alzheimer's Association establishes the Nancy and Ronald Reagan Research Institute.

1995-1996 Transgenic mouse models developed for Alzheimer's Disease, improving ability to study the disease.

1996 Second drug for Alzheimer's, donepezil, also a cholinesterase inhibitor, approved by FDA.

1996 The "nun study" finds a possible connection between poor linguistic ability in early life and cognitive function in late life.

1997 Prospective study shows estrogen reduces Alzheimer's Disease risk more than 50% by protecting nerve cells from Alzheimer's Disease's damaging effects.

1997 Nonsteroidal anti-inflammatory drugs (NSAIDs) linked with 30% to 60% reduction in Alzheimer's Disease risk.

1997 High-dose vitamin E shows promise in slowing disease progression in moderate Alzheimer's Disease. Same study shows modest effects of selegeline.

1997 AMY plaques identified as separate but co-existent with amyloid plaques, yielding new set of mechanisms to explore.

1997 Human lymphocyte antigen-A2 gene implicated in common form of Alzheimer's disease.

1997 Mutations in d2 glutamate receptor gene implicated in nerve cell death.

1997 Seventeen drugs in human testing stage or awaiting FDA approval.

time hospitals were the only place for skilled care of chronic conditions. Today special units in nursing homes are taking over those cases, providing a more personalized care, freeing up hospital beds and although specialized care in nursing homes is expensive, providing care at lower cost than hospitals.

The Social Security Administration had once predicted there will be 15 million Alzheimer's- prone people age 85 and older by 2050, but new demographic data suggests that number is likely to be close to 31 million. Although many feel that the treatment and strategies now in place will not be sufficient to cope with the problem, others feel that new breakthroughs and new drugs will keep the number of functionally impaired people to a manageable number.

Many times HMO or other managed care providers will contract with nursing homes having specialized units to provide for clients who have special conditions. As mentioned, one home in Lynchburg has developed a unit for Lou Gehrig's disease. This is a complex condition, requiring special monitoring and a trained staff. Frequently regular nursing homes or even some hospital units are not familiar with specialized treatments and are not specifically trained to monitor patients. Other common specialized care units are respirator and infusion therapy units, ventilator units, dialysis care, quadriplegic, or comatose units.

One of the most important considerations in developing a specialized care unit is the environment and individuality of the facility. One assisted living home opened a skilled care unit. But after operating it for several months they found it did not fit in with the needs of other patients. Many of their active residents felt strongly that they appreciated the positive, active philosophy of the facility and did not think the new unit, with chronic cases, fit into the philosophy of the facility. Staff agreed. After a meeting between residents, staff and administration, it was decided that the skilled care unit did not fit in with the individual facility, although other assisted living properties owned by the same company were very successful with these specialized units. The unit was phased out and the facility returned to its original format.

Federal and State Regulations

Regulations for each state are developed by that state, and licenses are issued according to those regulations. From time to time these regulations change and as the industry develops they become more and more uniform across the country. There are still different definitions from state to state, however, and different facilities may be licensed and regulated under different state agencies even though an individual resident gets much the same care. One of the reasons for this is that facilities do not fall clearly into specific categories. Nursing homes provide care for a wide variety of residents. Assisted living or adult care residences (as they are technically called in Virginia) have extended their care upward and now provide some of the same services as nursing homes. A resident at certain levels of function might be accommodated in either, depending on the preference of the resident and his or her family. The major difference is that if the facility is licensed as an assisted living property it falls under the Department of Social Services and is regulated and inspected by that agency, even if it is providing care which might overlap that provided by a nursing home. Nursing Homes are licensed and inspected by the Department of Health.

Codes and regulations cover a multitude of issues. They regulate admissions and discharge procedures and record-keeping which includes careful notes for each patient, evaluations and reevaluations of patients' conditions, and goals set for recovery. They regulate the use and administration of drugs and what workers can administer various types of care. They define and license employees working in certain capacities and regulate requirements for professionals within the building.

HCFA, the Health Care Financing Administration, mandates each state to license and certify facilities. The state agency for each type of facility licenses and certifies those properties which fall under its authority. A license is issued to allow a facility to operate, covering the physical part of the residence. Fire and safety codes are enforced. A locked cabinet and proper handling and tracking of drugs must be provided. Sanitation and Food Service Health Codes must be met. There are no requirements for patient care plans or such things as activity directors. As long as a property is 100% private-pay, a license is all that it needs and there will be no survey teams evaluating the home.

Certification grows from the power of payment. If there is even a single resident who qualifies for and collects Medicare or Medicaid reimbursement, the facility must be certified.

Nursing Homes

In February 1970 the federal government published rules and regulations requiring that states receiving Medicaid Title XIX monies establish state programs to license nursing home administrators and establish State Boards for Education and Licensure of Nursing Home Administrators. The effect was to establish a national regulation program. Today persons wishing to become nurs-

Residents' Bill of Rights

- be informed of rights and responsibilities, orally and in writing, in a language they can understand.
- a dignified existence
- be free from discrimination
- know and understand their total health status
- self-administer their medications unless contraindicated
- be free from abuse
- receive a comprehensive assessment at admission and when a change in condition occurs
- have a comprehensive care plan developed with their participation
- be informed of care and treatments, and changes to care and treatments
- refuse treatment
- choose a personal attending physician
- know if they are entitled to Medicaid benefits
- be informed of items and services for which they will be charged
- a written statement of:
  - how their personal funds are managed
  - the procedure for filling a complaint with the state agency
  - the names, specialties, and way of contacting physicians responsible for their care
  - application process for Medicaid and Medicare and to receive refunds from these programs if entitled.
- be notified when there is a change in room or roommate
- refuse to perform services for the facility
- send and receive mail unopened
- privately use a telephone
- retain and use personal possessions, including clothing, as space permits
- share a room with a spouse if both spouses consent
- participate in resident and family groups
- examine health department survey results
- receive visitors and have privacy during visitation
- confidentiality of records
- not to be transferred or discharged without just cause and 30 days prior notice
- every other right granted a citizen of the United States

(From the Federal Register, Vol 54, No. 21, February 2, 1989)

ing home administrators must have experience in the field and must sit for and pass both federal and state examinations.

All nursing homes must have an administrator, licensed in the state of Virginia, who is responsible for the entire facility. There must also be a director of nursing working 40 hours each week. If a facility lacks either of these professionals, it may not operate for more than 90 days.

A dietary manager must be a registered dietician or have a B.A. in foods, nutrition, or a related field or have completed a ninety-hour training course. Smaller facilities without a full-time dietary manager may hire a consultant for a minimum of 8 hours a month.

Physical therapists, occupational therapists, and speech therapists must be licensed in the state by the board and organization governing their discipline. All nursing staff must be licensed or certified for the level at which they are required to function.

If a facility has more than 120 beds, a social worker must be on staff. This person must have a B.A. in Social Work, or a related human services field, with a specialty in geriatrics. If the facility has fewer than 120 beds a social worker may have had two years of related experience under the supervision of a geriatric social worker.

An activities director must be on staff. To qualify, this person must have a degree in recreation with emphasis on geriatric needs or have completed a 120-hour training course, and be certified by the National Association of Activities Professionals or have 5 years experience in a long-term care setting dealing with activities.

All facilities are required to have a resident's council which meets at least once a month. These may be very formal with a full slate of officers or informal with simply a chairman or a president. They meet monthly to talk about the facility, their concerns, and ideas. They may hear from other residents and may call staff members they wish to talk with. Usually the social service or activities director acts as the liaison between the staff and the council, but others may serve in that capacity. In accordance with the Resident's Bill of Rights, and in keeping with the pro-active approach to senior care, these councils make suggestions, voice opinions, and help set policy for the facility.

The National Fire Protection Association is a private, non-profit organization with headquarters in Quincy, Massachusetts. It is not a government agency, nor does it write federal regulations. However, because federal regulations for licensing nursing homes require adherence to the Life Safety Code®, these fire safety standards have the effective force of law for nursing homes. They were developed through studies on the part of the National Fire Protection Association which has been studying fires since 1913. The Code represents collected wisdom on fire prevention and fire containment. First published in the *Federal Register* in 1974, the Life Safety Code was mandated in the 1987 Nursing Home Reform Act, often referred to as OBRA '87.

All nursing homes and hospitals must have a plan for the protection of all persons on their premises. The plan must be written, with copies available to all supervisory personnel. Employees must be periodically trained and informed of their duties and at least 12 drills (one on each shift per quarter) must be held per year. These codes also restrict areas of smoking for both residents and staff and define fire-resistance standards for draperies, furnishing, and decorations.

There are state building code requirements. They also include the American National Standard Specifications for Making Buildings and Facilities Accessible to and Usable by Physically Handicapped People. These are so specific that they regulate the height of a drinking fountain! Besides the basic components of building codes, they also provide for the width of doors, protruding objects, alarms and detection systems, ramps, elevators, and grab bars. There are requirements for all bathroom facilities, work surfaces, eating areas, assembly areas, and dwelling units. The purpose of these standards is to make the building accessible to and usable by people with physical disabilities and limitations.

Nursing homes operate, as do all businesses, under the Occupational Safety and Health Act, known as OSHA. These standards deal with work-place safety for employees. OSHA inspectors examine the premises for compliance with regulations and the records of illnesses and injuries to employees. Citations may be issued at the end of the inspection or later by mail for violations of the standards, with one citation issued for *each* violation, be it serious or nonserious. Specific requirements for correction and a time limit for the correction are included. Citations may be *imminent danger,* which can close operations down; *serious,* which calls for a major fine; *nonserious,* which is a violation in which a direct and immediate relationship exists between the condition and occupational health but not such as to cause death or serious physical harm; and *de minimus,* which is a small violation where notification is given but no fine is leveled. The correction and time limit are specified. Fines may imposed, under OBRA 1990, from $5,000 to $70,000 per violation and may double after the first conviction. In recent years OSHA has begun to emphasize voluntary compliance and educational programs through which safety inspectors advise and provide an opportunity for correction before any official inspections are done.

The local health planning agency can issue an Certificate of Need, often referred to as a CON, if it believes there is a need for more nursing home beds in an area, or refuse to issue one if they feel there are already too many such beds. In effect, the agency could deny permission to build a new long-term care facility. This policy is now active on a state level and provides each state with the ability to determine the needs of its citizens. Virginia uses Certificates of Need. For much of this decade they have been refusing to issue such certificates due to an overbuilding in the late 1980's and early 1990's. Recently, however, the state has issued a Certificate of Need for approximately 1500 new beds to meet anticipated demand.

Assisted Living

In the state of Virginia, the Department of Social Services licensing program covers adult care residences. These are further defined as homes for aged, infirm, disabled, indigent, and incapacitated persons. Virginia uses the term "homes for adults" and classifies them as "residential," "non-ambulatory" or "assisted." In this book we have called these facilities "assisted living," though in Virginia they are often referred to as residential care homes. There is a wide range of services and types of facilities falling into this category, but whether they are termed **assisted living** or **residential care homes** makes no difference. Sometimes it is a matter of what term has been historically used for the facility or of the term used by the corporation which owns the facility. Although not all facilities are alike, the use of either of these terms is not necessarily an indication of how they differ.

The regulations for these facilities are much simpler. Their administrators must also be licensed, but under the Department of Social Services. This is a different administrative license than that of a nursing home administrator. There must be a designated Food Service Manager capable of determining nutritional needs and providing for special dietary needs. Most of the better facilities will have a dietary manager, but it is not required. The Department of Social Services will provide assistance in this field on a twice-a-year basis. Social workers are not required. An activities professional must be on site 15 hours a week. Most of the good facilities will have at least a full-time activities director and many also have social workers.

Fire Codes apply for these facilities which are defined as custodial care facilities or buildings used for lodging or boarding for four or more persons who are incapable of self-preservation because of age or physical limitation.

Criminal Tracking and Drug Handling

One of the greatest fears for health care professionals is criminals slipping into the system. This is the stuff that TV dramas are made of. Actually, most criminals are involved in use and abuse of drugs, and there are very few cases of suspected injury or murder of patients.

There are separate and very specific regulations which apply to all agencies handling drugs. They apply whether the facility is certified or simply licensed. These regulations set forth the handling of drugs, who can sign for them, the type of cabinet they may be held in, and the tracking system and double-check on that system. For certain drugs every gram which enters the building must be tracked and accounted for from the time the shipment is received until it is given to the patient.

The state regulates and maintains a system of tracking criminals. Needless to say, persons convicted of certain kinds of crimes are not eligible to work in any health care facilities. The problem is that sometimes these people move to another state and apply for work without reporting their records. The federal government is in the process of setting up a national clearing house of records on criminals. When completed and on-line, a person applying for a job would be automatically run through this national screening system. All employees must take a drug test when they are hired, regardless of the job they are doing, and are subject to periodic retesting.

Senior Housing

Since the late 1970's, the federal government has been a primary source of funding for low-income senior housing. In the directory in the second section of this book, some facilities will be listed as "subsidized." These residences operate under the U.S. Department of Housing and Urban Development, or HUD. Seniors applying for federal assistance must meet income requirements to be eligible for such housing and monthly rent is often on a sliding scale of need. Sometimes referred to as "Section 8," these residences by definition offer housing only. Therefore services such as housekeeping, transportation, and personal care assistance are not typically available. Seniors applying for such housing are required to submit supporting financial documentation according to HUD-specified guidelines. Rents are established at 30% of gross annual adjusted income, and the adjustment is made by a complex calculation of income, assets, pensions, and annuities. Federal and state governments may subsidize the property further or provide for some services such as transportation, emergency response systems, leisure activities, security, and even meals. Since 1981 the federal government has cut appropriations for new Section 8 housing and other subsidized programs, but local and state governments have come in to fill the gap. Often cities and counties now offer rental housing to low-income seniors where they once spent resources to repair owner-occupied housing.

Fairfax County, in northern Virginia, offers, for example, four independent living communities for seniors. Monthly fees are based on individual income levels, with some tenants subsidized by the county. These properties usually have a waiting list. The northern Virginia area and populated areas such as Richmond or the Tidewater have developed these kinds of senior housing properties much more than rural counties or small towns where the demand of low-income seniors is not as heavy and can be handled by other options.

Survey Teams

When a facility is certified, the state has the power to enter the facility unannounced and conduct an on-site survey or inspection. This power is granted to the state under HCFA, which also grants the states the power to issue licenses and certification. A property does not need certification if there are no residents receiving Medicare or Medicaid benefits. However, once the certification is issued, even if it is necessary due to a single patient, the state survey team has the right to inspect the entire property and scrutinize the files of every resident, even those who are private pay.

The state is required to conduct a minimum of one inspection per year on each certified facility in the state. They may do more, however. If there is a complaint or complaints filed with the state, they may decide to conduct a survey. If there is a history of deficiencies or the building has had a number of deficiencies at the last inspection, the survey team may visit more frequently until they are convinced the problems have been dealt with. Subacute care units are inspected every three months by special teams. Often, if the deficiencies are severe and fines have been imposed, the facility will have 30 days to correct the condition and then another inspection will be done to ensure there is compliance with the requested correction.

HCFA also has teams. These federal teams act as quality control for the states. They inspect approximately 15% of homes in the nation on a random basis each year to spot-check the state teams. Neither the facilities nor the state has any idea when or where they will inspect.

Thirty to forty-five inspectors work for the state in three teams. These teams travel throughout the state rather than have an assigned territory. This means that a facility will seldom have the same team inspect them twice in a row. There are several reasons for this.

First, whether a facility is cited for a deficiency is sometimes a matter of opinion. Like any other written document, the state regulations can sometimes be interpreted in different ways. Ambiguous words leave room for personal decisions. Degree is often the determination of whether a regulation is being met. In some cases, the outcome and limits are set out in the regulations but the actual implementation is left up to the facility. Some of the regulations can be measured in black and white terms, the rest of the regulations leave room for interpretation.

For example, if a facility "shall provide" activities of a varied nature for the residents, and those activities are planned in consideration of the abilities, physical condition, needs, and interests of the residents, it may be up to the inspector to decide exactly how varied a program must be to be considered "varied" enough for the regulations. Further, suppose there is a wide range of physical abilities, conditions, and interests within the resident population. The inspector must decide if the activities fit that population. One inspector might decide that most activities should be aimed at the level of the middle capabilities of the group, while another might feel that it is important to include activities for the two extremes so that every group gets something specifically for their needs. In contrast, when the regulations say activities records shall be kept of the activity schedules for at least three months, it is easy for an inspector to see whether there are three months of schedules in the folder or not.

An example of how the outcome is regulated but the implementation is not would be the new regulations on accommodations for residents who smoke. The regulation states that a facility may choose to go "Smoke-Free." But it prohibits the facility from requiring those residents who are smokers, and who were admitted prior to the ban on smoking, from being transferred to another facility or from being required to stop smoking. A facility may only implement the policy by requiring newly admitted residents to be nonsmoking. However, the facility does have the right to limit the smoking area for those residents who smoke. The regulation states that " careful consideration must be utilized in designating smoking areas so that residents will not be exposed to secondhand smoke." It lists as an example that "a TV lounge used by both smokers and nonsmokers would not be an acceptable designated smoking area. However, the designated smoking area should maintain the quality of life for residents who smoke. Requiring residents who smoke to go outside is not an appropriate accommodation." But a facility may "limit a resident's access, i.e., staff available to accompany a resident for the duration of a smoking break." Here are just a few things which are not stated in the regulation but would be left up to the decision of the facility, and later to the survey team.

1. What if two people are roommates, one smoker and one nonsmoker? Should the room be smoke-free? What if the smoker needs assistance to get out of bed? What if the two have been friends and roommates for a long time? What if the nonsmoker does not mind?

2. What if a smoker complains because he needs help moving to the smoke-free area, but there is not enough staff to take him when he desires? How long should he have to wait after he requests a smoke-break?

3. The designated smoking area is a room at the end of the hall, but because there are not many smokers it is not very large. Does this room have to be larger? How many smokers may it hold at one time? All the smokers in the building? Half of the smokers? Must the room be comfortable in terms of decorating to insure the "quality of life" for the smoker?

Second, there are hundreds of regulations covering everything from food and care to visitation from family and residents' rights. It is nearly impossible for a team to completely evaluate every detail of every regulation. Therefore each inspector, just as each teacher in a school, will have a different area where he or she places importance. This is the area that inspector will inspect most closely or first. By rotating inspectors, there is a balance of emphasis.

Recently the emphasis in inspections has changed in an effort to humanize a very long and rigid set of rules and regulations. This is in keeping with new moves to give residents a proactive role in their living situation and enforce the Residents' Bill of Rights. Inspections are now considered "outcome driven," which means that observation of the residents and staff, their attitudes and morale, have a lot to do with the survey. In a facility where everyone seems happy and feels they are a part of what is going on around them, it is hard for an inspection team to be very picky about details which might not be in perfect order. However, if the residents are not happy, if they have complaints, if they are not in good physical and/or mental condition in relation to their level of function, the inspectors will be looking at the details much harder in an effort to determine why the facility is not providing the maximum level of support and care for each resident.

An example of this is the staff to patient ratio. There is no fixed staff-to-patient ratio in Virginia. If a facility is operating with what might be considered a high staff to patient ratio, but the patients are still not considered to be well cared for, they will be cited for insufficient staff. Another home might have a lower staff-to-patient ratio but its residents are happy and in good condition, and they would not be cited even though they have a lower number of staff people for the same number of residents. Management and morale are part of the responsibilities of the administrator and it is the reason why they must be licensed.

Third, rotating teams eliminates personality problems. It keeps bonds of friendship from interfering with the objectivity of the survey, and it allows personalities which do not work well together to have relief on the next inspection.

Finally, the rotation of teams is its own quality control. One team automatically monitors the team in front of it as the survey is conducted.

What Happens When a Survey Team Arrives At a Home

A survey team may arrive at any time on any day of the week. In reality, they will usually — but not always — arrive in the morning and, for the larger homes, in the first three days of the week. There will be two to five inspectors on a team, determined by the size of the home (number of beds defines the size of the home).

The first thing the team will do is simply walk around the facility and talk with the residents. They will identify patients they see who fall outside certain parameters. For example, suppose they see a fifty-five-year-old man in a wheelchair. They speak with him and see that he is mentally alert, responsive, and competent. He has good upper body control. But they observe he is strapped into his chair. They would want the staff to explain why he is restrained when there is no obvious condition which warrants the restraint.

Then they will meet with the staff. At one time, the survey team would pull and inspect charts on a random basis. It was usually every third or forth chart or some other pattern they had devised for random selection. Today they do a more complete surface evaluation of the entire home but a less detailed evaluation of random charts.

They will request a ***Resident Case Mix Matrix*** be provided for them. This matrix identifies each resident within the building and tracks them in fourteen different categories of care. From this matrix they will identify patients who are: 1) at risk for some reason, 2) have multiple medical issues, 3) have critical medical needs, and 4) those who appear to be in contradiction in some way across the fourteen categories Those are the charts they request for further inspection.

They will meet with the resident council to find out their feelings, hear their complaints, and consider their attitude toward the home and its staff. Based on what they hear, they may return to inspect other specific charts or they may excuse what might otherwise be a citation.

The same is true when they inspect a chart and find a problem, but the resident is fine. For example, suppose Mrs. Brown is a diabetic with high blood pressure. Regulations require her blood sugar be tested and recorded on a daily basis. The chart shows no record of this twice in the past month. But when the survey team member finds Mrs. Brown she is in the recreation room, looking fine, and playing an animated game of bridge. Other reports on the chart are in order, and the levels of blood sugar which are recorded are stable and within the proper range. The team will point out the error and request that it be corrected in the future, but there will not necessarily be a fine or a severe citation of deficiency or, if issued, it will not be as severe.

If there have been complaints filed or even a call made about an alleged problem in the home, the survey team will take time to look carefully at that particular area.

Virginia has growing pains as far as their survey teams are concerned. Relative to some states, Virginia was late to move inside the national parameters for inspections. This means that although there were regulations, Virginia inspection teams fell outside the average for the nation in issuing citations and did not close homes or impose heavy fines at the same rate as other states. This was followed by a period of heavy activity. Richmond had at least two homes closed, for example, which made the news because many seniors and their families were upset when the residents were displaced. But also many citations have been overturned at appeal. The pendulum has swung back to a more reasonable approach, with inspectors trying to work with facilities to fix problems rather than simply impose severe sanctions. Legislators have become much more involved in the process. Recently Commonwealth Senator Emily Couric heard a wide range of administrators, doctors, patients, and their families in meetings about the care and quality of homes in Virginia.

Assisted Living Surveys

Assisted living facilities which receive Medicaid or Medicare must also be certified, though they fall under the Department of Social Services. These survey teams are smaller and the surveys less detailed. Typically their survey team will be two people, and they are often finished in less than a day.

They are not required to have Interdisciplinary Patient Care Plans and they do not present a Matrix. They will look at the dietary program but do not get much deeper into detail than to see if the menus are nutritional and if the meals meet the special needs of those residents who require dietary support for medical conditions such as high blood pressure or diabetes. These survey teams will look at the plan of care for each patient, the general resident attitude, and they will hear complaints from residents. A plan of care for an assisted living facility is much more general than those required for a nursing home, even when the patient is receiving medical care.

With many assisted living homes taking over care which was at one time assigned to nursing homes, many health care professionals are concerned about the review process. Look for both regulations and surveys for assisted living facilities to tighten up considerably within the next decade.

The Real Meaning of Complaints and Deficiencies

It is nearly impossible for a home of any size to operate for many years without some complaints. As with any human interaction there will be misunderstandings and ill feelings somewhere along the way. When investigating a property take a look to see if there has been a history of complaints over some period of time. Were they all at one time, perhaps by one family or under one administrator?

Likewise, if you have pulled the information on deficiencies, take a look at what they represent. There is such a multitude of details that, as one health care professional said, with determination he could walk into any home in the state and find a deficiency at any time.

Although all regulations and all deficiencies of the same level are equal in the state's eyes, people who work in the industry have a tendency to divide deficiencies into categories — paperwork and those which affect the patient.

Suppose, for example, we go back to Mrs. Brown and her bloodwork. If the bloodwork has not been done, if her diet is not correct and does not support her condition, or if her medication is not given properly those are all things which will affect her health. If, however, the blood sugar was not recorded in the chart, if it was recorded in the wrong place, or if her medication was given but not supported by the right documentation that is a paperwork problem. Although both are important in order to assure the best possible care for the patient, quality control, and the ability to study residents and their response, some health care professionals see them as two different things. In fact, many professionals have resisted the new documentation requirements because they take so much time. In larger homes it will take the equivalent of a full-time nurse to make the notations on the charts. Those who resist the system argue that this is time and money taken away from direct patient care.

Every year each state will focus on an area or areas it wishes to promote within the nursing home community. Last year, for example, Commonwealth of Virginia survey teams were paying particular attention to "restraint free buildings." Focusing on one issue forces buildings to upgrade their staff and patient management and bring it into line with other buildings within the Commonwealth and the nation.

Management and Transfer of Information

This year the emphasis will be on the management and transfer of data for each resident.

HCFA regulations are multifaceted. Not only are they designed to monitor patient care, the information they record is sent to HCFA on a regular basis and compiled into studies. Data patterns are analyzed. In this way HCFA can track the success of different programs and the overall care and response of the senior population in this country.

Agencies also use the data to maintain quality within parameters. For example, seniors who are given freedom and dignity also are at some risk. Every home will have some residents fall. If, however, a home has a higher number of falls per capita than other homes, a survey team will be sent to find out why and to work on ways of correcting the situation. This "alarm bell" for problems which fall outside the typical parameters of most facilities is sounded only because the state and federal agencies have the data to be able to analyze what is "average" or "normal" and to spot those which do not fit the norm.

Although it was not a requirement, most nursing homes have been on computerized systems for several years. The software, written especially for nursing home management, is available from several different companies. This year, data from the 17,000 nursing homes across the country will be electronically downloaded to the state agencies on every resident, from every certified facility in each state. Once a month, all of the state data will be downloaded to HCFA. Virginia is scheduled to go on-line by March 22.

This attempt to control the data flow will likely occupy a good deal of time within the next year. The sheer mass of information is staggering. This program has been delayed for a year and a half and, as of the first of March, 1998, there were still a good number of bugs to iron out.

The information and studies which will be possible from this will be very helpful. It will mean that changes in regulations or practices can be analyzed within a few months instead of it taking years to collect and analyze data. Typically studies have lagged several years behind. It is hoped that problems can be spotted and corrected much more quickly with the new system.

On the other hand, many administrators fear that the time involved and the staff and equipment required to support the electronic transfer of data will further remove them and their funding from their primary duty — taking care of residents.

The Best Quality Assurance

Survey teams and the HCFA data transfer are two of the means state and federal governments have implemented to assure the quality of care for residents of assisted living and nursing homes. In their traditional role these governmental agencies are providing for seniors who have no one to look after them. If you have a senior family member who needs nursing home care, requesting ombudsman reports, looking at survey records, and inquiring about past performance of the home through various agencies may be a good place to start.

But remember that everyone is an individual and what makes some people happy may not be right for another. Your best assurance that the facility will be right for your senior family member is to visit it, ask questions, and form your own opinion. Nursing homes are not the type of business which can hide a great deal and often the personal feeling you form will be correct. By making your own observations, talking to staff and residents, and looking at the general building you will probably have a better understanding about the property than you would have from spending hours and hours going over reports.

Once you have a family member in such a facility, keep in touch. Talk to your senior and the staff. Visit often and take the time to read the bulletin board and talk to others, both staff and residents. If you are far from them, use the services of a geriatric care manager or other form of visitation service. We found that almost all facilities have newsletters and regular family meetings. Read the newsletter and attend the meetings. You are still the best form of quality control for your senior. You may not be able economically, physically, or emotionally to care for them in your home. But you can make the time to see that they are happy and healthy.

Administrators indicated that when lawsuits are filed, they are often filed by families with very little contact. Often these lawsuits are as much from guilt or ignorance on the part of the family as they are on substantive issues of care.

Governmental Protections

Caring for our aging population has been a concern of civilizations for hundreds of years. Services and programs to serve and protect them have grown up over the years until today there are several agencies and organizations which overlap.

Each state, under the direction of the federal government, sets up Area Agencies on Aging. These geographic divisions within a state facilitate the adoption and coordination of federal, state, and local programs to fit the needs of the community and individuals within the community. Often the AAA's coordinate, or work in conjunction with, other programs to analyze services and to institute policies and programs to fill gaps in services. The Area Agency on Aging serves as a focal point of programs for the aging and is responsible for advocacy on behalf of the elderly, assessing the needs and priorities for services, focusing the delivery of services for older persons with greatest economic and social need, planning and coordination of existing services, developing of new services and resources for the elderly whenever possible, and awarding grants and contracts for the provision of social and nutrition services.

The following two protective services can be located through the Area Agency on Aging.

Ombudsman

The Long-Term Care Ombudsman Program is designed to be an advocate for persons receiving long-term care in a nursing facility, home for adults, or in the community. Its goal is to improve the quality of life for recipients of long-term care. The program's objectives are to provide a point of entry for concerns and issues relating to long-term care services, to mediate complaints, to integrate existing services, and to provide complaint resolution. The program investigates and resolves complaints made by or on behalf of the individuals who are recipients of long-term care, relating to administrative action which may adversely affect the health, safety, welfare, and rights of such recipients. It monitors the development and implementation of federal, state, and local laws with respect to long-term care and provides information as appropriate to public agencies regarding the problems of older individuals receiving long-term care.

The local ombudsman assists patients and their families with concerns about patient care, serves as a link between patients and staff, lends an ear for patients who wish to express problems and concerns of a financial, social, family, or legal nature, and provides families and patients with information about rights, governmental benefits, and other agencies' services. This program, established nationally in 1979 to improve the quality of care in nursing homes, was expanded in 1983 by the Virginia General Assembly to include homes for adults and community-based long-term care services. In many areas this now extends to Adult Day Care facilities. Under Virginia law the ombudsman has the authority to enter long-term care facilities and review patients' records, to keep all records confidential, and to keep the complainant's name confidential, unless he or she signs a release.

In short, the ombudsman assists people who are both searching for long-term care services as well as those receiving them. For those who are seeking services, the ombudsman maintains information on home health services, nursing homes, and adult care residences. They provide data and details about facilities and services available in the area. They also maintain a complaint track record for ombudsman reports which include the complaint and the resolution, the time frame, and the appropriateness of the response. They can provide Virginia Department of Health licensure inspection reports (surveys). They can provide questions to ask and features to look for during the search. And they can provide particulars about what to expect in the admissions process and what will be needed in terms of paperwork.

For individuals receiving care in a nursing home or adult care residence, or from a home care provider, the ombudsman program handles problems and does counseling, usually by telephone. When there is a persistent problem, they will provide mediation to resolve the dispute. They can also provide formal complaint investigation aimed at achieving a resolution. They make regular visits to homes. In larger areas they are assisted in this process by volunteers who are also trained as ombudsmen.

The complaint investigation procedures are a focal point of their work and probably the area for which they are best known. Anonymous complaints are accepted and investigated. Complaint investigation written reports are kept confidential and are not subject to the Freedom of Information Act, which is sometimes important for those who feel they have something to lose by making the report. Signed waivers of confidentiality are required in cases where names will be used. The ombudsman addresses complaints of just one resident or problems affecting numerous residents. And they will address a very wide variety of complaint issues, unlike Adult Protective Services, which focuses only on abuse, neglect, or exploitation, and on specific individuals only.

Adult Protective Services

Another area of governmental service is available to individuals 60 years of age and older and their families who are at risk of abuse, neglect, or exploitation. Programs on elder abuse prevention are given periodically at nutrition sites, senior centers, senior clubs, and special events.

Although the most popular stereotype of senior abuse is the long-term care facility, in reality such cases are few and far between. There are several reasons for this. One is the overwhelming number of survey teams and state and federal regulations. With an emphasis on patients' rights and mandatory resident's councils meeting regularly with state inspectors, there is little probability that habitual abuse would slide by very long without discovery. Ombudsman programs provide a relief valve for frustration for both residents and their families. Another factor is simply an economic one. With increasing consumer awareness, facilities can ill afford a poor reputation within the community. Local newspapers carry the story of problems in this area as the attention of the community turns more and more to the field of aging and long-term care. As more corporations come into the field, they are more than ever concerned about how incidents with individual residents will reflect on the corporate name which has been built with care over years of expense. The potential for lawsuits for corporations, which are often seen as having deep pockets, make administrators and corporate offices very concerned with a bottom line of not only profit but resident satisfaction.

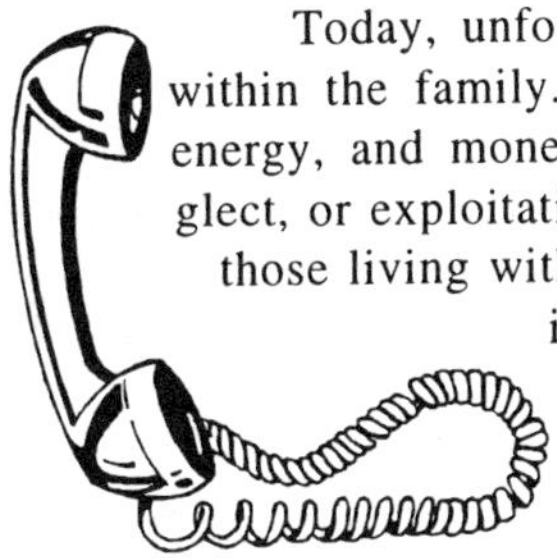

Today, unfortunately, the greatest potential for senior abuse exists within the family. Stress on the caregiver in terms of time, emotional energy, and money can all too easily feed a situation where abuse, neglect, or exploitation can take place. There are no regular inspections for those living with family. Training and education within the community is the only balance in place. Many communities maintain and advertise Abuse Hotlines for reports of suspected senior abuse or neglect.

Potential victims are most often female, those of advanced age, and those who are economically, physically, and even emotionally dependent. Isolation from neighbors, friends, or relatives allows the situation to build and continue. Often provocative behavior on the part of the elder person who may be demanding, ungrateful, and unpleasant will aggravate the already stressed caregiver. Sometimes excessive loyalty to the caregiver makes intervention difficult.

Those who are most likely to be abusers are substance abusers, those with mental illness who are unable to cope with elder family members, or advanced-age caregivers who may be frustrated because they cannot provide adequate care. Caregivers who are economically stretched, have been abused as a child or spouse, are isolated themselves, or who are depressed or frustrated are most likely to abuse or neglect seniors in their care.

Directory by Area Agencies on Aging

The Commonwealth of Virginia is divided into twenty-five Area Agencies on Aging. They differ from the seven divisions of the state as recognized by the Virginia Tourist Bureau. The Areas on Aging were designed to serve as a focal point of programs for the aging and are responsible for advocating on behalf of the elderly. They assess the needs and priorities for services, focusing on the delivery of services for persons 60 years of age or older, with the greatest economic and social needs. They plan and coordinate existing services, develop new services and resources for the elderly whenever possible, and they award grants and contracts for the provision of social and nutrition services.

Area Agencies on Aging are designated by the Virginia Department for the Aging in accordance with federal guidelines. They are governed by a board of directors appointed by local boards of supervisors. All services offered are provided without regard to race, sex, religion, disability, political belief or national origin. Some services are available to individuals regardless of age. Through outreach efforts Area Agencies on Aging identify the needs of an individual and/or the family caregivers. They run Employment Services and an Older Workers Program, Retired and Senior Volunteer Programs, and the SMILE (Seniors Maintaining Independent Living Environment) program maintains a listing of private-hire homemakers that is available to individuals or families seeking to hire someone to assist them in their homes. There are support and respite care programs for caregivers, legal programs, nutrition sites and centers, ombudsman programs, case management, transportation, home delivery of meals, elder abuse prevention programs, health programs, and pharmacy access. There is also the Virginia Insurance Counseling and Assistance Program where counseling and information is provided by certified volunteers to groups and individuals to better understand Medicare, Medicare Supplemental Insurance, Medicaid, health care options, patients' rights, and assistance in filing claims.

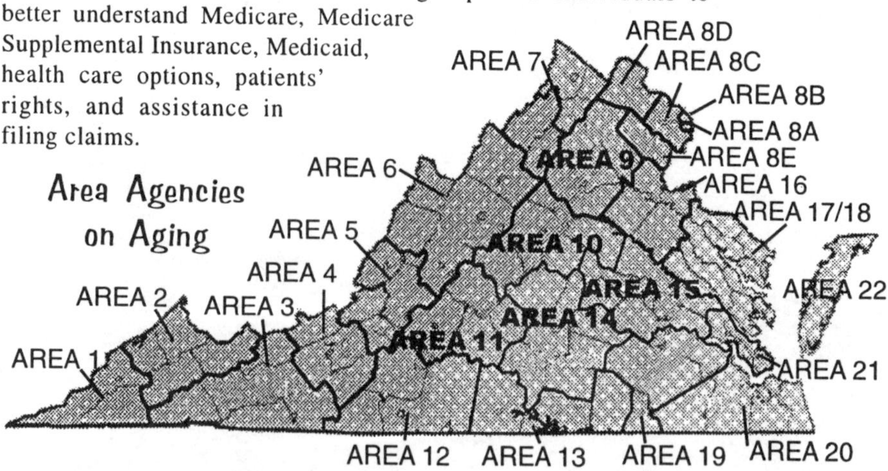

Immediately following the information on each area, a list of facilities has been included. Each facility within the state was contacted by phone and was sent a questionnaire. The returned information is compiled from the answers we received.

No recommendations, guarantees or warranties are expressed or implied as to any of the properties, facilities, or service providers appearing in this book, and none should be inferred.

The key to abbreviations used is as follows:

Types of rooms or units:
P - Private
SP - Semi-Private
W - Ward
For Independent Living:
Apts - Apartments, Cottage
TwnHm - Townhouses

The following abbreviations are used:
C *City location*
S *Suburban outside large city*
ST *Small town*
R *Rural*
Followed by nearest large city

Number of units or beds

Waiting list if any - Hours for Adult Daycare

Oak Ridge (540) 441-4444 **Assisted/Nursing**
P.O. Box 367, Duffield, VA 24244 **S** — Kingsport, TN 88 beds
1 story ❋ P/SP rooms ❋ 6-7 mos (8AM-7PM) ❋ **N/SCU** ❋ $1000-$1400mo (✢✙20%) — **SA-Sec-P-TD-ST-DTG-OTG-EX-CH-N-RFM-Ph-CB-W-K-CD-H-L-Rec**

The following abbreviations are used — always in the following order if they are available:

SA - Social Activities
Sec - Security
P - Pets Welcome
TD - Therapy/Resident Dog
ST - Shopping Trips
DTG - Day Travel Groups
OTG - Overnight Travel Groups
EX - Exercise Classes
CH - Craft or Hobby Classes
N - Newsletter
RFM - Regular Family Meetings
Ph - Private Phone Line
CB - Call Bell System
W - Wheelchair Accessible
K - Kitchens in units
CD - Community Dining
H - Housekeeping
L - Laundry Service
Rec - Recreation Program

Medical Care Available:
A *Daily Assistance*
N *Nursing Care/ Licensed Nurse on Staff*
SN *Skilled Nursing Care*
SCU *Special Care Unit*

Price range if available followed by:
$ - *Subsidies Available*
✢ - *Medicare*
✙ - *Medicaid*
__% - *Percent Private Pay*
✍ - *Contract required*

For senior housing:
R - *Rent*
L - *Lease*
P - *Purchase*

Area 1 — Mountain Empire Older Citizens, Inc
Serves the counties of Lee, Wise, Scott and the city of Norton.
Block 1-A Industrial Park — P.O. Box 888
Big Stone Gap, VA 24219 (540) 523-4202

This is Blue Grass and Country Music Country. In Hiltons, a small town which was the home of the Carter Family who made their first country music recording for national distribution in 1927, there is a Carter Family, Memorial Music Center; a 1,000-seat concert shed is carved from the side of a mountain and features buck dancing, clogging, and musical performances. In Big Stone Gap was the home of John Fox, Jr., the first novelist to sell a million copies of a book in the United States, and his novel is brought to life in a sentimental outdoor drama, "Trail of the Lonesome Pine." Norton, the largest town in the area, features a renovated community center which offers Blue Grass and Country Music performances. WAXM's Saturday night Virginia-Kentucky Opry is broadcast live from a 247-seat theater with balcony and dance floor. The *Mountain Wonder* is a publication of the *Coalfield Progress* and *The Post*, a guide to living in this area includes a feature for Mountain Empire older citizens.

The programs offered in this area include a Foster Grandparent Program which offers volunteer opportunities for low income men and women to work one-on-one with children who have special needs. Hot meals can be delivered or are available at specific sites. An information and assistance line determines needs and links the person with the appropriate service. Mountain Empire Transit provides transportation to people of all ages on a demand/response basis. Older Worker Programs promote and provide useful work experience opportunities. A wide variety of socialization and recreation services provides older people with opportunities to participate in constructive social experiences and leisure-time activities. And the Retired and Senior Volunteer Program has developed opportunities for the community to do volunteer work in aging programs and services. There are many other services to aid those in the community and to provide support for caregivers.

Duffield Adult Residential and Nursing Facility (540) 431-4244 **Asst/Nursing**
P.O. Box 367, Duffield, VA 24244 **S** — Kingsport, TN 88 beds
1 story ❋ P/SP rms ❋ **N/SCU** ❋ $1000-$1400 mo(✚) — **SA-Sec-P-ST-DTG-EX-CH-N-RFM-Ph-CB-W-CD-H-L-Rec**

Heritage Hall - Big Stone Gap (540) 523-3000 **Nursing Care**
2045 Valley View Dr., Big Stone Gap, VA 24219 **ST** 180 beds
1 story ❋ P/SP rms ❋ **N/SN/SCU** ❋ (+✚) — **SA-Sec-TD-Ph-CB-W-CD-H-L-Rec**
See page 156

Heritage Hall - Wise (540) 328-2721 **Nursing Care**
9434 Coeburn Rd (P.O. Box 1009), Wise, VA 24293 **ST** 97 beds
1 story ❋ P/SP/W rms ❋ **N/SN** ❋ (+✚) — **SA-Sec-TD-Ph-CB-W-CD-H-L-Rec**
See page 156

Area 2 — Appalachian Agency for Senior Citizens, Inc.

Serves the Counties of Dickenson, Buchanan, Tazewell and Russell.
P.O. Box 765
Cedar Bluff, VA 24609 (540) 964-4915

Here the country is rural and often mountainous. Small towns are spread out most of the roads are small and scenic. Tazewell sports the Historic Crab Orchard Museum and Pioneer Park which displays the history of southwest Virginia from prehistory to the present.

This Area Agency on Aging has been in operation since 1975. Marsha Garrett is the Public Relations person and she is very helpful. They have a wide variety of programs available and a very active volunteer program. They have a lovely package which has been carefully put together by hand. This is an area which is big on humanity even if it is short on population. The programs include FAN CARE — where fans are provided for persons 60 or older with limited income who need a fan for air circulation and cooling. The fans are made possible through a grant from Appalachian Power Company and local contributors. The Access and Acquisition staff provides assistance in coordinating and advocating for benefits and services needed by individuals.

They have a newsletter, published every four months and distributed free of charge to any senior citizen in the service area. It includes articles concerning federal, state and local programs, news and pictures from local nutrition sites/centers and senior clubs. They maintain a Volunteer Action Center and maintain a volunteer skills bank.

Some of their more unique programs include senior IDs for persons over 60 and arrangement of participating merchants who offer discounts with the ID. This program brings seniors and their needs in touch with the community. The Tele-N-Touch Program is a joint project between the Agency, Cumberland Mountain Community Services Board, and Dickenson County Community Services Board. This program is a special service provided by Agency staff and Community Services Board Club House members to make regular prearranged telephone calls to homebound elderly or other disabled persons. Some of these individuals are at great risk and need to be checked on routinely; others simply like to have a friendly telephone visit. The program is designed to relieve the loneliness of individuals whose circumstances may deprive them of social participation by providing some contact with the world outside their homes. The program also acts as a safety measure to promote feelings of security. And there is the Centennial Birthday Recognition, a special recognition for persons celebrating their 100th or greater birthday. Agency staff make a special visit for the birthday and cakes, balloons, and other items are donated by local businesses.

There are ten senior centers in the area which run programs and offer hot nutritious meals, recreational and socialization activities, and fourteen Senior Clubs throughout the four counties. Grundy Senior Center and Hurley Senior Site operate in Buchanan County. Clintwood Senior Site and Clinchco Senior Center serve Dickenson County. Russell County is served by Swords Creek Senior Site and Dante Senior Site. Finally, Tazewell County is home to the Pocahontas Senior Site, Richlands Senior Site, Tazewell Senior Center, and Day Out Group Respite.

Heritage Hall - Tazewell (540) 988-2515 **Nursing Care**
121 Ben Bolt Ave., Tazewell, VA 24651 **ST** 180 beds
1 story ❋ P/SP rms ❋ **N/SN** ❋ (+✙) — **SA-Sec-TD-Ph-CB-W-CD-H-L-Rec** **See page 156**

Heritage Hall - Grundy (540) 935-8144 **Nursing Care**
Route 5, Box 104, Grundy, VA 24614 **ST** 120 beds
1 story ❋ P/SP rms ❋ **N/SN** ❋ (+✙) — **SA-Sec-TD-Ph-CB-W-CD-H-L-Rec** **See page 156**

Heritage Hall - Clintwood (540) 926-4693 **Nursing Care**
Route 607, P.O. Box 909, Clintwood, VA 24228 **ST** 100 beds
1 story ❋ P/SP rms ❋ **N/SN** ❋ (+✙) — **SA-Sec-TD-Ph-CB-W-CD-H-L-Rec** **See page 156**

Area 3 — District Three Governmental Cooperative
Serves the Counties of Washington, Smyth, Wythe, Bland, Grayson and Carroll and the Cities of Galax and Bristol.
305 South Park Street
Marion, VA 24354-2999 (540) 783-8158 or (800) 541-0933

Area 3 runs along Interstate Highway 81, one of the two main north-south arteries of Virginia. Bristol straddles two states, Virginia and Tennessee, and Rt. 77 drops from Bluefield, West Virginia to North Carolina across this area. Bristol is often called the birthplace of country music and boasts a mural recognizing the Carter Family — who traveled to Bristol to make their first recording for national distribution in 1927. In Galax, the Old Time Fiddlers' Convention is held each August and draws tens of thousands of musicians and onlookers. Monthly, the Galax Mountain Music Jamboree is held. Abingdon is a town rich in history, and craft shops are filled with mountain folkart.

The District Three Governmental Cooperative offers a variety of opportunities for senior citizens who want to remain active in their communities. There are volunteer and paid job opportunities. The Retired and Senior Volunteer Program incudes nearly 1,000 members providing valuable community services in hospitals, libraries, senior centers, and other public facilities. Sixteen congregate nutrition sites and a number of other senior groups provide fellowship, informational programs, crafts, recreation, nutritious meals, health screening, shopping outings, and other social activities.

In addition, there are ample services for those with specific needs. Seniors can be linked with people and organizations who can meet their needs either on an emergency basis or for more long-term help. These services can help the frail and homebound elderly maintain their independence. They provide health insurance and legal counseling, chore and minor home repair, and senior discount cards.

Asbury Center at Birdmont (540) 228-5595 **Indep/Asst/Nurse**
990 Holston Rd., Wytheville, VA 24382 **S** 70 indep, 22 asst, 152 nurse
1 story ❋ P/SP/W rms ❋ **A/N** ❋ $1036-1860 indep, $1300-1600 asst mo(✛✚20%)
—SA-Sec-P-TD-ST-DTG-OTG-EX-CH-N-RFM-Ph-CB-W-K-CD-H-L-Rec

George B. Kegley Manor (540) 688-4141 **Nursing Care**
Rt. 1, Box 105, Bastian, VA 24315 **R** — Wytheville/Bluefield 57 beds
2 stories ❈ P/SP rms ❈ 2 wks ❈ **N/SN** ❈ $102-125 day (✛✙16%) —**SA-Sec-P-TD-ST-DTG-OTG-EX-CH-N-RFM-Ph-CB-W-K-CD-H-L-Rec**

Laurel Meadows (540) 398-2117 **Nursing Care**
Route 1, Box 181-B, Laurel Fork, Va 24352 **S** 60 beds
1 story ❈ P/SP rms ❈ **N/SN** ❈ (✛✙) — **SA-Sec-TD-Ph-CB-W-CD-H-L-Rec**
See page 156

Valley Rest Home, Inc. (540) 944-5497 **Indep/Asst Living**
P.O. Box 129, Meadowview, VA 24361 **R** 27 residents
1 story ❈ SP rms ❈ 2 wks ❈ **A** ❈ $900-950mo (100%) — **SA-P-ST-EX-CH-RFM-CD-H-L**

Area 4 — New River Valley Agency on Aging

Serves the Counties of Giles, Floyd, Pulaski and Montgomery and the City of Radford.

141 E. Main Street
Pulaski, VA 24301 (540)980-7720

The New River Valley includes the college towns of Blacksburg, home of Virginia Tech, and Radford, home of Radford University. As mentioned previously, many college towns are experiencing an influx of retirees who like the small town atmosphere and the excitement and attractions provided by the college. Virginia Tech is a large university with Division 1 sports programs and a high enrollment. Over many years of operation, it has produced hundreds of thousands of graduates, some of whom find their way back to spend their retirement years in the town of their youth.

Mountain beauty, forests, rolling hills, and the ancient New River fill the area with the wonders of nature. Dublin offers narrated cruises on the continent's oldest river. The Museum of Geological Sciences at Virginia Tech displays fossils, minerals, and gemstones of the area. Pulaski is the gateway to two state parks.

The New River Valley Agency on Aging operates a full range of services.

Heritage Hall - Blacksburg (540) 951-7000 **Nursing Care**
3610 S. Main St., Blacksburg, Va 24060 **ST** 194 beds
1 story ❋ P/SP rms ❋ **N/SN/SCU** ❋ (✢✣) — **SA-Sec-TD-Ph-CB-W-CD-H-L-Rec** **See page 156**

MacArthur House (540) 726-7272 **Assisted Living**
17 MacArthur Lane, Narrows, VA 24124 **ST** 27 units
2 stories ❋ P/SP rms and suites ❋ **A/N** ❋ $725-1700mo (100%) — **SA-ST-EX-CH-N-RFM-CB-CD-H-L-Rec**

Area 5 — LOA Area Agency on Aging

Serves the Counties of Roanoke, Craig, Botetourt and Allegany and the Cities of Salem, Roanoke, Clifton Forge and Covington.

P.O. Box 14205
Roanoke, VA 24038 (540) 345-0451

The LOA Area on Aging runs from the Jefferson National Forest on the west to the Shenandoah Valley. Interstate Highway 81 runs the length of the Area and the cities of Salem and Roanoke fall within its boundaries. High in the mountains, near Covington, Humpback Bridge State Wayside has a picnic area and the only surviving curve-span covered bridge in the nation and the oldest surviving covered bridge in Virginia. Dixie Caverns are near Salem. Roanoke boasts festivals galore, museums, and attractions such as the Museum of Transportation with an impressive collection of old railroad cars. Among other attractions are the Mill Mountain Zoo and the Mill Mountain Theater, the Roanoke Valley History Museum, The Rescue Museum of National Emergency Medical Services, and the Birthplace of Booker T. Washington.

There are a number of very good facilities in the area at all levels of senior living. And the location seems to make it an attractive area for corporate headquarters for a number of assisted living and nursing home chains. Interstate Highway 81 gives easy access to Tennessee, North Carolina, Washington, D.C., Maryland and Pennsylvannia. A good size airport has regular flights which link the area with major air hubs across the country. If travel is a factor, either for the active senior who likes to travel and explore, or for visiting family of a senior resident, this area has a lot to offer.

LOA provides service in five different areas. In-Home services include Case Management which provides intensive work with individuals and families to develope a care plan and arranging services and monitoring that care. Meals-on-Wheels deliver nutritious hot lunchs to homebounds and "Are You Okay?" is a weekday telephone reassurance call at a scheduled time to seniors who live alone. In the area of Elder Rights LOA maintains Legal Assistance, Ombudsman and a Volunteer Ombudsman service. In Consumer Service areas LOA provides information and referral for services, Health Insurance and Tax assistance and counseling. VMAP is the Voluntary Medicare Assignment Program which lists physicians who have agreed to accept Medicare assignment. Finally Health Promotion provides educational programs and information about products to promote physical and mental well-being.

As part of the Critical assistance, LOA provides transportation to appointments and Prescription Assistance which provides financial help getting prescription medications for those who cannot afford them.

As part of the Life Enhancing activities, LOA maintains a Retired and Senior Volunteer Program which puts the life experiences of those over 55 to work in the community. The Employment and Training service provides job referrals, training and job placement for eligible individuals. The Foster Grandparent Program provides volunteer opportunities to work with children who have special needs. The Senior Safety Program is funded by the Allstate Foundation and conducts home safety surveys and community education of how to make the home safer for aging residents. Finally, the Senior Companion Program matches elder persons with peers who remain at home. And the Diners Clubs allow seniors to get together for lunch and activities at neighborhood sites. Transportation is provided if necessary.

Adult Care of Roanoke Valley (540) 983-1026 **Adult Day/Respite**
VAMC Bldg 76-1, Salem, VA 24153 **C** 75 seniors
1 story ❋ (7AM-6PM — 7 day a wk) ❋ **A** ❋ (✚) — **SA-Sec-P-ST-DTG-EX-CH-N-RFM-W-L-Rec**

AVANTE AT ROANOKE (540) 345-8139 NURSING AND REHAB
324 King George Ave., Roanoke, VA 24016 City
This 130 bed facility can provide skilled nursing care and rehabilitation as well as traditional nursing services at affordable prices. Social activities and a garden maintain the quality of life with the help of a qualified activities director on staff. All religious affiliations are welcome and special attention is paid to family. Avante provides complex medical care including respiratory and IV therapy and wound care. Come and see how our family can help provide excellent care and comfort for your family and family member. **For other Avante facilities see page 192**

Berkshire Health Care Center (540) 982-6691 **Nursing Care**
705 Clearview Dr., Vinton, VA 24179 **ST**— Roanoke 180 beds
1 story ❋ P/SP rooms ❋ **N/SCU** ❋ $1000-$1400mo (✚ ✚30%) — **SA-P-EX-CH-N-RFM-Ph-CB-W-CD-H-L**

Brandon Oaks (540) 776-2600 **Continuing Care**
3804 Brandon Ave., SW, Roanoke, VA 24018 **C** 154 apts, 18 Duplex, 23 asst, 62 nurse
1 story ❋ P/SP rms ❋ **A/N/SN** ❋ (100%) — **SA-Sec-ST-DTG-OTG-EX-CH-N-CB-W-K-CD-H-L-Rec**

Cave Creek (540) 992-4599 **Indep/Assisted**
2140 Lee Highway, North, Troutville, Va 24175 **ST** 55 gentleman residents
1 story ❋ bedrms ❋ yes ❋ **A** ❋ Veteran Administration Special Care Facility (✛)
— **SA-Sec-TD-ST-DTG-OTG-CH-N-RFM-Ph-CB-W-CD-H-L-Rec**-**See page 162**

Friendship Manor Retirement Community (540)265-2100 **Indep/Asst/Nurse**
327 Hershberger Rd., Roanoke, VA 24012 **C** 350 units indep/373 beds
1 story ❋ efficiency, 1,2,3 bdrm units - P/SP rms ❋ varies ❋ **A/N/SCU** ❋ $275-925mo/nursing: $855-1705. (✛✚) — **SA-Sec-TD-ST-DTG-OTG-EX-CH-N-RFM-Ph-CB-W-K-CD-H-L-Rec**

Highland House (540) 862-4271 **AssistedLiving**
3501 Longdale Furnace Rd., VA 24422 **ST** — Roanoke 30 residents
1 story ❋ P/SP rms ❋ **A/N** ❋ $42-101 per day — **SA-Sec-P-ST-DTG-EX-CH-N-RFM-Ph-CB-W-CD-H-L-Rec**

Park-Oak Grove Retirement Community (540) 989-9501 **Indep/Asst Living**
4902 Woodmar Dr., SW, Roanoke, VA 24018 **C** 93 apts/30 beds
3 stories ❋ Papts ❋ yes ❋ **A/N** ❋ $1351-1839 mo + asst living services — **SA-Sec-P-ST-DTG-OTG-EX-CH-N-RFM-Ph-CB-W-K-CD-H-L-Rec**

Richfield Retirement Community (540) 380-4500 **Indep/Asst/Nursing**
3615 West Main St., Salem, VA 24153 **C** 193 units/172 res/327 beds
1 story ❋ apts/cottage/P/SP rms ❋ **A/N/SN** ❋ $485-$2310mo (✛✚) — **SA-Sec-P-ST-DTG-EX-CH-N-RFM-Ph-CB-W-CD-H-L-Rec**

Winchester Manor (540) 774-4263 **Assisted Living**
2965 Colonnade Dr., Roanoke, VA 24018 **S** 75 beds
1 story ❋ 1 mo ❋ **A** ❋ $1900-$2300mo —**SA-P-TD-EX-CH-N-RFM-CB-W-CD-H-L-Rec**

Area 6 — Valley Program for Aging Services

Serves the Counties of Rockingham, Rockbridge, Augusta, Highland and Bath and the cities of Buena Vista, Lexington, Staunton, Waynesboro and Harrisonburg.
P.O. Box 817
Waynesboro, VA 22980-0603 (540) 949-7141 or (800) 868-8727

The Shenandoah Valley lies between two mountain ranges. Natural caverns dot the ranges on either side of the valley. Several colleges lie along Interstate Highway 81, including James Madison University in Harrisonburg, Bridgewater, Virginia Military Institute and Washington and Lee University. The Homestead, with its hot springs and golf courses, is one of the best resorts in the country. Historic towns such as Lexington offer such interesting things as a Ghost Tour and carriage rides. The Theater at Lime Kiln provides plays and concerts. Staunton boasts the birthplace of Woodrow Wilson and the very interesting Museum of American Frontier Culture which features working farms brought from England, Germany, and Northern Ireland.

Senior housing is plentiful. Many realtors specialize in senior housing and property is not as costly as it is east of the mountains in Charlottesville and along Route 29. There are thirteen active senior centers. These community meeting places offer an opportunity for older adults to be with friends and neighbors, take part in recreational and social activities, and get involved. They feature hot meals at noon, recreation, field trips, entertainment, limited transportation, and opportunities to serve others. Vans are available for participants for trips to and from the centers.

Volunteer opportunities allow skills and time to be put to excellent use. For those low-income seniors over 55, there are job programs to help increase monthly earnings and independence. Help and information about problems that face older people are always available from the Valley Program for Aging Services. Home delivered meals, care, insurance, and legal advice and assistance for the aging are just part of the services for seniors. Respite care and adult day care centers help caregivers balance the needs of their senior family members with the demands of everyday life.

Gypsy Hill House (540) 886-8661 **Independent Living**
500 "C" Street, Staunton, VA 24401 **C** 100 units
3 stories ❋ apartments ❋ **SA-P-ST-DTG-EX-Ph-K**

Heritage Hall (540)464-8181 **Nursing Care**
205 Houston St., Lexington, VA 24450 **C** 60 beds
1 story ❋ P/SP rms ❋ **N/SN** ❋ $99 -$104 day (✚✚20%) — **SA-Sec-P-ST-DTG-EX-CH-N-RFM-Ph-CB-W-CD-H-L-Rec** **- See page 156**

The Mayflower (540) 463-3161 **Assisted Living**
409 South Main St., Lexington, VA 24450 **C** 38 residents
3 stories ❋ private suites ❋ **A** ❋ $42-$188 day — **SA-Sec-P-ST-DTG-EX-CH-N-RFM-Ph-CB-W-CD-H-L-Rec**

BRIDGEWATER RETIREMENT COMMUNITY **(540) 828-2531**
315 N. 2nd St., Bridgewater, VA 22812 **Indep/Asst Living**
Affiliated with the Church of the Brethren, this is a Christian, life-lease and rental community located in the beautiful Shenandoah Valley. The community offers a continuum of services including retirement housing, assisted living (Adult Care Residence), licensed short-term and long-term nursing care, therapy services, and restorative care. Bridgewater Retirement Community includes Bridgewater Home, Bridgewater Village and Bridgewater Health Care Foundation.

Oak Hill Center (540) 886-7459 **Nursing**
512 Houston St, Staunton, VA 24401 **ST** 189 residents
1 story ❋ P/SP/W rms ❋ **N/SN/SCU** ❋ (+✚15%) — **SA-P-TD-ST-DTG-EX-CH-RFM-Ph-CB-W-CD-H-L-Rec**

Shenandoah Nursing Home (540) 949-8665 **Nursing Care**
803 Westminister Dr., (P.O. Box 406) Fishersville, VA 22939 **ST** 60 beds
1 story ❋ P/SP rooms ❋ 1-3 mos ❋ **N/SCU** ❋ $114-$138 day (+✚) — **SA-TD-N-RFM-Ph-CB-W-K-CD-H-L**

Summit Square (800) 586-5499 **Life Care**
501 Oak Ave, Waynesboro, VA 22980 **ST** **See page 132**

Sunnyside Presbyterian Retirement Community (800) 586-5499 **Life Care**
100 Sunnyside Dr., Harrisonburg, VA 22801 **ST** **See page 132**

Area 7 — Shenandoah Area Agency on Aging, Inc

Serves the Counties of Page, Shenandoah Warren, Clarke and Frederick and the City of Winchester.
207 Mosby Lane
Front Royal, VA 22630 (540) 635-7141 or (800) 883-4122

The upper end of the Shenandoah Valley stretches from New Market, site of a major Civil War Battle, to the West Virginia border. Col. John Mosby, the legendary "Gray Ghost" slipped out of the fog which gathered in the hills and struck at supply trains of the Union just over the border. Here were Stonewall Jackson's headquarters, George Washington's office, and the birthplace of Patsy Cline. Apple orchards fill the area, and each year there is the well-known Apple Blossom Festival. Antiquing, art exhibits, wineries, and shopping in historic old town areas attract people of all ages. Here the George Washington Forest, the Blue Ridge Mountains, and the Skyline Drive end as the land flattens out to the north.

The Shenandoah Area Agency on Aging is very active and helpful. Their mission is to provide a variety of high quality services and opportunities that will enhance the dignity and independence of older persons and will promote their continued contributions to the community. From time to time they also provide short term, or special programs that continue to further the mission of providing needed services in the homes of older persons.

SAA produces a Senior Resource Directory which lists organizations, health services, support groups, pharmacies, physicians, and financial and legal services. There are recreation programs, food and nutritional programs, and volunteer and employment programs. The Retired and Senior Volunteer Program offers adults a recognized role in the community and a meaningful life in retirement through volunteer service. RSVP volunteers work in a wide range of services including entertainment, arts and crafts, tutoring, visiting, child care, tax and insurance assistance and libraries.

There is a strong ombudsman program which works to promote the highest possible quality of life and care for persons residing in nursing homes, living in adult care residences and receiving home care services.

There are six Senior Centers, each of which provides well-balanced meals in a fellowship setting. It is their belief that sometimes older people do not pay attention to their nutritional needs. A well-balanced meal coupled with stimulating activities often meets the needs of those who have become isolated.

Heritage Hall - Front Royal (540) 636-3700 **Nursing Care**
400 West Strasburg Rd., Front Royal, VA 22630 **ST** 60 beds
1 story ❋ P/SP rms ❋ **N/SN** ❋ (+✚) — **SA-Sec-TD-Ph-CB-W-CD-H-L-Rec** **See page 156**

The Home (540) 722-3011 **Assisted**
124 Valley Vista Dr., Woodstock, VA 22664 **ST** 40 units
1 story ❋ P/SP rms ❋ **A** ❋ $1200-$1800mo (100%) — **-SA-TD-EX-CH-N-RFM-CB-CD-H-L-Rec**

Mayfair House (540) 459-2525 **Assisted Living**
935 Ox Rd., Woodstock, VA 22664 **C** 48 units
1 story ❋ **A** ❋ (100%) — **SA-ST-DTG-EX-CH-N-RFM-Ph-CB-W-CD-H-L-Rec**

Rose Hill Nursing Center (540)955-9995 **Nursing Care**
110 Chalmers Court, Berryville, VA 22611 **C** 120 beds
5 stories ❋ Cottages/Apts/P/SP rms ❋ **A/N/SN** ❋ **SA-Sec-P-Tcat-ST-EX-CH-N-RFM-Ph-CB-W-CD-H-L-Rec**

Shenandoah Valley Westminster-Canterbury (540) 665-0156 **Life Care**
300 Westminster-Canterbury Dr., Winchester, VA 22603 **C** 128 indep/40asst/40nurse
1 story ❋ P/SP rooms ❋ yes ❋ **N/SCU** ❋ $1600-$3400mo (✛✚20%) — **SA-Sec-P-TD-ST-DTG-N-Ph-CB-W-K-CD-H-L**

The Southerlands (540) 636-2800 **Indep/Assisted Living**
600 Mt. View St., Front Royal, VA 22630 **C** 50 indep res/22 asst res
3 stories ❋ P/SP rooms ❋ **A** ❋ $1290-$2575mo (✛) — **SA-Sec-P-ST-DTG-EX-CH-N-Ph-CB-W-K-CD-H-L-Rec**

Susan B. Miller Nursing Home (540) 459-2118 **Nursing Care**
118 N. Muhlenberg St., Woodstock, VA 22664 **C** 51 beds
P/SP/W rms ❋ **N/SN** ❋ (✛✚20%) — **Rec**

Area 8A — Alexandria Agency on Aging

Serves the City of Alexandria.
2525 Mt. Vernon Avenue, Unit 5
Alexandria, VA 22301-1159 (703) 838-0920

Alexandria is one place that can honestly say, "George Washington slept here." This lovely old town is an integral part of the Washington D.C. complex. It has a special feeling, filled with the charm of a romantic seaport, unique art galleries, gourmet dining and an abundance of attractions and shopping. It is refreshing, intimate, contemporary and rich in history.

Tourboats prowl the Potomac from the wharves of Alexandria. Parks are pleasant and historical sites and markers are everywhere. See the boyhood home of Robert E. Lee, the Carlyle House, home of wealthy merchant and landowner John Carlyle and the historic Friendship Firehouse. It is a small town. It is a large town. It is an old town. It is a modern city.

The Alexandria Agency on Aging remarks that it is a close knit neighborhood where people are concerned with each other. A full 50% of all seniors in the area live in high rise developments. The Department of Housing has several high-rise subsidized housing developments. The biggest problem for active seniors in this area is that there is frequently a waiting period. Seniors who are looking for senior housing would do well to plan ahead. Nursing home beds are sometimes difficult to find and often expensive. Nursing homes in areas 7, 9 and 16 often care for former residents of Alexandria who cannot find space in an emergency.

The Alexandria Agency on Aging produces a very nice booklet called *Services for Older Alexandrians* every year. They also do a quarterly newsletter, *Vintage.* Two senior centers provide a variety of activities and hot meals The agency operates a wide variety of programs, many aimed at helping low-income seniors. Fund-raising for these programs is a regular part of the work done by the Agency. Programs include services for home care to employment training and counseling through two federal older worker programs. There are Special Transportation and Volunteer Programs. In-Home and Respite Care Programs assist persons with dementia and their caregivers. A 21-citizen member Commission on Aging is appointed by the City Council to study, make recommendations and coordinate existing and proposed programs to serve the aging and provide advocacy for aging issues.

The Jewish Council for Aging is active with a wide range of services and maintains the Senior Helpline. The Eldercare Locator is a Nationwide service to

The **Northern Virginia Senior Olympics** is held in September for participants 55 and older. The Area Agencies on Aging designated as 8 A-E and the city, county, parks and recreation departments, and community services programs of these areas participate to make the event readily available to all seniors. These events promote physical fitness and recreation and provide an enriching social atmosphere.

help families and friends find information about services for older people. Counseling is provided for those who need help and include Mental Health, First Step, Legal and Financial Counseling. The Northern Virginia Family Service Grandparenting Program provides support for grandparents raising grandchildren. The National Association of Retired Federal Employees Service Center is located here. A Senior Discount card allows seniors to save money at a number of businesses in the area and the Safe Return Program run by the Alzheimer's Association provides ID bracelets and assists police in identifying persons with memory loss who wander.

Goodwin House (703)578-1000 **Life Care**
4800 Fillmore Ave., Alexandria, VA 22311 **C** 179 combined
❋ P/SP rms ❋ some wait for certain units ❋ **A/N/SN** ❋ $1425-$2185mo (✢✚) — **SA-Sec-ST-DTG-EX-CH-N-RFM-Ph-CB-W-K-CD-H-L-Rec**

Lincolnian Residences (703) 914-0551 **Independent Living**
4710 N. Chambliss St., Alexandria, VA 22312 **C** 26 efficiencies
3 stories ❋ several years ❋ $120 or 30% mo (**$**) — **SA-Sec-P-ST-DTG-EX-CH-Ph-CB-W-K-CD-L-Rec**

Morris Glen Apartments (703) 719-7268 **Independent Living**
7010 Schoonmaker Court, Alexandria, VA 22310 **C** 60 apts
2 stories ❋ 6-9 mos ❋ $505-700mo (**$**) — **SA-Sec-P-ST-EX-Ph-CB-W-K-CD-L-Rec**

Surise Assisted Living of Alexandria (703) 212-9192 **Assisted Living**
3520 Duke St., Alexandria, VA **C** 95 beds
A ❋ $1680-$4110 mo **See page 150**

The Washington House (703)845-5000 **Life Care**
5100 Fillmore Ave., Alexandria, VA,22311 **C** 145 combined
10 stories ❋ P/SP rms ❋ some wait for certain units ❋ **A/N/SN** ❋ (+96%) — **SA-Sec-TD-ST-DTG-EX-CH-N-RFM-Ph-CB-W-K-CD-H-L**

Area 8B — Arlington Agency on Aging

Serves the County of Arlington

1801 North George Mason Drive
Arlington, Virginia 22207 (703) 358-5030

Arlington lies just outside Washington D.C., inside the Beltway, and between Alexandria and the capitol. Here is where the Custis-Lee Mansion crowns the hill overlooking Arlington National Cemetery. The U.S. Marine Corps War Memorial, Iwo Jima statue adorns the Washington Memorial Parkway. The Pentagon and National Airport lie along the banks of the Potomac and Crystal City rises up between them, filled with clean, modern high-rises. Ball-Sellers House is a rare 1750 colonist's log house with original clapboard roof. And the newest museum in the area is located in Arlington, the *Newseum.* Freedom Park surrounds Newseum and features icons that symbolize the worldwide pursuit of freedom including segments of the Berlin Wall.

This area also produces a nice Directory of Services for Senior Adults. There is a large and active Alzheimer group, with day care, respite care and support programs. The Adult Education Program offers varied classes with reduced tuition for adults 60 years of age and over. The *Leisure Review* is a twice a year publication for seniors.

FISH (For Immediate Sympathetic Help) is a group of church volunteers who provide transportation for "last minute" medical appointments as well as food and other services. Lifeline provides immediate 24-hour access to community medical and social services at the press of a button. It is a personal emergency response system that helps elderly or disabled persons maintain their independence. There are several groups such as Christmas in April and Hearts and Hammers that help with repairs of homes.

There are other services for seniors such as counseling. Three Senior Centers provide meals, social and recreation programs, six multipurpose senior centers provide recreation, education, arts, travel, wellness fitness and social services and twenty social clubs meet at various locations. The Senior Adult Newsletter is a free monthly newsletter with activities and trips. There are also several independent senior clubs such as the Association of Retired Administrators and Supervisors, the Arlington Retired Teachers Association and The Grandmothers Club as well as many senior clubs of religious affiliations.

Cherrydale Health & Rehabilitation Center (703) 243-7640 **Nursing Care**
3710 Lee Highway, Arlington, VA 22207 **C** 240 beds
5 stories ❋ none ❋ **A/N/SN/SCU** ❋ (✢✚) — **SA-Sec-DTG-EX-CH-N-RFM-Ph-CB-W-K-CD-H-L-Rec**

Surise Assisted Living of Arlington (703) 524-5300 **Assisted Living**
2000 N. Glebe Rd., Arlington, VA **C** 47 beds **See page 150**

Surise Assisted Living of Alexandria (703) 536-1060 **Assisted Living**
5910 Wilson Blvd., Arlington, VA **C** 47 beds **See page 150**

Area 8C — Fairfax County Area Agency on Aging

Serves the Counties of Fairfax and the Cities of Fairfax and Falls Church.

12011 Government Center Pkwy., Suite 720
Fairfax, VA 22035 (703) 324-5414

Fairfax County includes the growing suburban sprawl on the edge of the Beltway around Washington D.C. It bisects Dulles International Airport, Washington's second international Airport. Reston is the home for many industrial headquarters and trade centers including the Mid-Atlantic Gift Mart. Tysons Corners includes a very large shopping mall and Vienna is home to the Wolf Trap Performing Arts Center with some of the best entertainers in the country. The Reston Animal Park offers a unique look at domestic/exotic animals. There are educational programs, elephant, pony and haywagon rides for all ages. The Meadowlark Gardens Regional Park is just one of the fine parks in the area with natural and landscaped areas, this one covers 95 acres. Cherry Hill Farm is an 1845 furnished farmhouse and barn with antique tool collection.

In Fairfax Court House, George Washington's will was probated and is still on display today. Mount Vernon is located on the Potomac and nearby is Frank Lloyd Wright's Pope-Leighey house. Colvin Run Mill, Sully Plantation and several museums including the Fairfax Museum in an 1873 school building and the Railroad Museum make this an interesting area. Events throughout the year keep those who live here very busy without going very far from home.

This area has established the following priorities for services to the elderly and their caregivers: To Serve the Elderly who are vulnerable, disabled, socially or culturally isolated, or who need protection from abuse, neglect or exploitation; To promote physical and income self-sufficiency of the elderly to prevent or delay premature and unnecessary dependency that leads to costly services and greater demands on family and other caregivers; To prevent problems and crises for the elderly and their caregivers by early intervention; To strengthen family and community support through information, education, and planning of cost-effective services without losing quality. Their purpose and mission is to identify and promote better understanding of the problems of the aging and plan and promote activities that contribute to their well being. They provide information concerning services and activities for the aging. Acting as a clearinghouse and referral point for matters affecting the aging, they also serve as liaison between the County and other governmental, public and private groups concerned with aging issues. They inform the community of the needs of the aging and of the agencies and activities that exist to serve them. Stimulating programs for the benefit of the aging through public and private agencies are provided. **Learning In Retirement Institute** at George Mason University is part of a national association of teaching, studying and traveling adults.

The *Golden Gazette* is a newsletter for senior adults in the Fairfax Area and covers a range of issues from health care to a schedule of tours. Tours have something for everyone from dinner theatre, the Charlestown Races, shopping at the outlet centers of Pennsylvannia and to Williamsburg. Seminars cover a range of topics. Sixteen Senior Centers have active programs from Jazzercise, Line Dancing and Bingo to Blood Pressure Screening and hot lunches.

Two interesting programs are the Pets on Wheels which provides pets to visit nursing homes, providing residents with companionship and affection and the Seniors In Action (SIA) which coordinates with over 250 agencies and organizations to identify ways an older citizen might participate as a volunteer. A Telephone Reassurance program is a social calling program where a volunteer is matched with an elderly person and calls once a week to visit by telephone. Many other programs operate in this very active area for seniors, providing a wide range of information and services.

Ayr Hill Home for Adults, Inc. (703) 938-8200 **Assisted Living**
112 Ayr Hill Ave., N.W. Vienna, VA 22180 **C**
2 stories ❋ P/SP rms ❋ **A/N** ❋ $1450-$1750mo (100%) — **SA-Sec-TD-ST-EX-CH-RFM-Ph-CB-W-CD-H-L-Rec**

Burke Lake Gardens (703) 644-0061 **Independent Living**
9608 Old Keene Mill Rd., Burke, VA 22015 **ST** 100 apts
1 story ❋ 1 bdrms ❋ 2½yrs ❋ (**$**) — **SA-Sec-P-ST-DTG-OTG-EX-CH-N-RFM-Ph-W-K-Rec**

Evergreen House (703) 941-8707 **Independent Living**
6925 Columbia Pike, Annandale, VA 22003 **ST** 246 apts
6 stories ❋ 1½-2 yrs ❋ $0-$884mo (**$**) — **SA-Sec-P-ST-DTG-EX-CH-Ph-CB-W-K**

Greenspring Village (703) 913-1200 **Life Care**
7316 Spring Village Dr., Springfield, VA 22150 **ST**
opens fall of 1998

Lake Anne Fellowship House (703) 471-6474 **Independent Living**
11450 North Shore Dr., Reston, VA 20190 **S** 240 units
9 stories ❋ Effiency/1 bdrm ❋ 3-12 mos ❋ $269-$350mo (**$**) — **SA-Sec-P-ST-EX-CH-N-W-K**

Hunters Woods Fellowship House (703) 620-4450 **Independent Living**
2231 Colts Neck Rd., Reston, VA 20191 **S** 224 units
11 stories ❋ 1bdrms ❋ up to 12 mos ❋ 30% of adjusted income (**$**) — **SA-Sec-P-ST-EX-CH-N-RFM-Ph-CB-W-K-H-L**

Leewood Health Care Center (703) 256-9770 **Assisted/Nursing**
7120 Braddock Rd., Annendale, Va 22003 **S** 44 units/132 beds
1 story ❋ P/SP rms ❋ **A/N** ❋ $80-155day (**$+✚**) — **SA-Sec-TD-EX-CH-N-RFM-Ph-CB-W-CD-H-L-Rec**

Lewinsvile Center Residences (703) 442-9621 **Independent Living**
1609 Great Falls St., McLean, VA 22101 **S** 22 efficiencies
2 stories ❋ Several months ❋ $149or 30% income mo (**$**) — **SA-Sec-DTG-EX-CH-Ph-CB-W-K-CD-L**

Little River Glen (703) 503-8700 **Independent Living**
4001 Barker Court, Fairfax, VA 22032 **S** 120 apts
2 stories ❋ Several mos ❋ $605- $832mo — **SA-Sec-P-ST-DTG-EX-CH-Ph-CB-W-K-H-L-Rec**

Surise Assisted Living of Fairfax (703) 691-0046 **Assisted Living**
9207 Arlington Blvd., Fairfax, VA **C** 47 beds **See page 150**

Surise Assisted Living of Falls Church (703) 534-2700 **Assisted Living**
330 N. Washington St., Falls Church, VA **C** 53 beds **See page 150**

Surise Assisted Living of Gunston (703) 550-2400 **Assisted Living**
7665 Lorton Rd., Lorton, VA **C** 53 beds **See page 150**

Surise Assisted Living of Hunter Mill (703) 255-1006 **Assisted Living**
2863 Hunter Mill Rd., Oakton, VA **C** 95 beds **See page 150**

Surise Assisted Living of Oakton (703) 255-2050 **Assisted Living**
10322 Blake Ln., Oakton, VA **C** 47 beds **See page 150**

Surise Assisted Living of Springfield (703) 922-6800 **Assisted Living**
6541 Franconia Rd., Springfield, VA **C** 100 beds **See page 150**

Vinson Hall (703) 536-4344 **Life Care**
6251 Old Dominion Dr., McLean, VA 22101 **ST** 177res/42 beds/49beds
2 stories ❋ P/SP rms ❋ 6mos- 5yrs ❋ **A/N/SN** ❋ $866-$2312mo (✚ 100%) — **SA-Sec-ST-DTG-EX-CH-N-RFM-Ph-CB-W-K-CD-H-L**

The Virginian (703) 385-0555 **Life Care**
9229 Arlington Blvd., Fairfax, VA 22031 **S** 300 total res
5 stories ❋ P/SP rms ❋ **A/N/SN** ❋ (✚78%)

Area 8D — Loudoun County Area Agency on Aging

Serves the County of Loudoun
751 Miller Drive, SE, Suite D2
Leesburg, VA 22075 (703) 777-0257

The grand old country of foxhunts and rolling plantations, Loudoun county is still estates and fine living. This is horse country, with the famous Virginia Hunt, Steeplechases, quaint Bed and Breakfasts and mountain views. It is also large regional parks. Ball's Bluff, with its Civil War battle site, includes trails, interpretive displays, a national cemetery and natural areas. The charming historic Leesburg is a step back in time. Wineries dot the landscape. Historic homes and estates are all over including Morven and Oatlands Plantation. Antique shopping is almost endless.

This is an area much less densely populated than those closer to Washington D.C. *The Golden Grapevine* is a quarterly newsletter published by the Loudoun County Area Agency on Aging and covers tips on everyday living, health, activities and awards. A pet care project helps those over 60 if they are having difficulty feeding their pets. Transportation and a Senior Job Bank help seniors stay active and independent. The CAFE program welcomes seniors to Senior CAFE Centers and helps them maintain cost effective independent lifestyles through socialization, physical activity, information and referral assistance, volunteer community involvement, transportation needs, nutritious meals, self-help nutrition education and much more. The area designates its four senior centers as "Arcola CAFE," "Leesburg CAFE," "Purcellville CAFE," "Sterling CAFE," to represent *Companionship, Activities, Food, Education.* Book-By-Mail is a service that supplies books, large print books, audio cassettes and descriptive videos to people who are unable to use the library system.

The Loudoun County Department of Parks, Recreation and Community Services provide five senior clubs. The organize trips traveling as far as Virginia Beach. Fitness and sports programs include walking, aerobic aquatics and bowling and tennis.

The Area Agency on Aging provides planning, advocacy, information and programs for senior citizens and their families. The Commission on Aging is a citizen advisory body to the Area Agency on Aging and the County Board of Supervisors. This was one of the areas that were very friendly and helpful. The Area Agency on Aging provides Long Term Care programs, Senior Center Programs and Senior Services.

Heritage Hall Nursing and Rehab (703) 777-8700 **Nursing Care**
122 Morven Park Rd., NW, Leesburg, VA 20176 **ST** 164 beds
1 story ❋ P/SP rms ❋ very long ❋ **N/SN** ❋ $122-$138day (+✚20%+) — **SA-N-RFM-Ph-CB-W-CD-H-L** **See page 156**

Herndon Harbor House (703) 904-9444 **Independent Living**
783 Station St., Herndon, VA 20170 **S** 60 units phase I / 60 units phase II
3 stories ❋ 1 bdrm ❋ Developing ❋ $605-$677mo (**$**) — **SA-Sec-P-ST-DTG-EX-CH-Ph-CB-W-K-L**

Morningside House of Leesburg (703) 777-2777 **Assisted/Nursing**
316 Harrison St. S.E., Leesburg, VA 22075 **ST** 76 units
2 stories ❋ apts/suites ❋ **A** ❋ $1895-$3925mo (100%) — **SA-Sec-ST-DTG-EX-CH-N-RFM-Ph-CB-K-CD-H-L-Rec**

Sommerset Retirement Community (703) 450-6411 **Independent Living**
22355 Providence Village Dr., Sterling, VA 20164 **S** 105 units
3 stories ❋ apts ❋ 1-2 mos ❋ $1850-$2240mo (100%) — **SA-Sec-P-ST-DTG-OTG-EX-CH-N-RFM-Ph-CB-W-K-H-L-Rec**

Surise Assisted Living of Countryside (703) 430-0681 **Assisted Living**
45800 Jona Dr., Sterling, VA **ST** 47 beds **See page 150**

Surise Assisted Living of Leesburg (703) 478-1897 **Assisted Living**
246 W. Market St., Leesburg, VA **ST** 30 beds **See page 150**

Area 8E — Prince William Area Agency on Aging

Serves the County of Prince William and the Cities of Manassas and Manassas Park.

7987 Ashton Avenue, Suite 204
Manassas, VA 22110 (703) 792-6400

Prince William County was the site of the first battle of the Civil war. At the time, people drove out from Washington D.C. in their carriages with picnic baskets and parasols to see the battle. The Bull Run Battlefield is part of Bull Run Park. There are remnants of the two major battles known as First Manassas and Second Manassas. The park includes a planked handicapped trail. Every year there are many special events held here, including one of the largest AKC Dog Shows in the country.

There are eight championship golf courses open for public play. Quaint historic villages like Occoquan and Manassas offer antiques and handcrafted gifts. Potomac Mills Mall is Virginia's most visited tourist attraction and home of the largest outlet shopping center in the state. There are concerts at the Nissan Pavilion, Cellar Door's spectacular outdoor amphitheater and summer Shakespeare in the great outdoors. Auto racing at Old Dominion Speedway and Prince William Cannons Baseball are spectator sports complemented by a wide range of fishing and boating opportunities. Events during the year include Civil War Reenactments. Here also is Virginia's largest county fair.

The Area Agency on Aging produces a Directory of Programs and Services for Prince William Area Senior Adults. The Area Agency on Aging identifies needs and provides services, counseling and guidance in a number of areas and promotes social interaction. This area has a very active Caregivers Assistance program, maintains the Caregivers Resource Center to address the needs of local family caregivers by providing information, support and educational opportunities to assist them with their responsibilities. It provides information about health conditions including dementia and other related disorders and schedules education and training activities. They also provide a quarterly newsletter for Caregivers and a Resource Guide.

The Prince William Area Agency on Aging maintains the Bluebird Tour Bus Program which organizes educational and recreational day and overnight trips at nominal costs. A number of senior clubs are active for various groups, organized around interests, religious affiliation and profession. The Prince William Retired Teachers Association and the American Red Cross Walking Club are but two examples of the diverse interests reflected by these clubs. Several support groups offer help for caregivers and families. The Voluntary Action Center serves as a volunteer clearinghouse. It helps prospective volunteers find satisfying work and will help local agencies and groups find volunteers for their purposes. There are a number of assistance programs offering help with everything from health information to home care assistance and including meal delivery. Energy programs for the winter and the Fan Care program, both in partnership with Virginia Power, help seniors maintain the temperature of their homes at a healthy and comfortable level.

Lake Ridge Fellowship House (703) 690-3366 **Independent Living**
12800 Harbor Dr., Woodbridge, VA 22192 **S** 100 units
6 stories ❋ 1 bdrm ❋ 5 yrs ❋ 30% adjusted income (**$**) — **SA-Sec-P-ST-DTG-EX-CH-N-RFM-Ph-CB-W-K**

Area 9 — Rappahannock-Rapidan Agency on Aging

Serves the Counties of Orange, Madison, Culpeper, Rappahannock and Fauquier.
401 South Main Street
Culpeper, VA 22701 (703) 825-3100

This is rural country. In the north, it is a continuation of the horse and foxhunt country. Highway 29, connecting Washington D.C. with Danville on the North Carolina border, runs through the center of the piedmont, bisecting this Area. Warrenton, and Culpeper, the largest towns in the area, are both under 10,000 people. Orange, further to the east, has around 3,000. Wineries are abundant, and each year the largest wine festival in Virginia is held at The Plains in the town of Great Meadow. There are over forty wineries in Virginia, many of them located in the Piedmont. Wine growing was introduced in the state by Thomas Jefferson, but within the last decade vineyards have come into their own and today Virginia produces wines that are award winning the world over. The Virginia Gold Cup, a steeplechase, is also held at the Plains in May. Montpellier, past home of President and Dolly Madison is in Orange, to the south of this area. This estate, which later belonged to the DuPonts, is also the site of two steeplechase meets in the finest tradition of Virginia.

The Rappahannock Rapidan Community Service Board is unique in the state of Virginia. It is the only organization which serves both as an Area Agency on Aging and as a regional provider of mental health, mental retardation, and substance abuse services. This enables them to consolidate resources in many areas. For example, they have a consolidated transportation system that serves all of their clientele and coordinated case management programs. In other cases, they are able to pair their various clients, such as with the Chores for Seniors project, under which crews from the day support program for persons with mental retardation assist frail older persons in caring for their homes. They publish a nice newsletter, *Voice of Experience,* which covers a wide variety of issues for seniors. They maintain a strong volunteer program and active senior nutrition centers. Discount I.D.s are provided for all interested seniors who request them and discounts are offered by businesses and merchants throughout the area.

RRCSB provides a team of Senior Advocates who are available to meet with and counsel older persons who request help, in their homes if necessary. These Advocates determine the nature and extent of the need, identify services and elicit support or enrollment in the appropriate program. This Area also provides support services for families caring for Alzheimer's patients. Fauquier has a special day care service for Alzheimer's patients and the frail elderly which can provide relief for families. In other areas, in-home aides give families a needed break.

Culpeper Baptist Retirement Community (540) 825-2411 **Continuing Care**
P.O. Box 191, Culpeper, VA 22701 **ST** 92 units
3 stories ❋ $1391-$1648mo — **SA-Sec-ST-DTG-OTG-EX-CH-N-Ph-CB-W-K-CD-H-L-Rec** — **See page 137**

Meadowbrook Residential (540) 547-2333 **Assisted Living**
Rt 1 Box 421, Reva, VA 22735 **S** 36 units
A ❋ $1350-$1750mo (✚20%) — **SA-Sec-P-TD-ST-DTG-EX-CH-N-Ph-CB-W-CD-H-L**

Mountain View Nursing Home (540) 948-6831 **Nursing Home**
HC5, Box 186, Aroda, VA 22709 **S** 40 beds
1 story ❋ P/SP/Wrms ❋ **N/SN** ❋ $92.06day (✚) — **SA-P-ST-DTG-CH-N-RFM-Ph-CB-W-CD-H-L**

Oak Springs of Warrenton (540) 347-4770 **Nursing Home**
614 Hastings Ln., Warrenton, VA 20186 **ST** 108 beds
P/SP/W rms ❋ 2 wks-2mos ❋ **N/SN** ❋ appx $3500mo (✛✚20%) — **SA-Sec-CH-Ph-CB-W-CD-H-L**

Surise Assisted Living of Warrenton (703) 349-9001 **Assisted Living**
194 E. Lee St., Warrenton, VA **ST** 48 beds **See page 150**

Area 10 — Jefferson Area Board for Aging

Serves the Counties of Nelson, Albermarle, Louisa, Fluvanna and Greene and the City of Charlottesville.

674 Hillsdale Drive
Charlottesville, VA 22901 (804) 978-3644

Charlottesville, in the center of this area, and is the largest town in central Virginia. It was the home of Thomas Jefferson, who also built the University of Virginia. Because of that, it is a drawing card for active seniors who have attended UVA and are returning to enjoy the town and the lovely location. It is a town which attracts authors, artists and celebrities. There is nearby skiing at Wintergreen in Nelson County. Lake Anna provides water recreation. Golf courses abound, there is horse activity of every kind, and almost every weekend has something of interest. Some of the state's leading wineries give tours and the old town of Scottsville along the James River is a treat in itself. There are more newspapers, restaurants and lawyers per capita than almost any other place in the country. And it is just two hours from Washington D.C., an hour from Richmond. There are two excellent hospitals, Martha Jefferson and the University of Virginia Medical Center. Both have active programs designed for seniors.

Charlottesville has an active Area Agency on Aging. The Jefferson Board of Aging has programs for almost every interest. The Senior Center in Charlottesville plans trips, runs a gift shop which features handmade arts and crafts as well as interesting items from gift manufacturers. Inside, there are notices everywhere for tours, cruises and day trips. There are classes for almost every interest and dances. Entertainment and community volunteer programs are easy to find and become involved in. There are lists of service providers to help seniors maintain and manage their homes, and several continuing care and senior living communities in the area.

Center for Adult Rehab and Eldercare (804) 978-1417 **Adult Day Care**
674 Hillsdale Dr., Charlottesville, VA 22901 **R** 60 adults
1 story ❋ (7AM-5:30PM)+ respite care ❋ **A/N** ❋ $45day (✚) — **SA-Sec-ST-DTG-EX-CH-N-RFM-Ph-CB-W-CD-L-Rec**

ROSEWOOD MANOR **(804) 973-0239**
501 Park St., Charlottesville, VA 22902 **Residential/Asst/Intensive Assisted**
Rosewood Manor is an assisted living home designed for seniors who need help with some aspects of daily living, but do not require skilled nursing care. It is nestled among the trees and stately homes lining Park Street. Since 1983, Rosewood Manor's trained staff of professionals has provided personal care, assistance, and supervision, carefully prepared meals, exercise and activity programs, health monitoring, personal laundry, housekeeping and transportation, all to assure the comfort and security of their senior residents.

Evergreene Retirement Village (804) 985-4413 **Continuing Care**
422 William Mills Dr., Stanardsville, VA 22973 **ST** 178 total
1 story ❋ /Cottages/P/SP rms ❋ 1wk-3mos ❋ **A/N/SN/SCU** ❋ varies with level (✚✙) — **SA-Sec-ST-DTG-EX-CH-N-Ph-CB-W-K-CD-H-L-Rec**

Heritage Hall - Charlottesville (804) 974-7882 **Nursing Care**
505 West Rio Rd., Charlottesville, Va 22901 **ST** 120 beds
1 story ❋ P/SP rms ❋ **N/SN/SCU** ❋ (✚✙) — **SA-Sec-TD-Ph-CB-W-CD-H-L-Rec** **See page 156**

Lovingston Healthcare Center (804) 263-4823 **Nursing Care**
393 Front St. - P.O. Box 398, Lovingston, VA 22949 **ST** 60 beds
1 story ❋ P/SP rms ❋ **A/N/SN** ❋ (✚✙) — **SA-Sec-EX-CH-N-RFM-CB-W-CD-H-L-Rec**

Our Lady of Peace (804) 973-1155 **Indept/Asst Living**
751 Hillsdale Dr., Charlottesville, VA 22901 **C**
3 story ❋ 1,2bdrm apts/P/SP rms ❋ yes ❋ **A/N** ❋ $1841-$3500mo (**$✙**) — **SA-Sec-P-TD-ST-DTG-EX-CH-N-RFM-Ph-CB-W-K-CD-H-L-Rec**

Riverdale Assisted Living Facility (804)293-9845 **Assisted Living**
1329 Riverdale Dr., Charlottesville, VA 22902 **C** 30 residents
2 stories ❋ P/SP rms ❋ **A** ❋ $41-$112day (100%) — **SA-Sec-ST-DTG-EX-CH-N-RFM-Ph-CB-W-CD-H-L**

Sargent House (804) 973-9044 **Independent Living**
1264 Branchlands Dr., Charlottesville, VA 22901 **C** 44 units
1 story ❋ 1,2bdrm apts ❋ none ❋ $1200-$1775mo — **SA-Sec-P-ST-EX-CH-N-Ph-CB-W-K-H-L**

The Village Nursing Center (804) 842-2916 **Nursing Care**
Route 15, P.O. Box 669, Fork Union, VA 23055 **R** 60 beds
1 story ❋ P/SP rms ❋ varies) ❋ **N/SN** ❋ (✚✙) — **SA-Sec-Ph-CB-W-K-CD-H-L**

Westminster-Canterbury of the Blue Ridge (804) 980-9100 **Life Care**
250 Pantops Mtn Rd., Charlottesville, VA 22911 **C** 180 residents
1 story ❋ apts/cottages/P/SP rms ❋ 6mos-2 yrs ❋ **A/N/SN** ❋ varies — **SA-Sec-P-ST-DTG-OTG-EX-CH-N-Ph-CB-W-K-CD-H-L-Rec**

The Windham (804) 823-4307 **Assisted Living**
P.O. Box 310, 1220 Crozet Ave., Crozet, VA 22932 **ST** 153 units
6 stories ❋ rapid turn-over ❋ **A** ❋ $725-$2200mo — **SA-ST-DTG-EX-Ph-CB-W-CD-H-L-Rec**

Area 11 — Central Virginia Area Agency on Aging

Serves the Counties of Bedford, Amherst, Campbell and Appomattox and the Cities of Bedford and Lynchburg.
3225 Old Forest Road
Lynchburg, VA 24501 (804) 385-9070

Smith Mountain Lake, the largest lake in the state falls between this area and area 12. Bedford, an interesting old town, is surrounded by many sites that are well worth investigating. High in the Blue Ridge Parkway, Peaks of Otter is one of the most photographed spots in the state. Year round this lodge offers spectacular scenery, great dining and the famous waterwheel. Mansions including Avenel, built around 1838 features Civil War tales and ghosts and Poplar Forest is the octagonal house Jefferson designed as a year-round retreat.

Outside Lynchburg is Appomattox Courthouse National Historical Park, site of Robert E. Lee's surrender. Cloverhill Village is a living history museum with restored buildings. Lynchburg is the largest town in area. Educators and religious figures have been part of the town for many years. This is the home of Jerry Falwell and Liberty University.

There is a nice monthly newspaper of senior events, *Senior Times.* An active Habitat For Humanity program invites seniors to participate. They have built 130 homes between 1993 and 1995! There is a Central Virginia Community College program for seniors which provides free classes, several programs with the Parks and Recreation Department and senior centers host many events including parties and seminars as diverse as pet care and floral arrangements.

There is a Virginia Senior Games, sponsored by the Lynchburg Parks and Recreation which includes events from softball, volleyball, basketball and running everts. The AAA hosts an active Volunteer program which involves both seniors providing help throughout the community, and members of the community helping seniors. Many merchants in the area offer senior discounts and Lynchburg Bowl offers a daytime program where seniors can bowl for only 99¢. Health Programs provide exercise classes, preventative health education and screening.

Adult Care Center of Central Virginia (804) 847-8111 **Adult Day Care**
7th & Court St., P.O. Box 568, Lynchburg, VA 24505 **C** 20 adults
1 story ❋ none ❋ (7:30AM-5:30PM) ❋**A** ❋ $ $32day (✚) — **SA-Sec-DTG-EX-CH-N-RFM-Ph-W-CD-Rec**

Avante at Lynchburg (804) 846-8437 **Nursing Care**
2081 Longhorne Rd., Lynchburg, VA 24501 **C** 120 beds
1 story ❋ P/SP/W rms ❋ 3-6 mos ❋ **N/SN/SCU** ❋ $103-$400 (+✚10%) — **SA-P-CH-RFM-Ph-CB-W-CD-H-L** **See page 192**

The Briarwood (804) 947-6221 **Nursing Care**
3500 Powhatan St., Lynchburg, VA 24501 **C** 51 beds
1 story ❋ P/SP/W rms ❋ **N** ❋ (**$**+✚30%) — **SA-Sec-P-EX-CH-N-RFM-Ph-CB-W-K-CD-H-L-Rec**

Camelot Hall of Lynchburg (804) 239-2657 **Nursing Care**
5615 Seminole Ave., Lynchburg, VA 24502 **C** 180 beds
1 story ❋ P/SP/W rms ❋ **N/SN** ❋ $99-$118day (✛✚20%) — **SA-Sec-DTG-EX-CH-N-RFM-Ph-CB-W-CD-H-L-Rec**

Eden Pines Alzheimer's Special Care (804) 385-5102 **Assisted Living**
Lillian Lane, Lynchburg, Va 24506 **C** 32 beds
1 story ❋ usually has space available ❋ **A** ❋ — **SA-Sec-ST-DTG-EX-CH-N-RFM-Ph-CB-W-CD-H-L-Rec**

Elks National Home (540) 586-8232 **Independent/Assisted**
931 Ashland Ave., Bedford, VA 24523 **ST**
2 stories ❋ P rms, suites ❋ none ❋ **A** ❋ $660-$1045mo — **SA-Sec-ST-DTG-EX-N-Ph-CB-CD-H-L-Rec**

Guggenheimer Nursing Home (804) 947-5100 **Nursing Care**
1920 Atherhdlt Rd., Lynchburg, VA **C** 130 beds
3 stories ❋ P/SP rms ❋ yes ❋ **N/SN** ❋ $93-$175mo (✛✚40%) — **SA-Sec-P-ST-DTG-CH-N-RFM-Ph-CB-W-CD-H-L-Rec**

Heritage Hall - Brookneal (804) 376-3740 **Nursing Care**
633 Cook Ave., Brookneal, Va 24528 **ST** 60 beds
1 story ❋ P/SP rms ❋ **N/SN** ❋ (✛✚) — **SA-Sec-TD-Ph-CB-W-CD-H-L-Rec** **See page 156**

Mayfair House (804) 385-6077 **Assisted Living**
Lillian Lane, Lynchburg, VA 24506 **C** 48 beds
1 story ❋ space usually available ❋ **A** ❋ — **SA-ST-DTG-EX-CH-N-RFM-Ph-CB-W-CD-H-L-Rec**

Medical Care Center (804) 846-4626 **Nursing Care**
2200 Landover Place, Lynchburg, VA 24501 **C** 118 beds
3 stories ❋ P/SP rms ❋ **N/SN** ❋ (**$**✛✚) — **CD**

Runk & Pratt Residential Adult Care (540) 587-9387 **Assisted Living**
P.O. Box 503, 812 E. Main St., Bedford, VA 24523 **C** 44 beds
2 stories ❋ P/SP rms ❋ yes ❋ **A** ❋ $1280-$1680mo (✛✚) — **SA-Sec-ST-DTG-EX-CH-N-RFM-Ph-W-CD-H-L-Rec**

The Oaks of Lynchburg (804) 846-6611 **Assisted Living**
2249 Murrell Rd., Lynchburg, VA 24551 **C** 50 beds
1 story ❋ P/SP rms ❋ varies ❋ **A** ❋ $1595-$2095mo (100%) — **SA-Sec-ST-DTG-EX-CH-N-RFM-Ph-CB-W-CD-H-L-Rec**

St. Johns Nursing Home (804) 845-6045 **Indep/Asst Living**
3500 Powhatan S.t, Lynchburg, VA 24501 **C** 45 residents
1 story ❋ P/SP/W rms ❋ **A/N** ❋ starts at $1350 (100%) — **SA-ST-DTG-EX-CH-N-RFM-Ph-CB-W-CD-H-L-Rec**

Area 12 — Southern Area Agency on Aging

Serves the Counties of Patrick Henry, Franklin and Pittsylvania and the Cities of Martinsville and Danville.

433 Commonwealth Blvd.
Martinsville, VA 24112-4228 (540) 632-6442 or 1-800-468-4571

Further south along Hwy 29, Region 12 stretches to the North Carolina border. Danville was once a mill town for Dan River looms. Today the company is still a large presence in the city and a major employer. A factory outlet store sells the many fabrics and housewares produced by Dan River which became famous several decades ago for its gingham and county prints. This was the last capital of the Confederacy and there is a museum commemoration that event. There is also a new Science Center, a Fine Arts and History Museum and Museum of Natural History. Tobacco Auction Tours are interesting, and the tobacco auctioneer's chant rings through the six warehouses during the season.

Off of the main highway, Ferrum houses the Blue Ridge Institute and Farm Museum at Ferrum College with folklife exhibits. There is also an Art Gallery which shows professional and student exhibits throughout the year. Also to the west of the main road is Martinsville, home to the Martinsville Speedway billed as the world's most beautiful and comfortable race track. The State museum of natural history has an educational outreach program with changing exhibit galleries, traveling exhibits lectures and field trips. And Rocky Mount has the Hales Ford Academy, a restored one-room school museum.

Smith Mountain Lake sprawls into this area from the north and provides almost endless fishing, boating, golf, and camping. Shopping is rich in art galleries, antique shops, and country stores. Each year there are dozens of festivals. The Virginia Dare Cruise Boat offers brunch, dinner and sight-seeing cruises.

The mission of Southern Area Agency on Aging is to provide services that will help older people live independently in their own homes. The Agency on Aging furnishes information on a wide variety of age-related concerns. The eligibility age for most of the services is 60, though the Senior Employment Program extends to those 55 and older. Unfortunately, the Agency's funding has not kept pace with the demand for home-delivered meals, personal care and housekeeping for frail elders. Therefore there is a limitation or waiting list for services and those which are available are targeted to low-income seniors who lack family and friends to assist them and who are clustered in populated areas. Some outlying sections of the counties cannot be served.

There are nine service providers. The Danville and Martinsville Senior Centers provide transportation, health promotion and recreation activities. Danville also has telephone reassurance and a volunteer program. Franklin County Department of Aging Services provides transportation, health promotion and recreational activities and operates Residential Repair and Renovation Programs in all areas serviced by SAAA. Henry County Senior Services provides transportation, recreation activities and telephone reassurance as does Pittsylvania County Community

Action which also provides congregate meals at senior lunch sites and home-delivered meals and runs a volunteer program. Patrick County Senior Services provides transportation. There is an Adult Day Care Center in Martinsville and a Virginia Legal Aid Society in Danville.

Other services provided throughout the area are photo identification cards that qualify seniors for a 10% discount with participating merchants. There are also health promotion activities such as group exercise, walking clubs, health awareness programs and nutrition counseling.

Life Care
King's Grant Retirement Community
350 King's Way Rd (540) 634-1000
Martinsville, VA 24112 **ST** 30units
1 story ❋ P rms ❋ yes, varies according to unit ❋ **A** ❋ $91 day (✚) — **SA-Sec-P-ST-DTG-OTG-EX-CH-N-RFM-Ph-CB-W-K-CD-H-L-Rec** **See Page 132**

Assisted Living
Ashwood Assisted Living Residence
709 Betts St. (804) 793-8002
Danville, VA 24541 **C** 25 units
2 stories ❋ P/SP rms ❋ no ❋ **A** ❋ $33-$82/day — **SA-Sec-P-TD-ST-DTG-EX-CH-N-RFM-Ph-CB-W-CD-H-L-Rec**

Assisted Living
Abingdon Place of Danville
149 Executive Ct., (804) 799-1930
Danville, VA 24541 **C** 75 residents
1 story ❋ P/SP rms ❋ **A** ❋ $1150-$2850/mo (✚ 80%) — **SA-Sec-P-ST-DTG-EX-CH-N-RFM-Ph-CB-W-CD-H-L-Rec**

Area 13 — Lake Country Area Agency on Aging

Serves the Counties of Halifax, Mecklenburg and Brunswick and the City of South Boston.

1105 West Danville Street
South Hill, VA 23970-3501 (804) 447-7661 or 1-800-252-4464

Lake Country gets it's name from the lakes within its boundaries. The Roanoke River flows from Smith Mountain Lake to the East, through the Area and into John I Kerr Reservoir (Buggs Island Lake) which is a large body of water extending down into North Carolina. On the east, it is connected with the top of Lake Gaston, the main body of water in North Carolina. Outdoor recreation ranges from boating and fishing to camping, swimming, picnicking and hiking. Staunton River Battlefield State Park offers a Civil War Fort and guided trail across the railroad bridge with a museum and wetland. It is handicapped accessible.

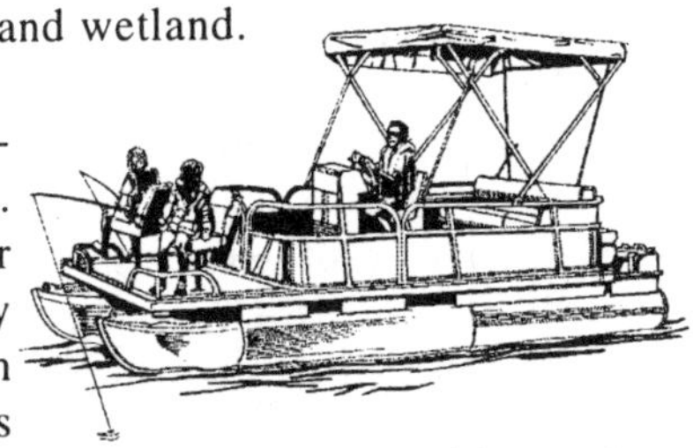

This is rural country, with no major interstate roads connecting it and no large cities. South Boston is the home of South Boston Motor Speedway, a NASCAR sanctioned speedway which hosts the Bush Grand National. South Hill offers tobacco farm and warehouse tours during the season and a Model Railroad Museum. For the feminine visitors, there is the Virginia Evans Doll Museum with more than 500 dolls and carriages from 1869-1980.

The Lake Country Area Agency on Aging began operating in 1975, although its Nutrition Program began in 1974. The two programs were consolidated in 1975. The primary objectives of the program are to serve as an advocate for persons 60 years and older by helping them to achieve a better quality of life; to secure and maintain independence and dignity in a home environment for older individuals who are capable of self-care when provided with the appropriate supportive services; to remove individual and social barriers to economic and personal independence for older individuals; and to provide a continuum of care to the vulnerable elderly, serving those older individuals most at risk of institutionalization. To that end LCAAA operates a checking program with the assistance of local police departments, senior citizens centers and volunteers to be sure that older citizens who live alone either call the town police department, senior centers or receive calls from volunteers on a regular basis. The Area also provides transportation to and from nutrition sites, for shopping and medical appointments. There is a Volunteer program, a senior employment program and senior I.D. cards for discounts at participating businesses.

Lake Country Area Agency on Aging also provides health screening, health and nutritional education programs, exercise and life style classes. They publish a newsletter and coordinate with the Emergency Food Bank for those with need. They operate five nutrition sites. Legal advice and representation is available for those who need it. For those who are homebound there are home care services, Case Managers, and Long Term Care available.

Boston Commons (804) 572-4959 **Retirement Residence**
1146 N. Main St., South Boston, VA 24592 **ST** 44 units
2 stories ❋ Suites/P/SP rms ❋ **A/N** ❋ $933-$2347mo — **SA-Sec-DTG-CD-Rec**

Mecklenburg House (804) 689-2291 **Assisted Living**
P.O. Box 700, South Hill, VA 23970 **ST** 24 units
1 story ❋ P/SP rms ❋ none ❋ **A/N** ❋ $42-$101day — **SA-Sec-P-ST-DTG-EX-CH-N-RFM-Ph-CB-W-CD-H-L**

North View Adult Home (804) 447-8892 **Residential/Asst/Intensive Asst.**
399 Saffold Rd., South Hill, VA 23970 **R** 12 residents
1 story ❋ P/SP rms ❋ **A** ❋ $737-$1474mo (✛✙) — **SA-Sec-P-TD-ST-EX-CH-RFM-Ph-CB-W-CD-H-L-Rec**

Area 14 — Piedmont Senior Resources, Inc.

Serves the Counties of Nottoway, Prince Edward, Charlotte, Lunenburg, Cumberland, Buckingham and Amelia.

P.O. Box 398
Burkeville, VA 23922 (804) 767-5588

Another rural area, this very central area has more going for it than would be apparent at first glance. Farmville is a home of two colleges, Longwood College and just outside of the town, Hampden Sidney College. Farmville is a quaint old town with 19th-century architecture and a Riverfront park, and very much a college town. Greenfront stores are the largest furniture and rug discount stores in the state and a Farmer's Market sells fresh produce. Prince Edward County Debtor's Prison was built in 1786 and is one of the few original "goals" for debtors remaining in the country. Sailors Creek Battlefield is the site of the last major Civil War battle. There are a number of state parks, nature trails and wildlife management areas which offer abundant outdoor recreation on all levels.

Peidmont Senior Resources, Inc., serves as the Area Agency on Aging and functions through the Advisory Council which provides it with information necessary to meet the needs of seniors in this area. It provides a number of services as needed from para-legal services to in-home services for the homebound which extend up to daily living assistance and education on adapting to cope with a new disability or illness. Home delivered meals are available for those with need. The Virginia Medical Assistance Program provides screening for Medicaid's long-term care and is designed to reduce inappropriate institutional placement by providing basic health-related services where it is cost-effective versus institutional care. There is also information and referral, employment services, nutritional centers in conjunction with other activities and I.D. discount cards.

Brookview Lodge (804) 392-4119 **Independent/Assisted**
2003 Cobb St., Farmville, VA 23901 **ST** 91 units
2 stories ❋ P/SP rms ❋ 2-3 mos ❋ **A** ❋ $10,900-$16,200yr — **SA-Sec-P-ST-DTG-EX-CH-N-RFM-Ph-CB-W-K-CD-H-L-Rec**

Heritage Hall - Dillwyn (804) 983-2050 **Nursing Care**
9 Brickyard Dr., Dillwyn, VA, 23936 **ST** 60 beds
1 story ❋ P/SP rms ❋ **N/SN** ❋ (✢✢) — **SA-Sec-TD-Ph-CB-W-CD-H-L-Rec** **See page 156**

Heritage Hall - Blackstone (804) 292-5301 **Nursing Care**
800 S. Main St., Blackstone, VA 23824 **ST** 180 beds
1 story ❋ P/SP rms ❋ **N/SN** ❋ (✢✢) — **SA-Sec-TD-Ph-CB-W-CD-H-L-Rec** **See page 156**

Holly Manor & Hollybrook Courts (804) 392-6106 **Residential/Nursing Care**
2003 Cobb St., Farmville, VA 23901 **ST** 115 beds
1 story ❋ P/SP/ward rms ❋ none ❋ **N/SN** ❋ $570-$1,025 mo to $22,000 yr (✢) — **SA-Sec-TD-ST-DTG-EX-CH-N-Ph-CB-W-K-CD-H-L**

Area 15 — Capital Area Agency on Aging

Serves the Counties of Goochland, Powhatan, Henrico, Chesterfield, Charles City, Hanover and New Kent and the City of Richmond.

24 East Cary Street
Richmond, VA 23219-3796 (804)0343-3000 or 1-800-989-2286

Richmond is the capital of the state, and once the capital of the Confederacy. Here was once the most inland port for the James River, and today riverboats offer brunch, dinner and special event cruises. Richmond has maintained its hold as the center of life in the state. Dance, theatre and art bring culture to the state with top companies on national tours, and top names in entertainment. The Richmond Ballet is well-respected far outside the state and the Virginia Opera is the 15th largest opera company in the nation. Dozens of smaller playhouses present everything from dinner theatre and mystery theatre to experimental. The Fine Art Museum has been home to top touring exhibits such as the Fabergé egg collection. The Science Museum, a Railroad Museum, an Aviation Museum and a Fire and Police Museum are only a sampling of the exhibits of interest. For sports enthusiasts there is the Richmond Braves, a successful minor league team which draws a big crowd throughout the season.

Strawberry Hill, the State Fairgrounds has something going on every weekend from RV and boat shows to horse shows and steeplechase events. Mansions such as the Wilton House, a 1753 mansion with period furnishings, Agecroft Hall, a 15th century Tudor Manor House imported from England and John Marshall House, the 1790 home of Chief Justice Marshall with its original furnishings are well worth visiting. The Edgar Allan Poe Museum is the world's largest Poe collection and is housed in Richmond's oldest house. Black history and culture are highlighted with the African Cultural Center, a Black History Museum and the Maggie Walker National Historic Site, among many other exhibits.

The state capitol was designed by Thomas Jefferson and includes the Houdon statue of George Washington. The White House of the Confederacy, the neighboring Civil War Museum and nearby battlefields represent the role Richmond played in that conflict. Scotchtown, one of Virginia's oldest plantations was Patrick Henry's home during the Revolutionary War. Parks, botanical gardens and a multitude of special events throughout the year make Richmond an interesting place to live or visit.

This is a very active Area Agency on Aging. They publish a bimonthly newspaper called *Mature Life,* which reports on issues, events and programs of the area. For the fourth year, CAAA has conducted a Serv-A-Thon which acts both as a community service event and a fund-raiser. It provides assistance to older persons who have needs that cannot be met through existing community resources which might range from painting, cleaning and yard work to building ramps and porch railings. Volunteers are matched with jobs that best meet their skills and preferences. Volunteers are encouraged to seek sponsorships for their time or sponsors for the projects undertaken.

They have an active Foster Grandparents volunteer program which provides help in public schools, hospitals, treatment centers, battered women's shelters, head start programs and day care centers where they work with vulnerable children. And they maintain a large base of volunteers from the community who help seniors in a variety of different ways.

There are a wide variety of health and education programs to help prevent medical problems or to help cope with them without giving up quality of life. Events such as the Goochland Heal Fair, a health fair at the fairgrounds featuring immunizations, screenings and information along with door prizes and refreshments. The CAAA promotes voter registration and voter education to make its seniors as politically effective as possible. They promote The Open University Program to provide an opportunity for people age 60 and over to come together for classes, individual lectures and to learn something new. And there are dozens of senior oriented events in each area from open houses of historic homes to craft classes, from trips to club meetings. Dances and art festivals, exercise classes and trips keep seniors active and social. There is also an active program for seniors thought the Parks and Recreation Department. It offers almost every type and level of exercise and recreation for seniors at a variety of locations throughout the area.

The Capital Area Agency on Aging makes sure that older Virginians have access to the services necessary to remain independent. In addition to the services usually provided by AAAs, there is also a Volunteer Money Management program for low-income persons age 55 and older and Partners in Guardianship where trained volunteers assist persons 50 and older with making responsible decisions regarding daily living and financial issues. Phone Pals is an outreach program offering telephone reassurance that brings together a caring volunteer with one who is alone and sometimes may need help.

Braxton (804) 275-2689 **Independent Living**
5700-A Hopkins Rd., Richmond, VA 23234 **S** 120 homes
1 story ❋ $145,000-$225,000 — **SA-Sec-P-N-Ph-W-K**

Eden Pines Alzheimer's Special Care (804) 746-7370 **Alzheimer Care**
7080 Brookes Farm Rd., Mechanicsville, VA 23111-4686 **S** 32 residents
1 story ❋ usually available ❋ **SCU** ❋ — **SA-Sec-ST-DTG-EX-CH-N-RFM-CB-W-CD-H-L-Rec**

Ginter Hall West (804) 741-9494 **Assisted Living**
12411 Gayton Rd., Richmond, VA 23233 **C** 185 residents
3 stories ❋ P/SP rms ❋ 1 mo ❋ **A** ❋ $1,500-$2,500mo — **SA-Sec-ST-DTG-EX-CH-N-RFM-Ph-CB-W-CD-H-L-Rec**

Heritage Oaks Retirement (804)323-3800 **Independent Living**
1100 German School Rd., Richmond, VA 23225 **C** 121 units
4 stories ❋ varies ❋ $1,200-$2,200mo — **SA-Sec-ST-DTG-EX-CH-N-CB-W-CD-H-L-Rec**

The Hermitage (804) 355-5721 **Life Care**
1600 Westwood Ave., Richmond, VA 23227 **C** 242 residents
waiting list ❋ **A/N/SN/SCU** ❋ (100%✍)— **SA-Sec-ST-DTG-EX-CH-N-RFM-Ph-CB-CD-H-L-Rec**

The Hermitage at Chedarfield (804) 968-5520 **Life Care**
2300 Cedarfield Parkway, Richmond, VA 23233 **C** 550 residents
1 story ❋ indep/P/SP ❋ about 300 ❋ **A/N/SN/SCU** ❋ several plans (100%✍)— **SA-Sec-P-ST-DTG-OTG-EX-CH-N-RFM-Ph-CB-W-K-CD-H-L-Rec**

Lakewood Manon Baptist Retirement Community, Inc., (804) 740-2900 **Life Care**
1900 Lauderdale Drive, Richmond, VA 23233 **C** 265 units
3 stories ❋ apartments ❋ several months ❋ **A/N/SN** ❋ $62,600-$105,100 entrance, $1,431-$1,991 mo (100%✍) — **SA-Sec-ST-DTG-OTG-EX-CH-N-Ph-CB-W-K-CD-H-L** **See page 137**

The Laurels of Willow Creek (804)379-4771 **Nursing Care**
11611 Robious Rd., Midlothian, Va 23113 **S** 120 beds
1 story ❋ P/SP rms ❋ depends on level of care ❋ **N/SN/SCU** ❋ (+✚30%) — **SA-Sec-TD-EX-CB-W-CD-H-L**

St. Mary's Woods (804) 741-8624 **Indep/Assisted**
1257 Marywood Ln., Richmond, VA 23229 **C** 118 units
3 stories ❋ apts ❋ 4-6 mos ❋ **A** ❋ $1,400-$2,771mo — **SA-Sec-ST-DTG-OTG-EX-CH-N-Ph-CB-W-K-CD-H-L-Rec**

Westminster Canterbury - Richmond (804) 264-6256 **Life Care**
1600 Westbrook Ave., Richmond, VA 23227 **C** 640 residents
Prms ❋ varies by unit desired ❋ **A/N/SN/SCU** ❋ seven contract options (+✚100%✍) — **SA-Sec-P-ST-DTG-EX-CH-N-RFM-Ph-CB-W-K-CD-H-L-Rec** — **This Facility is pictured on the front cover. For more information see page facing Table of Contents.**

Area 16 — Rappahannock Area Agency on Aging

Serves the Counties of Caroline, Spotsylvania, Stafford and King George and the City of Fredericksburg.

Bowman Center
11915 Main Street
Fredericksburg, VA 22408 (540) 371-3375

Between Richmond and Washington D.C. is Fredericksburg. Long before Union and Confederate cannons fired across the rolling hills of the area, Fredericksburg, Spotsylvania and Stafford were already rich in colonial and Revolutionary history. George Washington grew up here at Ferry Farm, the site of the famous "Cherry Tree." Later, in the area, five major battles of the Civil War were fought, including Chancellorsville, Lee's largest victory. It was after that battle that Stonewall Jackson was killed by a mistaken shot from one of his own troops.

Today, this is a city which maintains the air of a small town, while accommodating residents and tourists from far outside the area. Mary Washington College is now co-ed and occupies a lovely campus near the downtown area. Antique stores abound. Over 350 original buildings from the 18th and 19th century occupy the 40-block National Historic District. There are many homes where Washington and his family lived. Fine dining, unique bed and breakfasts, wineries and excellent shopping fill the area. To the north is Potomac Mills, the largest outlet center in the state. Events throughout the year include a fabulous 4th of July celebration and fireworks display and the Virginia Renaissance Faire, a 16th century celebration of Elizabethan entertainment, games, food and handcrafts.

Surrounding areas include parks with picnicing and camping, boating and fishing along the Rapidan and Rappahannock Rivers, the Potomac River and Lake Anna. Dozens of lakes and reservoirs dot the area. And Caledon Natural Area on the Potomac River is a bald eagle nesting area.

The Rappahannock Area Agency on Aging (RAAA) offers a wide range of programs beginning with Access and Acquisition which assesses the eligibility and need for services of a senior citizen. Information and referral will make families and caregivers aware of available opportunities, services and resources that will assist them with their needs. Nutritional programs include home delivered meals, education, and congregate meals. The meal centers accommodate the entire service area and encourage fellowship and social interaction. Telephone reassurance is designed to determine on a daily basis if persons living alone are safe and well. A daily call is followed by a personal check of the property if there is no answer. Other services include employment, home repair, legal and insurance counseling and transportation.

RAAA publishes a *Senior Resource Directory*. This includes names and numbers of Delegates and Representatives as well as city and county officials and their numbers. Seniors are encouraged to vote and make their concerns known to elected officials at all levels. There are also numbers and addresses for local and national organizations which are of interest to seniors.

Commonwealth Retirement Center (540) 891-5540 **Assisted Living**
9300 Onyx Ct,, Fredericksburg, VA 22407 **C** 48 rms
1 story ❋ P/SP rms ❋ intermittent ❋ **A** ❋ — **SA-Sec-ST-DTG-EX-CH-N-RFM-Ph-CB-W-CD-H-L-Rec**

Chancellor's Village Retirement Community (540) 786-5000 **Life Care**
12100 Chancellor's Village Ln,, Fredericksburg, VA 22407 **C** 121 units
2 stories ❋apts ❋ yes ❋ **A** ❋ $67,000-$128,000 entry, $1200-1955mo — **SA-Sec-P-ST-DTG-OTG-EX-CH-N-RFM-Ph-CB-W-K-CD-H-L-Rec**

Heritage Hall - King George (540) 775-4000 **Nursing Care**
8443 King Highway (P.O. Box 495), King George, VA 22485 **ST** 130 beds
1 story ❋ P/SP rms ❋ **N/SN** ❋ (+✚) — **SA-Sec-TD-Ph-CB-W-CD-H-L-Rec** **See page 156**

Marion Manor of Stafford (540) 659-6375 **Assisted Living/Extended Care**
P.O. Box 412, Stafford, VA 22555 ❋ 177 Old Potomac Church Rd,, Stafford
2 stories ❋ P/SP rms ❋ **A/N** ❋ $2500-$3500mo — **SA-Sec-P-TD-ST-DTG-OTG-EX-CH-N-RFM-Ph-CB-W-CD-H-L-Rec** — **This facility is pictured on the back cover.** **For more information see page facing Table of Contents.**

Area 17/18 — Northern Neck-Middle Penninsula Agency on Aging

Serves the Counties of Westmoreland, Northumberland, Richmond, Lancaster, Essex, Middlesex, Matthews, King & Queen, King William and Gloucester.
P.O. Box 610
Urbanna VA 23175 (804) 758-2386

These ten counties line the peninsulas between the Potomac River and the Rappahannock River and between the Rappahannock and the York Rivers. The York is fed by the Pamunkey River which feeds out of Lake Anna and the North Anna River and the Mattaponi River which feeds from the foothills south of Fredericksburg. It is said that the riverbank is always only ten minutes away. George Washington's birthplace stands just a few miles from Robert E. Lee's birthplace and Stratford Hall. Cruises to remote Tangier Island leave from Reedville between May and October. It is a step back in time to this village where even English sounds different. Reedville also has a Fishermen's Museum representing life in the area and a Victorian Historic District. There are 1120 miles of shoreline along the rivers, creeks and Chesapeake Bay. Working waterfront villages still look to the sea for their livelihood, and blue crabs are a dietary staple served in the smallest of restaurants.

Natural areas are scattered throughout the area and the Mattaponi Indian Reservation is one of the few Indian Reservations in the Mid-Atlantic. Ingleside Plantation Vineyards and Winery has a tour, a museum and special events. The Northern Neck abounds with resorts and waterway traffic. The resorts offer golf, boating, yacht mooring and all kinds of water recreation. Marinas dot the rivers and many of them offer week long or weekend packages of dining and dancing to fine bands reminiscent of a bygone era. Fishing is some of the finest in the state, with striped bass and bluefish on the Potomac River, catfish, bream and crappie at Rock Spring Pond. There is excellent birdwatching along the shores. There are also several archaeological sites and fossils can be found along the shoreline.

Essex House (804) 443-5921 **Assisted Living**
Rt 3, Box 324, Tappahannock, VA 22560 **ST** 20 residents
1 story ❋ P rms ❋ none ❋ **A** ❋ $60-$104day — **SA-Sec-P-ST-DTG-EX-CH-N-RFM-Ph-CB-W-CD-H-L-Rec**

Gloucester House Retirement Home (804) 693-3116 **Assisted/Nursing**
7657 Meredith Dr., Gloucester, VA 23061 **S** 96 residents
1 story ❋ P/SP rms ❋ yes ❋ **A/N** ❋ $1,700-$2,500mo — **SA-Sec-P-ST-DTG-EX-CH-N-RFM-Ph-CB-W-CD-H-L**

Mayfair House (804) 435-9896 **Assisted Living**
460 S. Main St., Kilmarnock, VA 22482 **ST** 48 residents
1 story ❋ usually available ❋ **A** ❋ — **SA-ST-DTG-EX-CH-N-RFM-Ph-CB-W-CD-H-L-Rec**

Rappahannock Westminster-Canterbury (804) 438-4000 **Life Care**
132 Lancaster Dr., Irvington, VA 22480 **R** - Northern Neck
1 story ❋ apts, cottages ❋ **A/N** ❋ — **SA-Sec-P-ST-DTG-EX-CH-N-RFM-Ph-CB-W-K-CD-H-L-Rec**

Sanders Nursing Home, Inc. (804) 693-2000 **Indept/ Asst/Nurse**
7385 Walker Ave., Gloucester, VA 23061 **S** 55 beds
2 stories ❋ P/SP rms ❋ **N** ❋ $81.10-$99.50day (100%) — **SA-Sec-P-ST-DTG-EX-CH-N-RFM-Ph-CB-W-CD-H-L**

Area 19 — Crater District Area Agency on Aging

Serves the Counties of Dinwiddie, Sussex, Greensville, Surry and Prince George and the Cities of Petersburg, Hopewell, Emporia and Colonial Heights.

23 Seyler Drive
Petersburg, VA 23805 (804) 732-7020

Just South of Richmond, this area features a wide variety of interesting attractions for almost every interest. Hopewell has a historic walking tour with restored antebellum buildings and Civil War sites. It also features a self-guided driving tour of 1920's mail order Sears cottages and homes. This is one of the most diverse examples of these homes found in the United States. There are boat tours of plantations along the James River which may include brunch, lunch and dinner. Flowerdew Hundred is a historical and archaeological museum and the Virginia Alliance of Quilters museum exhibits contemporary, traditional and antique quilts and does demonstrations, classes and sales of quilts.

Emporia features Village View 1790's mansion displaying family life in the rural Southside before and during the confederacy. Weston Plantation is a rare example of a Georgian River Plantation with period furnishings. And Petersburg has the Centre Hill Mansion, a magnificent 1823 mansion which has been host to three U.S. Presidents. The Farmers Bank was built in 1817 and is one of the oldest banks in America. There are several other noteworthy mansions and plantations in the area. One of the most interesting is Trapezium House with its legends of ghosts.

We tried on a number of occasions to contact this Area Agency on Aging. We were referred to their web page, but frankly, it was less than enlightening. It simply listed the services they offered and the area they served. The services are: Information and Referral, Employment, Socialization and Recreation, Adult Day Care, Meals Program, Homemaker/Home Care Companion Services, Transportation, Elder Abuse, Repair and Renovation, Health Promotion, Long Term Care Ombudsman, Legal Assistance, Volunteer Programs, Foster Grandparents Program, and Tax Counseling for the Elderly. Even with an E-mail message, we were unable to get any more personalized information.

Bloom Retirement Center (804) 348-4004 **Assisted/Nursing**
308 Weaver Ave, Emporia, VA 23847 **ST** 65 residents
1 story ❋ P/SP/W rms ❋ none ❋A ❋ $38-$104day — **SA-Sec-P-ST-DTG-EX-CH-N-RFM-Ph-CB-W-CD-H-L-Rec**

Eden Pines Alzheimer's Special Care (804) 861-4358 **Assisted Living**
550 Flack Rd, Petersburg, Va 23805 **C** 32 residents
1 story ❋ usually available ❋ **A/N** ❋ — **SA-Sec-ST-DTG-EX-CH-N-RFM-CB-W-CD-H-L-Rec**

Mayfair House (804) 861-6977 **Assisted Living**
590 Flack Rd, Petersburg, VA 23805 **C** 48 residents
1 story ❋ usually available ❋ **A** ❋ — **SA-Sec-ST-DTG-EX-CH-N-RFM-Ph-CB-W-CD-H-L-Rec**

Area 20 — Southeastern Virginia Area Wide Model Program, Inc. (SEVAMP) Serves the Counties of Southampton and Isle of Wight and the Cities of Franklin, Suffolk, Portsmouth, Chesapeake, Virginia Beach and Norfolk.

7 Koger Executive Center, Suite 100
Norfolk, VA 23502-4121 (804) 461-9481

Virginia has literally thousands of miles of waterways and coastline. Along the Potomac, the James River up to Richmond, the York River and the Rappahannock River up to Fredericksburg. The Atlantic Ocean, Chesapeake Bay and wealth of costal waterways have defined the area since 1607 and offer an overwhelming number of water-related activities. The tidewater area is dotted with marinas of every kind, providing space for every size and shape of vessel. There is everything from deep sea fishing and whale and dolphin watching to calm rides from one point to another in the local water taxis. Virginia Beach is the world's longest resort beach, with twenty-eight miles of sand and surf. Portsmouth features a paddle wheeler for sight-seeing tours of the Hampton Roads area, or cruise the Chesapeake Bay on an overnight excursion boat. The Dismal Swamp Canal is the oldest operating artificial waterway in the United States. Smithfield and the Isle of Wight, both located on the Pagan River, just off the James River are havens for water sports. Museums focus on the lifestyle of the sea and prosperous homes of local merchants were financed by trade and shipping. This is one of the largest seaports in the country, and home to the Atlantic Fleet and Naval Yards and the world's largest naval base. Resorts, shopping and restaurants cluster along the waterfront.

This sprawling area is the largest population center in the state, covering the cities of Suffolk, Portsmouth, Norfolk, Chesapeake and Virginia Beach. There are a number of theatre companies, performing arts centers which draw top talent, the Virginia Symphony with more than 100 performances from September to June and the Chrysler Museum, recognized as one of the nation's top twenty art museums. Museums for almost everything from tugboats and the Nauticus, the National Maritime Center to Air and Space can provide something interesting for almost everyone. Parks and special events provide activities throughout the year.

SEVAMP is one of ten national programs designed to plan and administer a full range of services for the elderly. It was established in 1965 as the Senior Citizens Service Center, and incorporated in 1968. It was changed to the Southeastern Virginia Area wide Model Program in 1972, and designated as the Area Agency on Aging for Planning District 20 in 1973. It offers a wide variety of programs that help meet the many different needs of families across a diverse region, for this area is both urban in the south and rural in the north. Services are available through partnerships with public agencies and an active private sector. Its mission is to promote development of a comprehensive and coordinated system for the delivery of services to the elderly and their families. This area focuses heavily on families facing questions for which they are unprepared. They are critically aware of the stress of helping older family members and still meeting other responsibilities.

SEVAMP maintains numerous senior centers throughout South Hampton Roads. They provide information and referral via telephone for meeting needs. The Case Management program serves older persons and their families in their homes through assessment of need, care planning and coordinating services. A Case Manager will then monitor the status of the senior on a regular basis. Senior Housing Service Coordination is provided to elderly housing complexes which coordinates services which will assist housing managers and residents.

Transportation is available for medical visits, adult day care and to senior centers. Many organizations are coordinated to provide group health education and exercise programs, and individual medication review and health screening are available. Senior volunteer services and employment, primarily in part-time positions, is available through employment programs.

Autum Care of Great Bridge (757) 547-4528 **Nursing Care**
821 Cedar Rd., (P.O. Box 15224), Chesapeake, VA 23328 **C** 55 beds
1 story ❋ P/SP/W rms ❋ varies ❋ **N/SN/SCU** ❋ $84.50 day (✛✙) — **SA-Sec-Ph-CB-W-CD-H-L**

Autumn Care of Norfolk (757) 857-0481 **Nursing Care**
1401 Halstead Ave., Norfolk, VA 23502 **C** 120 beds
1 story ❋ P/SP rms ❋ varies ❋ **N/SN** ❋ $100-$110day (✛✙) — **SA-Sec-TD-Ph-CB-W-CD-H-L-Rec**

Autumn Care of Portsmouth (757) 397-0725 **Nursing Care**
3610 Winchester Dr., Portsmouth, VA 23707 **C** 108 beds
1 story ❋ P/SP/W rms ❋ 2-3wks ❋ **N/SN/SCU** ❋ $82-$130day (✛✙10%) — **SA-Sec-TD-Ph-CB-W-CD-H-L-Rec**

Baypointe Medical and Rehabilitation Center (757) 481-3321 **Nursing Care**
1148 First Colonial Rd., Virginia Beach, VA 23454 **ST** 118 beds
2 stories ❋ P/SP rms ❋ **N/SN** ❋ (**$**) — **SA-Sec-P-ST-DTG-EX-CH-N-RFM-Ph-CB-W-CD-H-L-Rec**

Brighton Gardens by Marriott (757) 499-4800 **Assisted Living**
5620 Wesleyan Dr., Virginia Beach, VA 23455 **C** 114 units
2 stories ❋ 3 mos ❋ **A** ❋ $1500-$2300mo — **SA-Sec-ST-DTG-EX-CH-N-RFM-Ph-CB-K-CD-H-L-Rec**

Courtland Healthcare Center (757) 653-0908 **Nursing Care**
23020 main St., Courtland, VA 23837 **ST** 90 beds
1 story ❋ P/SP rms ❋ usually ❋ **N/SN** ❋ (✛✙7%) — **SA-Sec-P-ST-EX-CH-N-RFM-CB-W-CD-H-L-Rec**

First Colonial Inn Retirement Community (757) 428-2884 **Independent/Assisted**
845 First Colonial Rd., Virginia Beach, VA 23451 **C** 184 apts
3 stories ❋ studio/1&2bdrm ❋ depends on unit ❋ **A** ❋ $1480-$2900mo (100%✍) — **SA-Sec-ST-DTG-OTG-EX-CH-N-RFM-Ph-CB-W-K-CD-H-L**

Ghent Arms Retirement (757) 627-8758 **Assisted Living**
641 Redgate Ave., Norfolk, VA 23507 **C** 45 residents
3 stories ❋ P/SP rms ❋ yes ❋ **A** ❋ $1,750-$3,300mo — **SA-Sec-P-ST-DTG-OTG-EX-CH-N-RFM-Ph-CB-W-CD-H-L-Rec**

Harbour Pointe Medical and Rehabilitation Center (757) 623-5602 **Nursing Care**
1005 Hampton Blvd., Norfolk, VA 23507 **C** 170 beds
4 stories ❋ P/SP rms ❋ yes ❋ **N/SN/SCU** ❋ $1,000-$1,400mo (**$**+✚15%) — **SA-Sec-P-ST-DTG-EX-CH-N-RFM-Ph-CB-W-CD-H-L-Rec**

Heritage Hall — Virginia Beach (757) 499-7029 **Nursing Care**
5580 Daniel Smith Rd., Virginia Beach, VA 23462 **C** 90 beds
1 story ❋ P/SP rms ❋ **N/SN** (+✚) — **SA-Sec-Ph-CB-W-CD-H-L-Rec -**
See page 156

Kings Grant House (757) 431-8825 **Assisted Living**
440 N. Lynnhaven Rd., Virginia Beach, VA 23452 **C** 48 residents
2 stories ❋ P/SP rms ❋ 1 mo ❋ **A** ❋ $1638-$2520mo — **SA-Sec-P-ST-DTG-EX-CH-N-RFM-Ph-CB-W-CD-H-L**

Lydia H. Roper (757) 622-6979 **Independent Living**
127 E. 40th St., Norfolk, VA 23504 **C** 27 units
3 stories ❋ **A** ❋ $790-$1,305mo — **SA-Sec-DTG-EX-CH-N-CB-CD-H-L-Rec**

Lynn Shores Chateau (757) 498-0187 **Assisted Living**
350 Lynn Shores Dr., Virginia Beach, VA 23452 **C** 16 units
1 story ❋ studio apts ❋ 0-3 mos ❋ **A** ❋ $1860mo — **SA-Sec-ST-EX-CH-CB-CD-H-L-Rec**

Mayfair House (757) 826-3728 **Assisted Living**
1030 Topping Lane, Smithfield, VA 23666 **S** 48 residents
1 story ❋ usually available ❋ **A** ❋ — **SA-Sec-ST-DTG-EX-CH-N-RFM-Ph-CB-W-CD-H-L-Rec**

Nansemond Pointe Rehabilitation and Health Care Centre (757) 539-8744 **Asst/Nurse**
200 W. Constance Rd., Suffolk, VA 23434 **C** 194 residents
1 story ❋ P/SP rms ❋ yes ❋ **A/N/SN** ❋ $55-$135day (**$**✛✚50%) — **SA-Sec-P-CH-RFM-Ph-CB-W-CD-H-L**

Riverside Assisted Living/Convalescent Center (757) 244-7008 **Asst/Nurse**
200 Lumar Rd., Smithfield, VA 23430 **C** 155 residents
1 story ❋ none ❋ **A/N/SN** ❋ $1700-2400 mo asst -$120day (**$**✛✚) **See page 227**

The Village at Woods Edge (757) 562-3100 **Indept/Assisted**
1401 N. High St., Franklin, VA 23851 **C** 44 units
2 stories ❋ sometimes ❋ **A** ❋ buy ❋ — **SA-Sec-ST-DTG-OTG-EX-CH-N-RFM-Ph-CB-W-K-CD-H-L-Rec**

Virginia Beach Healthcare & Rehabilitation Center (757) 481-3500 **Nursing Care**
1801 Camelot Dr., Virginia Beach, VA 23454 **C** 240 beds
1 story ❋ P/SP/W rms ❋ yes ❋ **N/SN/NCU** ❋ (✛✚16%✍) — **SA-Sec-P-TD-DTG-EX-CH-N-RFM-Ph-CB-W-CD-H-L-Rec**

Windermere at Virginia Beach (757) 496-3939 **Nursing Care**
1604 Old Donation Parkway, Virginia Beach, VA 23454 **C** 60 beds
1 story ❋ P/SP rms ❋ none ❋ **N/SN** ❋ $114-$121day (**$**✛✚) **See page 227**

Westminster-Canterbury in Virginia Beach (757) 496-1100 **Life Care**
3100 Shore Dr., Virginia Beach, VA 23451 **C** appx 500 residents
3 stories ❋ apts/condo/P/SP rms ❋ 6mos-2yrs ❋ **A/N/SN** ❋ $varies (✍) — **SA-Sec-ST-DTG-OTG-EX-CH-N-Ph-CB-W-K-CD-H-L-Rec**

Area 21 — Peninsula Agency on Aging

Serves the Counties of James City and York and the Cities of Williamsburg, Hampton and Poquoson.
739 Thimble Shoals Blvd.
Executive Center Building 1000, Suite 1006
Newport News, VA 23606-3562 (804) 973-0541

This is a relatively small Area in terms of square miles, but very active with the senior community. This is the birthplace of English speaking America and a major area in both the Revolutionary and Civil Wars. Jamestown, the first permanent English settlement in the New World began in 1607. Costumed interpreters tell about life on the ships during the five-month journey across the Atlantic. Here is the first manufacturing in America at the Jamestown glass factory, and nearby Poor Potter Site, the remains of a furnace run by colonial entrepreneur William Rogers. Williamsburg, once the capital of Virginia is maintained as probably the most outstanding example of colonial life in the country The Yorktown Battlefield Colonial National Historical Park celebrates the final battle of the Revolutionary War and the Victory Center tells the story of the American Revolution through galleries, timeline walkway, film and living history including an 18th century farm and recreated Continental Army camp. There is Nelson House, home of Thomas Nelson, Jr., signer of the Declaration of Independence.

Fort Wool in Hampton is a Civil War era island fortress and near the last struggle between the great ironclads. Fort Monroe was Confederate President Jefferson Davis's prison cell after the war and includes an exhibit of period weapons. Fort Monroe is America's only active-duty moat-encircled fort.

Williamsburg boasts fine dining, great resorts, dozens of golf courses and fantastic shopping at specialty shops or the Williamsburg Pottery Factory outlet center. Historic sites stand side by side with waterparks and theme parks such as Busch Gardens. The college of William and Mary carries on a tradition as one of the oldest colleges in the country. Dozens of plantations offer a look at a time well past. A driving tour of nine fascinating Jefferson sites begins here and stretches to Charlottesville and down to Natural Bridge and Poplar Forest. There is even a historic air tour over James River plantations, battlefields and naval shipyards! And Hampton features a self-guided tour of African-American heritage sites. Langley Speedway features NASCAR/Winston Cup Racing every Saturday night.

The Elderhostel program under the College of William & Mary in Williamsburg is an educational program which offers inexpensive, short-term academic programs on a variety of topics at varied locations throughout the world. This program is specifically designed for seniors.

The Peninsula Agency on Aging is dedicated to helping older Americans retain dignity and independence. PAA was established in 1974 and provides programs in cooperation with other community agencies in the tidewater area. The stated goal is a quote from the 1965 Older Americans Act, "...to secure and maintain maximum independence and dignity in a home environment for older individuals, to remove individual and social barriers to economic and personal independence and to provide a continuum of care for the vulnerable elderly."

It provides an active case management program which locates needed services on an individual basis. With a single phone call, and a few simple questions, a case manager begins to determine what services would be of importance to the client. This may be followed by a home visit and a discussion in depth of problems the client is having, the kinds of help already being received and available resources. The case manager may coordinate multiple services. This kind of individual case management is particularly useful to persons whose families live outside the local area, those who need additional services or those living alone and are unable to access available community services.

In home nursing assistants are available on a temporary or permanent basis for nursing care of daily living assistance. Home delivered meals are delivered to homebound individuals by a large corps of volunteers. Senior Centers provide group dining and the opportunity to socialize with others and stay in touch with the community. Recreation, blood pressure monitoring, bingo, exercise programs, shopping trips and even line dancing are served up in addition to the lunch programs at the eleven locations in the PAA. Special events, health and nutrition education, and van transportation are available. This area uses its centers as hubs for volunteer programs, case management and insurance and tax assistance when needed.

The Chesapeake (757) 599-6623 **Life Care**
955 Harpersville, Rd., Newport News, VA 23601 **C** 278 units
3 stories ❋ apts ❋ depends on unit ❋ — **SA-Sec-P-ST-DTG-OTG-EX-CH-N-Ph-CB-W-K-CD-H-L-Rec** **See page 137**

Eden Pines Alzheimer's Special Care (757) 826-5415 **Special Care**
1034 Topping Ln., Hampton, VA 23666 **C** 32 beds
1 story ❋ usually available ❋ **N/SCU** ❋ — **SA-Sec-ST-DTG-EX-CH-N-RFM-CB-W-CD-H-L-Rec**

Riverside Convalescent Center - Hampton (757) 722-9881 **Nursing Care**
414 Algonquin Rd., Hampton, VA 23661 **C** 160 beds
2 stories ❋ none ❋ **N/SN** ❋ $124-$130day (**$+✚**) **See page 227**

Riverside Regional Convalescent Center (757) 875-2000 **Nursing Care**
1000 Old Derbigh Blvd., Newport News, VA 23602 **C** 385 beds
1 story ❋ **N/SN** ❋ $119-$320day (**$+✚**) **See page 227**

Area 22 — Eastern Shore Area Agency on Aging/Community Action Agency

Serves the Counties of Accomack and Northampton on the Eastern Shore.

P.O. Box 8
49 Market Street
Onancock, VA 23417 (804) 787-3532

The Eastern Shore is a quiet place, filled with natural beauty and the timelessness of the Chesapeake Bay. It is accessible from the west by boat, or by car from the south over the twenty-one mile Chesapeake Bay Bridge Tunnel. From the north the two routes would be to cross the Chesapeake Bridge near Annapolis and travel down the Eastern Shore of Maryland through Salisbury. For the faint hearted who do not wish to traverse the rather formidable bridge with its low guard rails and narrow lanes, a trip north to Delaware and then down the straight Route 13 is probably the most direct way to reach this furthest barrier against the Atlantic Ocean.

Here there is flat rural land, with only one main highway. There are no major cities in either of the counties. As a community which depends on the sea for its livelihood, unemployment during the summer is almost nonexistent, but it soars during the winter. Almost twenty-five percent of the people live at or below the poverty level and more than one fourth of the population is over the age of fifty-five. These people, whose roots go deep into the past, are tied to the land and the sea and the broad, flat marshlands.

There are no large hospitals. The community hospital on the Eastern Shore offers limited services. Skilled nursing such as dialysis or Cancer treatments are referred over the bridge to Virginia Beach, or north to Salisbury.

But the area is rich in tradition and warmth. Though this is the poorest district in Virginia, it also has two private country clubs with golf courses and yacht moorings have been a drawing card for more affluent seniors. There is a small but steady flow of younger, active seniors moving into the area from the northern states. Several real estate companies handle senior properties.

George Podelco, the Executive Director of the Eastern Shore Area Agency on Aging is very friendly and helpful. He talked at length to us and was happy to be of service. He sent us to David Parker, the President of the Chamber of Commerce, where we were again greeted with enthusiasm.

Their AAA program interacts with the Community Action Agency. Together they work to utilize the community's own resources in a coordinated and efficient manner to reduce the effects of poverty and alleviate the problems of aging. Primary is the concern to promote the most cost-effective use of all available resources and to work with Federal, State and County governments, as well as local public and private agencies to achieve that end.

With innovation, the AAA has created both a thrift shop and "Country Makin's," a craft co-op to showcase the skills of the residents. With this shop they educate, encourage and advise people over 55 on the making and marketing of fine handicrafts to supplement their income, perfect their skills and increase their sense of independence and self worth. Through this they perpetuate the local cottage crafts and exchange ideas between senior citizens and other groups.

Another innovation is the Literacy Education for the Elderly Program (LEEP). This one of only twenty sites nationwide which provides one-on-one tutoring in basic literacy for elderly persons. The program has been featured in national training events and in a videotape as a model rural project. Reading centers provide a variety of books and materials for loan to help supplement the resources of the public library.

They provide Daily Living Seminars to help seniors become better informed on issues affecting their daily lives: safety, nutrition, proper use of medications, preventive health care and controlling medical conditions through diet and lifestyle.

There are a number of other programs. In an area of great need and limited resources, the AAA and the community has managed to do a great deal and truly make a difference in the quality of life for many senior residents of the area.

Heritage Hall - Nassawadox (757) 442-5600
Nursing Care
9468 Hospital Ave. (P.O. Box 176,) Nassawadox, VA, 23413 **ST** 145 beds
1 story ❋ P/SP rms ❋ **N/SN/SCU** ❋ (+✚) — SA-Sec-TD-Ph-CB-W-CD-H-L-Rec **See page 156**